MW01680649

HEROES

This book is provided by

TRUTHFORLIFE®

THE BIBLE-TEACHING MINISTRY OF **ALISTAIR BEGG**

At Truth For Life, our mission is to teach the Bible with clarity and relevance so that unbelievers will be converted, believers will be established, and local churches will be strengthened.

Since 1995, Truth For Life has aired a Bible-teaching program on the radio, which is now distributed on over 1,600 radio outlets each day, and freely on podcast and on the Truth For Life mobile app. Additionally, a large content archive of full-length Bible-teaching sermons is available for free download at www.truthforlife.org.

Truth For Life also makes full-length Bible-teaching available on CD and DVD. These materials, and also books authored by Alistair Begg, are made available at cost, with no markup, so that price is not a barrier to those seeking a deeper understanding of God's Word.

The ministry connects with listeners at live listener events, pastor events and conferences across the U.S. and Canada in cities where the radio program is heard.

Contact Truth For Life
In the U.S.:
PO Box 398000, Cleveland, OH 44139 1.888.588.7884
www.truthforlife.org letters@truthforlife.org

In Canada:
P.O. Box 19008, Delta, BC V4L 2P8 1.877.518.7884
www.truthforlife.ca letters@truthforlife.ca

And also at:
www.facebook.com/truthforlife www.twitter.com/truthforlife

HEROES

Iain H. Murray

THE BANNER OF TRUTH TRUST

THE BANNER OF TRUTH TRUST
3 Murrayfield Road, Edinburgh EH12 6EL, UK
P.O. Box 621, Carlisle, PA 17013, USA

*

First published 2009
This paperback edition 2013

ISBN: 978 1 84871 367 3

*

Typeset in 11/15 pt Sabon Oldstyle Figures at
The Banner of Truth Trust, Edinburgh

Printed in the USA by
Versa Press, Inc.,
East Peoria, IL

To

JEAN MACINTYRE MURRAY
AND JOHN HERBERT MURRAY

MUCH LOVED SISTER
AND BROTHER-IN-LAW

CONTENTS

FOREWORD

The definition given for the word 'Hero' in the *Shorter Oxford English Dictionary* has the words, 'A man who exhibits extraordinary . . . greatness of soul, in connection with any pursuit, work or enterprise.' That is close enough to how I feel about the men included in this volume. Nor do I doubt that, in its feminine form, the word is equally applicable to many women. I think, for example, of Mary Slessor of Nigeria and Amy Carmichael of Dohnavur, South India. It is spiritual, Christian greatness with which I am concerned, and with the help it can be to see it in others. More than we can tell, we are all affected by examples, especially when we are young; and figures from the past, rediscovered in their biographies, may influence us deeply. A new biography of John Knox stirred Scotland two hundred and fifty years after his death. Many books have had a similar effect.

Lytton Strachey set a different fashion for the writing of biography with his *Eminent Victorians* in 1918. He meant his readers to understand that his subjects were not so 'eminent' after all. Since then the idea of presenting lives as models to be followed has fallen into discredit. Modern biographers generally do not need the caution to include 'warts and all' that Oliver Cromwell once gave to his portrait painter. This same approach to biographical writing sometimes appears in Christian circles. The suspicion that a book does not give sufficient prominence to a Christian's failures and blemishes is enough, with some, to consign it to the category of 'hagiography'. Even the biographies of John Stott and James Packer have been so described.[1] The label is intended as a put-down, yet it is a strange word to use in a pejorative sense. It derives, of course, from the Greek *hagios*, meaning 'holy' or 'consecrated to God'. It is the word which the New Testament applies more than sixty times to Christians: they are 'the saints' or 'the holy ones'. The word does not imply a present moral perfection, but it does attribute something extraordinary to Christians. They belong to God. Christ lives in them. When a heathen judge demanded of Ignatius of Antioch, why he spoke of himself as *theophorus* ('bearer of God'), the martyr replied that it was because he was 'one who has Christ in his breast'. In Christians, he declared, the promise was fulfilled, 'I will dwell in them, and walk in them, and they shall be my sons and daughters, says the Lord Almighty.'

To believe this ought to affect the writing of Christian biography. Every Christian believes, with the apostle Paul, that, 'In me (that is, in my flesh,) dwells no good thing' (*Rom.* 7:18). But Paul had not forgotten that confession when he also wrote, 'Be followers [imitators] of me' (*1 Cor.* 4:16; *Phil.* 3:17). He knew the grace of Christ was in him, and making him all that he was: 'I will not dare to speak of any of those things which Christ has not wrought by me' (*Rom.* 15:18). This is the focus when examples are held up for us in Scripture, and we see it in Luke's account of Paul. It does not mean that significant faults are to be hidden; but it is the outworking of what Henry Scougal called 'the life of God in the soul' that qualifies chiefly for record and for imitation. 'They glorified God in me', Paul could say of the Judean Christians

[1] By Rob Warner, *Reinventing English Evangelicalism 1966–2001: A Theological and Sociological Study* (Milton Keynes: Paternoster, 2007), p. 39.

to the Galatians (*Gal.* 1:24). Christ is the author and the finisher of the life of the believer. The faith given, the talents allocated, the spiritual ambition, and the measure of usefulness are all from him. This should rule out any adulation. To recognize heroes is not the same as 'hero-worship'. Spurgeon could speak of taking Whitefield as his model, yet he also wrote:

> We read the biographies of former worthies with great wonder and respect, but we do not attempt to follow in their steps with equal strides. Wherefore not? It has pleased the Father that in Jesus all fulness should dwell, a fulness for Paul, a fulness for Luther, a fulness for Whitefield, and blessed be God, a fulness for me, a fulness for you. All that Jesus has given forth has not exhausted him.[2]

That there is a danger of thinking and writing too highly of men I do not deny.[3] It is all because of Christ that 'the righteous shall be had in everlasting remembrance.' True Christian biography should therefore concentrate on what is edifying and for the praise of Christ. The desire of those who write such books should be that their readers should know something of what F. W. H. Myers felt when he rose from reading the life of Paul, with the words:

> Christ! I am Christ's! And let the Name suffice you,
> Ay, for me too He greatly hath sufficed;
> Christ is the end, for Christ was the beginning,
> Christ the beginning, for the end is Christ.

[2] *Metropolitan Tabernacle Pulpit,* 1874 (vol. 20), pp. 233–4.

[3] The Scottish leader, John Livingstone, speaking of the failure of the church in his day, wrote: 'Our ministers were our glory, and I fear our idol, and the Lord hath stained the pride of our glory.' *Scottish Puritans – Select Biographies,* ed. W. K. Tweedie (Edinburgh: Banner of Truth, 2008), vol. 1. p. 250. The danger of a wrong regard for men arises particularly when our heroes all come from one place and one period of time.

Having said this, I should explain that all these pages are by no means meant to be biography. In cases where lives are already well known – as Whitefield's and Spurgeon's ought to be – I have concentrated on aspects of their thought. These eight men I admire greatly. I have learned much from them all, but I do not mean them to be understood as my special heroes. The history of the Christian church offers a whole galaxy of men and women whose lives are worthy to be held up for imitation, and I have written on a number of them elsewhere. There are others whose biographies are so attractive that they need addition from none – I think, particularly, of the *Life of Robert Murray M'Cheyne* by Andrew Bonar.[4]

The first chapter in this book arose out of my need to return to the study of Jonathan Edwards for the bicentenary commemorations of his birth at Northampton, Massachusetts, and Minneapolis, in 2003. That was sixteen years after the publication of my biography of Edwards; the intervening years had seen several more volumes of Edwards, previously unpublished, from Yale University Press, as well as George M. Marsden's valuable biography from the same publishers in 2003. The only pages in this book which have appeared in print earlier are those on John Newton (*The Banner of Truth* magazine, August/September 2007), and Thomas Charles (in *Thomas Charles' Spiritual Counsels*, 1993).

I am particularly indebted to the libraries of the Presbyterian Historical Society at Montreat, North Carolina, and of Reformed Theological Seminary, Jackson, Mississippi, for

[4] This can be bought separately or in the larger volume, *Memoir and Remains of Robert Murray M'Cheyne* (repr. London: Banner of Truth, 1966). Of this title Spurgeon said: 'This is one of the best and most profitable volumes ever published. Every minister should read it often.' But *Robert Murray M'Cheyne: In the Footsteps of a Godly Scottish Pastor* by Derek Prime (Leominster: Day One, 2007), with over 150 colour photos, is a worthy addition.

material relating to Charles Colcock Jones, and to Steve Martin of Fayetteville, and Tom Ellis of Kansas City, for doing so much to interest me in this little-known Christian leader of Georgia.

My hope is that these pages may give young Christians a relish for old authors, and encourage younger ministers of the gospel in the assurance that the Saviour of yesterday is the same today and tomorrow. The study of history is vital to the health of the church. As Thomas Fuller wrote long ago:

> History maketh a young man to be old, without either wrinkles or grey hairs; privileging him with the experience of age, without either the infirmities or inconveniences thereof. Without history a man's soul is purblind, seeing only the things which almost touch his eyes.

IAIN H. MURRAY
Colinton,
Edinburgh
September 2008

ILLUSTRATIONS

I

JONATHAN EDWARDS: THE MAN AND THE LEGACY

Jonathan Edwards (1703–58)

Next to the Holy Scriptures, the greatest aid to the life of faith may be Christian biographies.

A. W. Tozer

There are times when the discovery of an author makes such an impact that the date is never forgotten by the reader. Thus for the date, June 22, 1832, Robert Murray M'Cheyne marked in his diary, 'Bought Edwards' Works'.[1] They became his companions for life. One day early in the year 1929, Martyn Lloyd-Jones, with time to spare as he waited for a train in Cardiff, visited the second-hand bookshop of John Evans. 'There', he said, 'down on my knees in my overcoat in the corner of the shop, I found the two-volume 1834 edition of Edwards which I bought for five shillings. I devoured these volumes and literally just read and read them. It is certainly true that they helped me more than anything else.'[2] John Piper has written about a little pantry, 8 by 5 feet, in Munich, where in the early 1970s the writing of Edwards so took hold of him that it turned a pantry into the vestibule of heaven.[3] Others could speak similarly.

[1] *Robert Murray M'Cheyne: Memoir and Remains,* Andrew Bonar (London: Banner of Truth, 1966), p. 17.

[2] *D. Martyn Lloyd-Jones: The First Forty Years,* Iain H.Murray (Edinburgh: Banner of Truth, 1982), pp. 253–4.

[3] *God's Passion for His Glory: Living the Vision of Jonathan Edwards,* John Piper (Wheaton: Crossway, 1998), pp. 90–1.

Sometimes the biographies of Christians may have a depressing effect, and that was how the life of Jonathan Edwards first appeared to M'Cheyne. He felt, 'How feeble does my spark of Christianity appear beside such a sun!' Then he added these significant words, 'But even his was a borrowed light, and the same source is still open to enlighten me.'

The abiding importance of Edwards and his writings lies in this 'borrowed light'. It is true that numbers have found an interest in him for other reasons. Through a lengthy period until the 1950s, he was chiefly remembered as a philosopher and eminent eighteenth-century thinker. Given that image, it is no wonder his works ceased to have any appeal in the churches. It was the rediscovery of him as a Christian and teacher of the Word of God that led to the extraordinary resurgence of his influence in more recent times. As a preacher of divine revelation he commands attention today and that because, as he says, 'The wisdom of God was not given for any particular age, but for all ages.'[4]

Early Life

Edwards was born a little over seventy years after the first Puritan settlement of New England and, at the time of his birth, October 5, 1703, there were some 130 towns in the colony. Some were well established, others were small and on the frontiers of the wilderness. From his birth, he spent his first twelve years in his parents' home at East Windsor, close to the Connecticut river. His father, Timothy Edwards, was pastor of the local church, a good student and preacher, as well as a part-time school teacher and farmer. His mother,

[4] *The Salvation of Souls: Nine Previously Unpublished Sermons by Jonathan Edwards*, eds. R. A. Bailey and G. A. Wills (Wheaton: Crossway, 2002), p. 120.

Esther, had eleven children—four girls, then Jonathan, to be followed by six more girls, and all of them six feet in height. Then there was the larger family circle. Both his grandfathers were born in the 1640s; both were still alive in Jonathan's youth, and both remained representatives of what was best in the Puritan age. One of them, his maternal grandfather, Solomon Stoddard, was pastor of the largest church in New England, some thirty-five miles away at Northampton.

Jonathan Edwards would appear to have had a healthy and happy childhood, spent largely in female company. When he was not quite thirteen he was sent down river to the Collegiate School of Connecticut. Two years later the School settled at New Haven and became Yale College. The Head was one of Edwards' many cousins, Elisha Williams. Edwards graduated Bachelor of Arts in 1720, and it was decided he would stay a further two years to become a Master of Arts. One year later, however, in the Spring of 1721, something far more important happened. Edwards at this time was already religious but despite 'repeated resolutions' it was not a religion that had changed his heart or humbled his natural pride. But now, he says, 'I was brought to that new sense of things', to an 'inward, sweet delight in God and divine things . . . quite different from any thing I ever experienced before.' 'I began to have a new kind of apprehensions and ideas of Christ, and the work of redemption, and the glorious way of salvation by him.' When he went home in the summer of 1721 he tells us that he saw the fields around the parsonage as he had never seen them before:

> As I was walking there, and looking up on the sky and clouds, there came into my mind so sweet a sense of the majesty and grace of God, that I know not how to express—I seemed to

> see them both in a sweet conjunction . . . holy majesty and also a majestic meekness; a high, and great, and holy gentleness.[5]

It was now that Edwards' concern to see Christ's kingdom extended was born.[6] Before concluding his M.A. studies he went to serve a congregation in New York at the age of nineteen. This was a joyful time for him and there is record of it in his diary and 'Resolutions' that have survived. Sermons he preached in New York are now in print and show him to be remarkably mature.[7] But there were those, including his father, who wanted him back in Connecticut and from 1724 to 1726 he joined the staff at Yale as a tutor. These were years of preparation and 1726 brought the great milestone of his life, for that year saw him invited to join his grandfather, Solomon Stoddard, now aged eighty-three, and still the minister at Northampton.

Meanwhile something even more significant had happened. As a teenager he had fallen in love with a girl who lived with her mother close to the College Green in New Haven. She was Sarah Pierrepont, and, on July 28, 1727, seventeen years old

[5] I quote from the *Memoirs of Edwards* in the two-volume edition of his *Works* (Edinburgh: Banner of Truth, 1974), p. xiii. These volumes remain in print and provide the largest amount of Edwards' material in affordable compass. Hereafter referred to as *Works*. A Yale edition of Edwards, commenced in 1953 has now been completed in 23 volumes, and is of especial value in the volumes of sermons and correspondence from MS not previously published. I will distinguish these volumes by adding 'Yale' in brackets after *Works*. For long there were no biographies sympathetic to Edwards in print; there are now George Marsden, *Jonathan Edwards, A Life* (New Haven: Yale University Press, 2003; my own, *Jonathan Edwards, A New Biography* (Edinburgh: Banner of Truth, 1988); and, more briefly, Stephen J. Nicholls, *Jonathan Edwards, A Guided Tour of his Life and Thought* (Phillipsburg, N.J.: P&R, 2001).

[6] He wrote in later life: 'If I know my own heart, I have for more than thirty years, set my heart on the advancement and enlargement of Christ's kingdom on earth, as a kingdom of light, love and peace, and have preferred these things to my chief joy.'

[7] *Sermons and Discourses, 1720–1723*, ed. Wilson H. Kimnach, *Works* (Yale), vol. 10.

and dressed in pea-green satin brocade, she married Jonathan and became his inseparable helper. Northampton, a town of some 200 homes, mostly clustered together for defence, had a population of about a thousand men, women and children. The first settlers had all been assigned four acres beyond the village, with shared common pasture, but, with a rising population, land resources were growing scarce. Given his status, Edwards had no problem in that regard. The couple set up home on a rural lane (later King Street), and they were given ten acres and a further forty, five miles away. A year later the first of their children was born, and in the next twenty-two years the family grew until there were eight daughters and three sons.

The first seven years at Northampton were ones of hard work and happiness as Edwards settled into the habits of a lifetime. One concern, however, was to deepen as he grew to understand his congregation. His people made up the only church in the town and—according to the early New England pattern—the whole population regarded it as their own. When Stoddard died in 1729 the oversight fell entirely on Edwards. The Northampton church was as eminent as any in the land but it seems that it had come to rely too much on what it had been. Its spiritual condition did not come up to Edwards' expectation and his sermons increasingly revealed that he saw too many of his hearers as no more than nominal believers: 'They come to meeting from one Sabbath to another and hear God's word, but all that can be said to 'em won't awaken 'em, won't persuade 'em to take pains they may be saved.'[8] Often, he feared, such people were not even listening, 'They are gazing about the assembly minding this and the

[8] *Works* (Yale), vol. 17 (New Haven: Yale University Press, 1999), p. 178.

other person that is in it, or they are thinking of their worldly business.'[9]

Revival

This state of affairs came to an end in one of the best-known events of Edwards' life, the revival of 1734–5, when, in his words, 'A great and earnest concern about the great things of religion, and the eternal world, became universal in all parts of the town.' 'The world was only a thing by the bye.' He thought it probable that 300 had been converted within six months, and it was his hope that 'the greater part of persons in this town, above sixteen years of age, are such as have the saving knowledge of Jesus Christ.'[10] These were months when the crowded meetinghouse was filled with praise, but there were to be other consequences that were not anticipated. In a letter to Benjamin Colman in Boston, Edwards gave an account of the awakening. Colman asked for a fuller narrative and, when he got it, he sent it on to London where it was published under the title, *A Faithful Narrative of the Surprising Work of God.*

The book drew widespread attention and instantly put Edwards and the Northampton church on the world stage. This appears to have been the occasion of a family quarrel that was to go on through the rest of Edwards' lifetime. Solomon Stoddard had twelve children, of whom Edwards' mother was one. From his mother's side of the family Edwards thus had numerous cousins, of whom the most influential were the Williamses. New England society, it has to be remem-

[9] Ibid., p. 179.

[10] *Works*, vol.1, p. 350. The quotation is from *A Narrative of Surprising Conversions*, which is also published separately by the Banner of Truth Trust, and is in *Works* (Yale), vol. 4.

bered, was hierarchical according to the English pattern, and all the descendants of Stoddard were conscious of their position among the elite. Perhaps some of them now resented the celebrity of the young man who had succeeded their grandfather; whatever the reason, from about the time of the publication of *A Faithful Narrative*, Edwards had critics from amongst the Williamses. His cousin, Colonel Israel Williams of Hatfield, for example, was critical of Edwards' preaching and was to pass his doorstep for the next fourteen years without ever calling in.

One biographer says that Edwards, in his inexperience at this date, looked upon the continuance of revival as proof that 'God was still with them.'[11] The assertion cannot be proved; there may have been an element of it in his thinking when he was thirty-three years old. The revival did not continue. It is clear that by 1736 he was again struggling with the difficulties of more normal church life, and there was cause for some disappointment as his anticipations of the permanent results of the revival were not all fulfilled. Party strife, long endemic in the village, reappeared. In 1740, however, a work of grace, much wider in scale than in 1734–5, began along the eastern seaboard. It was the beginning of 'the Great Awakening', which would touch several places in the thirteen colonies of the fledgling nation.

It is impossible here even to sketch the Great Awakening years. For Edwards they were exhausting times which brought him 'to the brink of the grave'. Besides the care of his own people, he was now itinerating widely to preach for other men. Correspondence multiplied, and yet somehow he

[11] Ola Elizabeth Winslow, *Jonathan Edwards 1703–1 758* (New York: Macmillan, 1940), p. 164.

was also preparing two of the most significant books ever written on the subject of revival, *Distinguishing Marks of a Work of the Spirit of God,* and *Thoughts on the Revival in New England.* No wonder he speaks of a 'prodigious fullness of business'. Yet these were happy years, indeed, at one point, there was fear lest his wife Sarah would die of sheer joy. Perhaps the closest Edwards comes to summarizing what happened in 1740–2 are in these words:

> God is pleased sometimes, in dealing forth spiritual blessings to his people, in some respects to exceed the capacity of the vessel in its present scantiness; so that he not only fills it, but makes their 'cup to run over' (*Psa.* 23:5) . . . It has been with the disciples of Christ, for a long season, a time of great emptiness on spiritual accounts. They have gone hungry and have been toiling in vain, during a dark night of the church; as it was with the disciples of old (*Luke* 5:5; *John* 21:3). But now, the morning being come, Jesus appears to his disciples, and gives them such an abundance of food, that they are not able to draw their net; yea, so that their net breaks, and their vessel is overloaded. [12]

Edwards the Preacher

Among the myths that grew up about Edwards none has been more often repeated than his appearance as a preacher. It is said he was a man who, as he preached, stood motionless, with a candle in one hand and his manuscript lifted up to his eye in the other. How such a delivery failed to bore people to death is then regarded as something of a miracle. This is a portrait which Edwards's hearers would not have recognized. It is, however, with the distinctive content of his preaching that I am here concerned.

[12] *Works,* vol. 1, pp. 368–9.

First, *Edwards had a truer understanding of human nature than had many of his contemporaries.*

Today 'sin' has almost dropped out of common speech. People have been happy to embrace the philosophy that denies the corruption of the human race. In so doing they have become fools, for the Word of God says, 'He that trusts in his own heart is a fool' (*Prov.* 28:26).

For Edwards a true understanding of the condition of the natural man has to be the starting point of preaching. There are not a few in the churches today who would question this starting point. They would say, 'Edwards was living in a New England possessed of a Bible-believing tradition. But to talk today about the fall of man and sin would be incomprehensible to most people. The starting point has to be somewhere else.'

That is a dangerous mistake. God has not left every generation of preachers to find the right starting point; there is not one for the first century, another for the eighteenth and another for our own. What the Bible says about human nature dictates the starting point: it has to be conviction of sin and it is the same for all generations because no one by nature or education has a true sense of sin. 'There is no fear of God before their eyes' (*Rom* 3:18) is a universal statement. Edwards' problem was exactly our own:

> How unreasonable is the security of multitudes of men . . . they seem to live easy and undisturbed. Yea, and many of those that have been well instructed in this doctrine of the necessity of being born again . . . they don't trouble themselves about it. They have something else to mind: they mind the world, are concerned to increase their estates, or mind their pleasures and their company, and let this matter of their being born again be as it will.

What the natural man needs before everything else is conviction of sin and therefore the preacher must begin where God begins with men: 'The fear of the LORD is the beginning of wisdom' (*Psa.* 111:10). Or, in New Testament language, 'When [the Holy Spirit] is come he will reprove the world of sin, of righteousness, and of judgment' (*John* 16:18). So for Edwards it was an axiom, 'You can't be saved without convictions.'

How then did Edwards understand conviction of sin?

1. *It is the experience which proves to men the kind of deliverance that they need.* Without any conviction of sin people may believe that they have some sins that need forgiveness. They admit they have done and said things that they would wish to be forgotten. But conviction brings home to us more than our wrong *actions*. We have a wrong *nature*, and it is only in the light of the holiness of God that the extent of our corruption begins to be seen.

Conviction of sin discovers to men their ignorance of God, and the knowledge of God teaches them that their problem is more than the need of forgiveness; the heart and nature is wrong. A new start cannot meet this need. There has to be a new life and a new nature.

2. *Conviction of sin shows to men the rightness of obedience to God and to his law.* This is a point where Edwards, and the whole Puritan tradition, diverges widely from much of our own. He believed that making known the moral character of God involves preaching the duty of sinners to obey God's holy commandments. God has not suspended his requirement of perfect obedience to the law that was written on man's heart at his first creation (*Rom.* 2:15). That law was given anew in the Ten Commandments, and the standard

remains in force for all mankind. All are to love God with all their heart and soul and mind and strength. All are to love their neighbours as themselves. Thus the prophets up to John the Baptist preached the law of God; Jesus preached it; and the apostles preached it. The law of God demands an entire change of life; that is what repentance means. Every sin is to be given up, and nothing retained that is contrary to God: 'If thy hand or thy foot offend thee, cut them off and cast them from thee: it is better for thee to enter into life halt or maimed, rather than having two hands or two feet to be cast into everlasting fire' (*Matt.* 18:8). And it is not simply some sins that are to be given up; nothing less than the denial of self is the obligation that Jesus imposed. 'Cast away from you all your transgressions, whereby ye have transgressed; and make you a new heart and a new spirit' (*Ezek.* 18:31).

But what, it may be asked, is the purpose of such preaching? Is preaching in this way not a return to salvation by works? Not at all. The purpose is exemplified in the words of Christ to the Rich Young Ruler, 'If thou wilt enter into life, keep the commandments' (*Matt* 19:17). Jesus went on to demand complete obedience from the young man; no other obedience was what he owed to God.

Christ's words are the plainest demonstration that the law comes before the gospel. The law tells men what they *ought* to do, not what they *can* do. Conviction of sin teaches the rightness of giving full obedience to God (*Rom.* 7:7). When a man first becomes concerned about salvation, he commonly thinks he can do what is needed. Conscience and the Word of God tell him that he must radically change his life, and so he embarks on the quest to improve himself. But the more he seeks to obey and to be holy, the more hopeless he finds his position to be. Instead of getting better he finds he grows worse. What God requires begins to look like an impossibility. The recognition of that impossibility is exactly what the Spirit of God intends to bring about.

When the disciples observed the way Christ dealt with the Rich Young Ruler, and saw the man go away sorrowful, 'they were astonished out of measure, saying among themselves, Who then can be saved?' Then Jesus told them why he had spoken as he had, 'With men it is impossible, but not with God' (*Mark* 10:27). The Rich Young Ruler was never convinced of this or he would have recognized that he was truly lost and in need of a deliverance from outside himself.

Preaching the law and the holiness of God is the God-given means to bring men to an end of themselves:

> Such earnestness and thoroughness of endeavours, is the ordinary means that God makes use of to bring people into an acquaintance with themselves, to a sight of their own hearts, to a sense of their own helplessness, and to a despair in their own strength and righteousness . . . It is experience of ourselves, and finding what we are, that God commonly makes use of as the means of bringing us off all dependence on ourselves . . . It is therefore quite a wrong notion that some entertain, that the more they do, the more they shall depend on it. Whereas the reverse is true; the more they do, or the more thorough they are in seeking, the less will they be likely to rest in their doings, and the sooner will they see the vanity of all that they do.[13]

3. *Conviction of sin often makes real to men their danger of the wrath of God*. Sin not only ruins men, it dishonours God. The love and the wrath of God are not opposed in Scrip-

[13] *Works*, vol. 1, pp. 656–7.

ture. God loves his own infinite excellence and perfection; it is his glory, in which he delights. Wrath is not a passion in God, it is the unchanging response of holiness to the monstrosity of sin. We underestimate the demerit of sin because we know so little of the glory of God. If God were not implacably opposed to all that dishonours him, he would cease to be God. Judgment to come and hell are the righteous response to all who continue in sin. 'Upon the wicked he shall rain snares, fire and brimstone, and an horrible tempest . . . For the righteous LORD loveth righteousness' (*Psa.* 11:6–7).

At no point has Edwards' teaching been more attacked than here. While he was alive he was accused of trying to frighten people into religion and his reply is ignored. He wrote:

> The word *fright* is commonly used for sudden, causeless fear, or groundless surprise; but surely a just fear, for which there is good reason, is not to be spoken against under any such name.[14]

The criticism is in reality a rejection of Scripture. The wrath of God is not a fiction. There are truths intended to convict and alarm the careless, and one reason there is so little sense of the seriousness of sin today is that these truths are little preached. The cross of Christ is a message with no relevance for the careless.

In a personal note, written before 1731, Edwards observed that it was God's 'ordinary way', in convicting of sin, to show 'the danger of it before conversion'. And yet he did not make a sense of the danger of sin and of the wrath of God an essential stage preparatory to true conversion. It had troubled him as a young Christian that he had known little of such an experience

[14] *Works*, vol. 2, p. 266.

before his conversion. He came to see that there is no one pattern to which all experience should conform. All he would have insisted on was that men need to know they are lost before they can be saved.

Second, *Edwards preaching differs from that of today in that he had a stronger emphasis on the wonder of the love of God.*

At this point, more than any other, he differs from the legend that has been promoted about his preaching. It is supposed that the wrath of God was the staple diet of his hearers. He 'realized the Great Awakening', says a modern writer, by representing sinners as hanging by a thread over hell.[15] When commemorating Edwards' birth in October 2003, the Edwards Church at Northampton gave each attendee a 14 inch long pencil, inscribed with the words, 'That God that holds you over the pit of hell, much as one holds a spider . . . over the fire, abhors you.' The outcome of this sustained caricature has been that his sermon, 'Sinners in the hands of an angry God', is said to be the best-known sermon in American history.

The proponents of this view of Edwards are the liberal successors of those who sought to discredit his ministry in his own day. As early as 1741 he was defending himself against this misrepresentation: 'The law is to be preached only to make way for the gospel, and in order that it may be preached more effectively. The main work of ministers is to preach the gospel.'[16]

Far from wanting to keep his hearers in spiritual distress, Edwards was concerned that too many remained under need-

[15] M. X. Lesser in *Works* (Yale), vol. 19, p. 22.
[16] *Works,* vol. 2, p. 266.

less conviction, and he said so. He did not teach that a certain degree of distress gave individuals a warrant to entrust themselves to Christ; the warrant is in Christ's invitation, and *willingness* to come to him was all that is needed. So his hearers were encouraged

> immediately to go to God through Christ for mercy . . . the arms of mercy are open to embrace you . . . If your souls be burdened, and you are distressed for fear of hell, you need not bear that burden and distress any longer. If you are but willing, you may freely come and unload yourselves, and cast all your burdens on Christ.[17]

Men come to conviction by the law, but they come to faith through the knowledge of Christ and of the promises. The great end of preaching is therefore to make known the excellence and love of Christ. Legal fears awaken men, but they do not draw them to Christ. For that sinners need to know the welcome that awaits them in the Saviour. Men must learn the truth about him because, 'There never was any man that once came to understand what manner of man [Christ] was but his heart was infallibly drawn to him.'

Knowing this, Edwards' most important sermons were those that placarded Christ and appealed to his hearers to come to him.

> God has provided a Saviour that woos in a manner that has the greatest tendency to win our hearts. His word is most attractive. He stands at our door and knocks. He does not merely command us to receive him: but he condescends to apply himself to us in a more endearing manner. He entreats and beseeches us by his word and his messengers.[18]

[17] Ibid, p. 112.
[18] Ibid, p. 156.

The idea that Edwards succeeded because he preached a gospel of fear is misconceived. 'Sinners in the hands of an angry God' was not the tenor of his preaching. But he did believe that only as individuals know they are sinners can they truly come to understand the love of God.[19] The ultimate purpose of preaching is to draw men heavenwards, to a world of love, where,

> God is manifested and shines forth in full glory, in beams of love; there the fountain overflows in streams and rivers of love and delight, enough for all to drink at, and to swim in, yea, so as to overflow the world as it were with a deluge of love.[20]

The same note is foremost when Edwards speaks of the first qualification of a gospel minister. It is, he said, by divine love in the soul, 'especially, that a minister of the gospel is a burning light; a minister that is so has his soul enkindled with the heavenly flame; his heart burns with love.'[21] 'He who will set the hearts of other men on fire with the love of Christ, must himself burn with love.'[22]

I must add the words of two witnesses to the love of God in Edwards. The first is his English contemporary, John Wesley, who himself spoke much on the subject. In an issue of his periodical, the *Arminian Magazine,* Wesley included an article with the title, 'An Extract from a Sermon on "God is Love".' He introduced it with this note: 'The following is the most remarkable discourse I ever saw upon the subject; and gives

[19] 'The people who have appreciated the love of God the most have always been those who have realized their sinfulness most.' D. M. Lloyd-Jones, *Romans: Exposition of Chapter 5, Assurance* (London: Banner of Truth, 1971), p. 123.

[20] Quoted by Marsden, *Edwards,* p. 161.

[21] *Works,* vol. 2, p. 957.

[22] The words are those of Thomas Scott, another 18th-century preacher and admirer of Edwards, *The Force of Truth* (repr. Edinburgh: Banner of Truth, 1984), p. 60.

a full answer to one of the capital objections frequently made against Christianity.'[23] The author was Jonathan Edwards.

It is no less significant that George Marsden, in his recent biography of Edwards, should write: 'That God was in essence love was no novelty in Christian or Calvinist theology or in other thought of the era, yet Edwards' emphasis on this theme in a rigorously Reformed context was at the core of his revitalization of that tradition.'[24]

LIFE AFTER THE GREAT AWAKENING

The blessing of the early 1740s was followed by a longer period of difficulty when two major problems confronted Edwards almost simultaneously.

First, in the wider scene in New England, opposition developed to the very idea of the Awakening as a 'work of the Spirit of God'. Most of it could be explained, some began to say, by purely natural causes—people were suffering from over-heated imaginations, from mere excitement and hysteria, and the chief culprits were Edwards and those like him who manipulated people by preaching to their emotions instead of their reason. Fuel to this opposition came from a number who professed to be friends of the revival. They were very active in it, and yet by foolish behaviour and lives lacking in Christlikeness they gave just cause for criticism. Some of these people were fanatics, people who saw physical phenomena as sure proof of the Spirit's work and presence. The 'wild fire' they represented gave support to the arguments of those who wished to discredit the whole work. Thus Edwards found

[23] *Arminian Magazine*, ed. John Wesley, vol. 8 (London: Paramore, 1785).

[24] Marsden, *Edwards*, pp. 191-92. He adds, 'Because Edwards was so thoroughly Reformed there was no sentimentality in Edwards' love. To be loving God simply meant that one had to love what God loved and to hate what God hated.'

himself caught between two forces and in opposition to them both.[25]

In addition to this, in every revival there is a work of the Spirit on large numbers which ultimately proves to be no more than what the Puritans called a 'common work'. For a time such individuals express spiritual concern and their lives take on a new seriousness but it does not last, and in time there is a return to their former indifference and formal religion. With pain, Edwards had to recognize that in Northampton itself the number of true converts was not what he had once hoped. Some of the most significant words he ever wrote were these:

> It is with professors of religion, especially such as become so in a time of outpouring of the Spirit of God, as it is with blossoms in the spring; there are vast numbers of them upon the trees, which all look fair and promising; but yet many of them never come to anything.[26]

The other great difficulty which Edwards now experienced was much nearer home. Support from his own congregation was weakening and one cause of this was the hostility of certain members of his wider family circle. Although the Williams family were not in his church, they were near enough to exert influence. When the normal kind of pastoral difficulties arose in Northampton, the cousins outside were ready to foment them. At length a *cause célèbre* occurred which presented an opportunity to have Edwards removed altogether

[25] Many writers make no distinction between revival and revivalism. Thus Ola Winslow credits Edwards with establishing 'a technique of revival behaviour' and then says the blame for the excesses belonged 'upon his shoulders'. *Jonathan Edwards*, pp. 172–3.

[26] Edwards, *Select Works*, vol. 3, *Religious Affections* (London: Banner of Truth, 1961), pp. 113–4. Also *Works* (Yale), vol. 2, where the editor, John E. Smith, rightly says that this title 'has unquestionably been Edwards' most widely read book'.

from his pulpit. During the 1740s Edwards had come to disagree with his grandfather Stoddard's long-established practice of not requiring a profession of saving faith in Christ in order to be a communicant; communicants, Edwards came to see, *ought* to be believers. But Stoddard's name was already a legend, and when his grandson's disagreement with the great man became known there was uproar in the town, with the Williams family involved as usual. And now opposition to Edwards had a leader from his family within the congregation, another cousin by the name of Joseph Hawley. Edwards sought to explain his conviction, but he was not to be heard, and the final extraordinary outcome was his being voted out of his church. The great majority of the 230 male communicants voted for his removal; only some 23 wanted him to remain. We might suppose that the bulk of Edwards' opponents were 'stony-ground hearers', who had no business to be members at all, but he allows us no such thought. The tragedy deepens when he writes that 'most of them esteemed me to be the chief instrument in the hand of God of the eternal salvation of their souls'.[27] Thus one of the most fruitful pastorates in history ended on June 22, 1750.

Edwards was now forty-six. A month after his dismissal he wrote to a friend: 'I am now, as it were, thrown upon the whole wide ocean of the world, and know not what will become of me and my numerous and chargeable family.' No financial arrangement was offered to help them and for the best part of a year, apart from some temporary engagements, he remained unemployed. Then, just as parties in Virginia were making moves to secure him, he accepted a call to an

[27] *Works* (Yale), vol. 16, p. 647. The later repentance of the ring-leader, Joseph Hawley, confirms this.

improbable situation. Stockbridge was a village in the frontier wilderness, about sixty miles by trail from Northampton, and with a congregation of only about a dozen white families. This settlement alone in New England expressed interest in him. Edwards hesitated, but one factor that added to the appeal of Stockbridge was the presence of Indians and the existence of a school for Indian children. So, after difficulties in selling their Northampton home, the whole family was eventually settled on the frontier by October 1751.

For Edwards Stockbridge was a haven of peace compared with the turmoil he had left behind. Yet any hope that these later years would continue free from trial was soon disappointed.

One of the families in the little congregation, and the most influential in the area, were Williamses, and it was not long before they were showing all the prejudice and hostility that had marked the other members of the same clan. The Stockbridge Williamses had their own ambitious plans, in which material gain seems to have played no small part, and they wished for no oversight from anyone of Edwards' stature. For three years there was to be another painful struggle, but this time the congregation stood with their pastor, and so did the Indians, whom the Williamses had antagonized. Only in 1754 did the Williamses in Stockbridge give up, and the strife was over. Yet there were other trials, including persistent financial constraints, and, then, with the outbreak of war with the French, the whole frontier situation became exposed to attack.

One of Edwards' daughters, Esther, had married Aaron Burr, President of Nassau Hall, the College of New Jersey recently established at Princeton. In the summer of 1756 Esther visited her parents and family at Stockbridge and was filled with alarm at the danger of their situation. The next year Esther's husband died and Edwards was surprised to learn that the decision of the College trustees was that he should be his son-in-law's successor. Given the precarious nature of life at Stockbridge we might have expected him to welcome a return to a more civilized situation but that was not his response. He did not wish to accept, he wrote to the trustees, adding, 'We have scarcely got over the trouble and damage sustained by our removal from Northampton.' When the approaches to him continued, Edwards referred the decision to a council of friends. They concluded he should go to Princeton, the only time in his life that we read he shed tears. One major reason for his reluctance was that he now believed that he could be more useful by writing than by speaking and he had a number of potential books in hand.

Given the urgency of the need at Princeton, Edwards left Sarah and most of his family behind at Stockbridge when he left in January 1758. His text for his final sermon was, 'For here we have no continuing city, but we seek one to come.' As he left the home for the last time, his daughter remembered, 'When he had got out of doors he turned about,—"I commit you to God", said he.' Edwards was now fifty-four and he spoke of his health being stronger than previously, but the next month an inoculation against smallpox went wrong, and on March 22, 1758, he died at Princeton. A little before that event he wrote to one of his daughters at Stockbridge:

> It seems to be the will of God, that I must shortly leave you; therefore give my kindest love to my dear wife . . . And as to my children, you are now like to be left fatherless, which I hope will be an inducement to you all, to seek a Father that will never fail you.

Sixteen days after her father Esther also died at Princeton, leaving two orphaned children. Sarah hurried down from Stockbridge to care for them, only to die herself and be buried with her husband at Princeton in October 1758.

The Man

We turn now from the main events in Edwards' life to the man himself. For our information we are dependent on three sources. First, his friends. George Whitefield described him as 'a solid, excellent Christian. I think I have not seen his like in New England'; and after a weekend in the Northampton parsonage he noted, 'A sweeter couple I have not yet seen.'[28] Another visitor to the Edwards' home recorded, 'The most agreeable family I was ever acquainted with. Much of the presence of God here.'[29]

Tall and thin, he was never robust in health, despite his daily exercise in such things as horse-riding or wood chopping. Samuel Hopkins wrote of Edwards' closeness to his wife and of how his children loved him. As a pastor he seems to have given more than the usual time to the care of the young people of the congregation, and it may be that he was more relaxed with them than with adults. Hopkins says, 'He was not a man of many words, and was somewhat reserved among strangers.'[30] Undoubtedly he was what we would call a private person yet he was no recluse. We read of family gatherings in the parlour after tea and of the 'cheerful and animated conversation' in which he shared. Nonetheless, a quiet spirit was a leading feature. In the words of a friend at

[28] *George Whitefield's Journals* (London: Banner of Truth, 1960), p. 476.
[29] Joseph Emerson, quoted by Winslow, *Edwards*, p. 131.
[30] Samuel Hopkins, *Memoirs of Jonathan Edwards* (London: Black, 1815), p. 85.

his death, 'Always steady, calm, serene . . . as he lived cheerfully resigned to the will of Heaven, so he died.'[31]

Our second source of information is what Edwards reveals about himself as a Christian. This source is limited for he left no extended diary or journal, and his letters say little of a personal nature. We know enough to say that the pursuit of holiness and of closer communion with God was his life-long concern.[32] Friendship with God was, for him, the chief purpose of redemption. If, in this context, we were to ask what was the particular grace to which he most aspired, there might be a case for arguing that it was the grace of joy. Certainly he held that communion with God 'is the highest kind of pleasure that can possibly be enjoyed by the creature'.[33] Spiritual happiness is a pervasive note in his early sermons. In one sermon on that subject, written when he was still a teenager, he spoke of the tendency of godliness to 'maintain always a clear sunshine of joy and comfort in it'.[34] This was certainly Edwards' own experience as a young Christian, when his joy overflowed.[35]

But while he ever regarded joy as an important part of the Christian life, he came to see that it is not to be taken as an accurate measure of growth in grace. Experience was to teach him that there are other things God would have us

[31] Quoted by Winslow, *Edwards*, p. 372.

[32] George Marsden summarizes Edwards' spiritual life in these words: 'Edwards worked constantly to cultivate gratitude, praise, worship, and dependence on his Savior. Whatever his failings, he attempted every day to see Christ's love in all things, to walk according to God's precepts, and to give up attachments to worldly pleasures in anticipation of that closer spiritual union that death would bring.' *Edwards, A Life*, p. 490.

[33] *Works* (Yale), vol. 10, p. 640.

[34] Ibid., p. 302.

[35] I surmise that it was because he did not have this joy to the same degree that he later wrote, 'It seems in some respects I was a far better Christian, for two or three years after my first conversion, than I am now' (*Works*, vol. 1, p. xlviii).

learn. About thirty-seven years after writing the words about 'a clear sunshine', he referred to this subject in a letter to his daughter Esther. She had been recently blessed with a special happiness in the sense of God's love and nearness. After recording his thankfulness for this, her father went on: 'God will never fail those who trust in him. But don't be surprised, or think some strange thing has happened to you, if after this light, clouds of darkness should return. Perpetual sunshine is not usual in this world, even to God's true saints.'[36]

If joy was not the pre-eminent grace that Edwards sought, what was it? I think there need be no doubt on this point; it was the grace of love. 'All creature holiness', he insists, consists essentially and summarily in love to God and love to other creatures.' ''Tis manifest that love is . . . the very essence of Christianity.'[37]

Love was the growing theme and passion of his life. He regarded it as the sure proof of regeneration that saints love God for himself, for the loveliness they see in him, and not for what they expect to gain from him. And the evidence that this knowledge of God is true is that its possessors are humble before him and before men. This was the goal of Edwards' Christian vision. As yet, for himself, he spoke of knowing only of 'a little spark of divine love'.[38]

[36] *Letters and Personal Writings, Works* (Yale), ed. George S. Claghorn, vol. 16, p. 730. In another later letter, he expresses his belief that there is progress in the Christian life, 'if not in joys, and some other affections, yet in greater degree of spiritual knowledge, self-emptiness, trust in God, and solidity and ripeness of grace'. Ibid., p. 234. This volume of the Yale edition is particularly valuable for the previously unpublished material of a biographical nature it contains.

[37] Summarizing Edwards' thought, Marsden writes, 'God's very being is "love and friendship which subsists eternally and necessarily between the several persons of the Godhead." The ultimate end or purpose of creation is an expression of that love. Intelligent beings are created with the very purpose to be united in love with the Godhead.' *Edwards*, p. 467.

[38] *Charity and Its Fruits* (repr. London: Banner of Truth, 1969) p. 335.

But there is a third source of information on Edwards from contemporaries and it is in conflict with what I have already said.

'He was', said one relative, 'a very great Bigot',[39] while another called him 'a tyrant';[40] 'Haughty and morose', Timothy Cutler called him.[41] He was accused of acting from 'resentment, from implacableness of spirit, stiffness and willfulness of temper, or an assuming disposition, and fondness of rule and authority'.[42] In short, in the opinion of some, he was 'a person not a little obnoxious'.[43]

Akin to these views of his person were the criticisms of his beliefs: they were narrow, old-fashioned, and uncharitable—'He would not admit any person into heaven, but those that agreed fully with his sentiments.'[44] It was said that he belonged to a school of thought 'living in gloomy caves of superstition', teaching, 'the most absurd, silly, and monstrous opinions, worthy of the greatest contempt of gentlemen possessed of that noble and generous freedom of thought, which happily prevails in this age of light and inquiry'.[45]

In 1749, at the height of the controversy in Northampton, Edwards wrote to a friend, 'I have many enemies abroad in the country, who hate me for my stingy principles, enthusiasm, rigid proceedings.'[46]

Here indeed is strong disagreement. Personally, I do not think that the contradictory portrait of Edwards to be found

[39] Murray, *Edwards, New Biography*, p. 361.
[40] *Works* (Yale), vol. 16, p. 323.
[41] Murray, *Edwards, New Biography*, p. 407 n.
[42] *Works* (Yale), vol. 16, p. 677, and pp. 648-49.
[43] Ibid., p. 513.
[44] Murray, *Edwards, New Biography*, p. 361.
[45] *Works*, vol. 1, p. 89.
[46] *Works* (Yale), vol. 16, p. 284.

in such words need detain us long. What is important is the question how such a differing assessment is to be explained. The main answer lies not in the eighteenth century but in the Bible itself. The unregenerate mind, far from being attracted by truth and by Christlikeness, is antagonized by them. 'If ye were of the world', our Lord said to his disciples, 'the world would love his own' (*John* 15:19). Accordingly, Scripture lays down a principle necessary for the interpretation of all history, and Paul stated it in writing to the Galatians, 'As then he that was born after the flesh persecuted him that was born after the Spirit, even so is it now' (*Gal.* 4:29). This is not to argue that Edwards had no faults that could reasonably offend, but, whatever we may think they were, they cannot explain the *animus* against him. There was a deeper reason for the hostility and why he had 'many enemies'. At the heart of the dislike of Edwards was a thinly disguised attack on biblical revelation. Edwards taught something that many did not believe, namely, 'There is naturally a great enmity in the heart of man against vital religion.'[47]

What is really at stake here is the whole biblical teaching on salvation. Fallen man is in a condition from which he can only be saved by divine grace, received as a sovereign gift of God. The common name for that belief in the eighteenth century was 'Calvinism', and Edwards spent much of his life contending for that belief because, if it is denied, man sees himself as his own saviour. The real issue between the Christian faith and the thinking of the world is that of supernaturalism against naturalism, and it is certain that the world will always favour belief that does not see man as a sinner dependent upon divine grace. The attack on Edwards was,

[47] *Works*, vol. 1, p. 408.

at heart, an attack on biblical truth. Some superficial writers on Edwards have explained his doctrinal outlook in terms of his adherence to traditional beliefs, but in so doing they have overlooked a very significant fact: Edwards was himself, once, on the side of the critics of divine sovereignty. In the only piece of personal testimony we have from his pen, he wrote:

> From my childhood up, my mind had been wont to be full of objections against the doctrine of God's sovereignty in choosing whom he would to eternal life . . . It used to appear like a horrible doctrine to me.

But, in a way he could not explain at the time, he says, there came 'a wonderful alteration in my mind, with respect to the doctrine of God's sovereignty', so that now he had 'a delightful conviction' about its truth.[48] This radical reversal in his thinking, he came to see, was not of himself; he owed it to the 'extraordinary influence of God's Spirit'.

We should not, however, deduce from this that Edwards saw all who opposed him as non-Christians. At times it might have been easy for him to have done so, but Christian charity led him differently. In this regard a letter he wrote to Mrs Elizabeth Williams in 1755 is memorable. He had heard that Mrs Williams, recently married into the family of his opponents, had been spreading misrepresentations of his character, and he wrote to her at length, in an attempt to win her to see things differently. In the course of doing so, he conceded that, 'in this present state of imperfection, darkness and confusion', people of good character may come to 'diverse and even contrary opinions of persons and things'. After expressing his forgiveness for the injury she had caused him, he went on:

[48] Ibid., pp. xii–xiii.

> I shall comfort myself with hopes of the time when all God's people shall meet together in an unembarrassed, unalloyed charity, in a world of such clear and perfect light as shall abolish all misunderstandings, and even the strongest prejudices . . . through which many of them now view one another.[49]

The feelings expressed in this letter are characteristic. Given the hurt he had experienced, expressions of resentment would have been understandable. Instead grace prevailed, as it had done in his Farewell Sermon preached at Northampton in 1750. Rather than addressing his people in words of censure, their best interests remained his concern. An eyewitness who was present in Northampton in the dramatic days following his dismissal noted:

> That faithful witness received the shock, unshaken. I never saw the least symptoms of displeasure in his countenance the whole week but he appeared like a man of God, whose happiness was out of reach of his enemies.[50]

What Edwards Has Left Us

1. *Edwards left an immensely valuable witness to the nature of true Christian experience.*

Of all the subjects on which he wrote none was more important than this. How he came to write on it is one of the keys to understanding his life. It may appear strange to us that God permitted the setbacks and disappointments that followed the revival of 1734–5 in Northampton, and to a greater extent, the Great Awakening; yet without these things there would never have been the need for several of his most

[49] *Works* (Yale), vol. 16, p. 678.

[50] Murray, *Edwards, New Biography*, p. 327.

important books. It was the painful necessity of circumstances that drove Edwards to write on how true spiritual life is to be distinguished from false. We can see that divine providence shaped his circumstances and experience for our benefit. As early as 1737 we find him saying, 'I don't know but I have trusted too much in men, and put too much consideration in the goodness and piety of the town';[51] later he writes these poignant words:

> I once did not imagine that the heart of man had been so unsearchable as it is. I am less charitable, and less uncharitable than once I was. I find more things in wicked men that may counterfeit and make a fair show of piety; and more ways that the remaining corruption of the godly may make them appear like carnal men than once I knew of.[52]

Edwards' experience compelled him to focus his thought on discriminating between the true and the false, and this culminated in probably his greatest book, *A Treatise Concerning the Religious Affections* (1746). The title needs a little explanation. Edwards understood a person to have two governing faculties, the mind and the will. The mind perceives and understands things, the will inclines us for or against the things we perceive. So love or dislike are actings of the will, and when these actings or inclinations are vigorous he calls them 'affections'. Love, desire, and joy are affections, so are fear, grief, and anger. If you want to call these 'exercises of the heart', Edwards will not disagree with you; he recognizes that our vocabulary is imperfect. He gave his book the title

[51] *Works* (Yale), vol. 19, p. 677. But the element of disappointment should not be exaggerated. He could remind his congregation in 1738, 'The Spirit of God has been poured out wonderfully here. Multitudes have been converted.' *Charity and Its Fruits*, p. 49.

[52] *Works*, vol. 2, p. 276.

he did because the main argument is that there is an essential difference between the affections of the natural man—the non-Christian—and the true believer. Orthodoxy is not a sufficient test; a person may have a speculative knowledge of the truth that leaves his life unchanged: 'If we be not in good earnest in religion, and our will and inclinations be not strongly exercised, we are nothing.'[53]

So the key issue has to do with the nature of conversion. What is the evidence of a saving conversion? It is not, he says, a prior conviction of sin—men can have that and never be regenerate; it is not the speed at which the supposed conversion occurs—the stony-ground hearer of Christ's parable 'immediately' received the word with joy (*Matt.* 13:20); it is not whether conversion is attended by physical signs—Felix trembled; it is not whether texts of Scripture come wonderfully into our minds—the devil is able to quote Scripture. Positively, the test is whether or not conversion is the result of *regeneration*. That is to say, has the individual known a change of nature, has there been the introduction of a new principle? 'There are many that think themselves born again', he writes,

> that never have experienced any change of nature at all; that haven't had one new principle added, nor one sinful disposition mortified; that never saw one glimpse of divine light, never saw the least of God's or Christ's glory . . . They think themselves now renewed in the whole man that never have had one finger renewed, if I may use such an expression.[54]

Again he says:

> They that are truly converted are new men, new creatures; new

[53] *Religious Affections*, p. 28.
[54] *Works* (Yale), vol. 17, p. 194.

> not only within, but without; they are sanctified throughout, in spirit, soul and body; old things are passed away, all things are become new; they have new hearts, and new eyes, new ears, new tongues new hands, new feet . . . they walk in newness of life, and continue to do so to the end of life.[55]

Because this new life is the restoration of the life of God in the human soul, the chief characteristic of its possessor is God-centredness. The true convert is aware of God, admires God, loves God, lives for God. The false convert, whatever his language or experiences, remains self-centred: self is the one abiding interest of the unregenerate life. It is to demonstrate this that Edwards examines so closely the subject of affections.

'The affections of men', he argues, 'are the springs of motion.' The natural man is governed by what Edwards calls 'false affections'; he may think he has love for God but that is only because he thinks of God as profitable to him; self-interest is in control. But the regenerate person loves God for his moral excellence, that is, his holiness. It is holiness that appeals to the true believer, and attracts the believer, because that is his nature—he loves the way of salvation because it is a holy way; loves the commands of God because they are holy; loves heaven as a world of holiness.[56] Holy love, as we have already noted, is 'the chief of affections' in the Christian, and this grace, Edwards shows, has one inseparable companion, namely, a humble spirit. A person who is satisfied with his spiritual attainment, who has no longing for more grace, is not yet a Christian at all. A humble spirit, he writes, leads Christians

[55] *Religious Affections*, pp. 313–4
[56] Ibid., pp. 184–5.

> to look upon themselves as but little children in grace, and their attainments to be but the attainments of babes in Christ, and [they] are astonished at and ashamed of the low degrees of their love and their thankfulness, and their little knowledge of God . . . A truly Christian love, either to God or men, is a humble broken-hearted love. The desires of the saints, however earnest, are humble desires. Their hope is a humble hope; and their joy, even when it is unspeakable and full of glory, is a humble broken-hearted joy, and leaves the Christian more poor in spirit, and more like a little child, and more disposed to a universal lowliness of behaviour.[57]

Edwards' legacy was to teach the church again what a great thing conversion is; it is a real turning from sin to God, it is an end of the reigning power of sin, it is the recovery of the image of God in men. 'True grace reaches to the very bottom of the heart . . . Counterfeit grace never dispossesses sin of the dominion of the soul, nor destroys its reigning power there.'[58] As we have seen, Edwards not only taught this by word but he upheld it in practice. He might have lived and died in comfort as the respected minister of the church at Northampton had he not sought to bring the church into line with the higher standards of the New Testament. The conviction that church members ought to be converted people and people who live as saints was a costly one for him. It entailed suffering, but the consistency of his teaching and his practice made a profound impression on many and contributed immensely to the future health of the churches.

Professor John de Witt, of Princeton Theological Seminary, once spoke of this point as the distinctive contribution of Edwards. He wrote:

[57] Ibid., pp. 248, 266.
[58] *Charity and Its Fruits*, p. 292.

> Jonathan Edwards changed what I may call the centre of thought in American theological thinking . . . No one but a man of genius could have made this change of emphasis so potent a fact in American Church History . . . More than to any other man, to Edwards is due the importance which, in American Christianity, is attributed to the conscious experience of the penitent sinner, as he passes into the membership of the Invisible Church.[59]

In other words, Edwards was used to restore teaching on conversion to its true place in the church. Joseph Tracy rightly takes the point further when he traces the recovery not simply to Edwards but to the revival in which he played such a part. Tracy wrote:

> The influence of the revival in this respect can scarce be estimated too highly. It brought out and presented in bold relief, the idea, that conversion is a change, ordinarily discoverable by its effects, so that he who exhibits no evidence of it, may with propriety be regarded as an unconverted man; and then it created a demand in the public conscience, for evidence of conversion in church members; and the beneficial influence of this demand is felt in all evangelical churches.[60]

Tracy wrote those words in 1842. The tragedy is that a new form of evangelicalism was already emerging at that date. It would lower the idea of conversion and encourage the error that it is separable from living a holy life. Edwards' words, 'a

[59] 'Jonathan Edwards; A Study', in *Biblical and Theological Studies,* by Members of the Faculty (New York: Scribners, 1912), pp. 130–1.

[60] *The Great Awakening: A History of the Revival of Religion in the Time of Edwards and Whitefield* (1842; repr. Edinburgh: Banner of Truth, 1976), p. 412. Referring to the truth, revived by Edwards, that churches should be 'composed of members who made a credible profession of piety', Tracy adds, 'Those hostile to the revival, regarded that doctrine and practice as "divisive", as "uncharitable", as "censorious", as "an invasion of God's prerogative to judge the heart".' This is a particularly valuable volume.

holy life is the chief of all signs of grace',[61] would be forgotten and many would be hurried prematurely into a Christian profession and church membership. A renewed serious reading of Edwards on the true nature of the Christian life would work a purifying change in our modern evangelicalism.

2. *Edwards confirmed the churches in a framework with which to understand history and the future.*

We live in a time when the world at large sees no meaning in history and has no anticipation of the future. Fifty years ago Winston Churchill said, 'I am bewildered by the world; the confusion is terrible.' Many more are thinking that today, and an uncertainty has come even into our evangelical churches. A number of views about unfulfilled prophecy have come and gone, and now there are professed evangelicals who question whether God has any control over history or even knows what it will be. I am not about to suggest that we need to take up all of Edwards' views on unfulfilled prophecy; his views were heavily influenced by the belief that the book of Revelation gives a kind of chart for the course of history, set down in chronological order, so that the church can estimate approximately where we stand in the time-line. On the contrary, I believe it can be argued convincingly that the last book in the Bible is best not interpreted in that way.

But the legitimacy of Edwards' general framework does not depend on his interpretation of that one book of the Bible. It depends rather on the many Scriptures which, beginning in the Old Testament, speak of the triumphant increase of the kingdom of Jesus Christ. Psalm 72 says, 'He shall have dominion also from sea to sea, and from the river unto the

[61] *Religious Affections*, p. 327.

ends of the earth.' God has said to his Son, 'Ask of me, and I shall give thee the heathen for thine inheritance, and the uttermost part of the earth for thy possession' (*Psa.* 2:8). So it must be: 'The Gentiles shall come unto thee from the ends of the earth, and shall say, Surely our fathers have inherited lies, vanity, and things wherein there is no profit' (*Jer.* 16:19).

Edwards saw history in the light of such promises. The Protestant Reformation of the sixteenth century was part of the fulfilment of God's programme, as was the settlement of the Puritans in America, and the defeat of Catholic France in the 1750s. Yet let us remember that in his lifetime large parts of the earth were still unexplored. Captain Cook had not seen the Pacific and the modern missionary movement had not begun. He was sure that the greater success of the gospel still lay in the future, for Scripture speaks of the expansion of Christ's kingdom into all nations. 'There is a kind of veil now cast over the greater part of the world', he writes, but it will be taken away (*Isa.* 25:7) and, 'It may be hoped that then many of the Negroes and Indians will be divines, and that excellent books will be published in Africa, in Ethiopia, in Tartary, and other now the most barbarous countries.'[62]

On this subject also, Edwards' thinking was in part shaped by events in his own life. His personal experience of the outpouring of the Spirit showed him something of the power that attends the Word of God accompanied by the Holy Spirit. As he looked to the future, he was sure brighter times would come, and this would not be chiefly by scholarship, or education, or social and political progress, but by

> a glorious pouring out of the Spirit with this clear and powerful preaching of the gospel, to make it successful for reviving

[62] *Works*, vol.1, p. 609.

> those holy doctrines of religion which are now chiefly ridiculed in the world.[63]

Another event, however, shaped Edwards' thinking and contributed largely to the legacy he was to leave for others.

While he was still at Northampton, on May 28, 1747, a young twenty-nine-year-old man rode unexpectedly into the parsonage yard. The visitor had come from New Jersey and had spent the previous four years in wilderness areas among the Indians. Often without proper food or shelter, on occasion riding as many as four thousand miles in a year, having only one white person in four years come to visit him, dependent on an interpreter to be able to preach, he had been met generally with stolid indifference.

Then in August 1745, at Crossweeksung in New Jersey, a work of grace appeared among the Indians, which David Brainerd could only liken to 'the great mourning' prophesied in Zechariah 12. Suddenly, he says, 'upon a people given to worshipping devils and dumb idols, the power of God seemed to descend', and the conviction of sin was profound. No less marked was the rejoicing in God that followed as an Indian camp became a new creation. Amazed and delighted, Brainerd was tempted to make his permanent home among these young Christians. But his burden for those beyond, and still in darkness, would not allow him to do so. When he returned to Crossweeksung in March of the next year he could write of the young Christians, 'I know of no assembly of Christians, where there seems to be so much of the presence of God, where brotherly love so much prevails.'[64] But Brainerd was now worn out and suffering from tuberculosis. Compelled to

[63] Ibid., p. 606.
[64] *Works*, vol. 2, p. 407.

return to New England for medical help and, with his own parents dead, it was in the parsonage at Northampton that he found his last home on earth. There he died in October 1747.

Had Brainerd died anywhere else we might never have known of his name today. The reason we do know him is that among his very few possessions were his diaries and journals, and these he had committed to Edwards. As Edwards read them, he was convinced that they made a book which must go out to the world. So it was that the first full missionary biography came to be published in 1749 with the title, *An Account of the Life of the Late Reverend Mr David Brainerd.* The book was an up-to-date proof that the gospel, preached and lived by a man endued with the Spirit of God, could succeed among any people and overcome any stronghold of Satan. It carried a message that would circle the Protestant world.

Across the Atlantic, thirty years after Edwards' death, men such as William Carey read Brainerd's *Life*, and it was this, along with other writings by Edwards, that played such a major part in inspiring the new missionary era. There is a direct link between Edwards and Carey's famous Nottingham sermon on Isaiah 54 and its themes, 'Expect great things from God. Attempt great things for God.' With that sermon of 1792 the missionary movement had begun, and repeatedly in the lives of the subsequent missionaries who were raised up in such numbers it was Edwards' writings that God used to focus their vision. Like Carey, Henry Martyn carried his copies of Edwards with him to India and when, on one occasion, he was challenged by a Muslim with the question why Christianity was so weak in the world 'if the heathen nations had been given to Christ for an inheritance', his reply was just the one that Edwards would have given: 'I rejoined that he was not yet come to the end of things.'[65]

This missionary legacy of Edwards has remained down to our own days. Little more than fifty years ago, before a group of young men laid down their lives to bring the gospel to the Auca Indians of Ecuador, Jim Elliot, one of those missionaries, wrote in his journal, 'I see the value of Christian biography tonight as I have been reading Brainerd's *Diary* . . . much encouraged to think of a life of godliness in the light of an early death.'[66] The truth is that Christians who imbibe the best of Edwards are not likely to be moulded into academics, or lecturers in theology; they are more likely to become evangelists, pastors, and missionaries. To understand Edwards is surely to appreciate biblical priorities and gain fresh confidence that God is reigning in all history.

In speaking of Edwards and the future, however, it would be very wrong to give the impression that unfulfilled prophecy was his first interest. It was certainly of importance in his thinking, but something else was far more important. He did not believe that a Christian's attention is to be centred on what may or may not happen in the world; it is to the day of Christ's coming that we must look—to the consummation, the day of resurrection and final redemption, the day when 'he shall have put down all rule and all authority'. Much may happen before the end of time that may not affect us; other generations may rise and pass away like our own; and events occur that we will never see. While, therefore, we are to pray

[65] *Journals and Letters of the Rev. Henry Martyn*, ed. S. Wilberforce (1839), pp. 749–50.

[66] *Shadow of the Almighty*, Elisabeth Elliot (New York: Harper, 1958), p. 108. Quoted in Robert E. Davis, *Jonathan Edwards: His Message and Impact* (Oswestry, Shropshire: Quinta Press, 2003), p. 42.

and work for future blessing in the earth we are not to live for these things, nor are we to be dismayed if God's calendar for outpourings of the Spirit is different from our own. We are to live for eternity and to do so in the certainty that we shall all very soon be there. Much that may happen in time is hidden from our view. What is not hidden is that we shall all stand before the judgment seat of Christ, to give account of the deeds done in the body. This transitory world, with all its history, is the night time, but the morning is coming: 'The night is far spent, the day is at hand.' If we are Christians at all, Edwards tells us, we are not to be occupied with this little span of life; this is not our rest; we are to look to the permanent and the eternal.

For Edwards, the life-breath of religion is the thought of the world to come. It was characteristic of him that his Farewell Sermon at Northampton after his dismissal was on the words of 2 Corinthians 1:14, 'As also you have acknowledged us in part, that we are your rejoicing, even as ye also are ours in the day of the Lord Jesus.' Listening to that sermon, few in the congregation would not have agreed with George Marsden's words, the eternal 'had always been Edwards' over-arching concern'.[67] The concern is everywhere in his preaching. For him, time is related to eternity as a porch is related to a house:

> Our present state and all that belongs to it, is designed by him that made all things, to be wholly in order to another world—This world was made for a place of preparation for another. Man's mortal life was given him that he might be prepared for his fixed state. And all that God has given us here, is given for this purpose. The sun shines, and the rain

[67] *Edwards, A Life*, p. 361.

> falls on us; and the earth yields her increase to us for this end. Civil, ecclesiastical, and family affairs, and all our personal concerns, are designed and ordered in subordination to a future world.[68]

This is a key to understanding Edwards. Take eternity out of the equation and his life looks very different. Think only of his trials — of his seeming lack of permanent success; of the way he was removed from serving the largest church outside Boston to live in a corner, on 'one side, far out of the way';[69] of his uncompleted writings; of the way his death 'in most American newspapers was recorded in a sentence'— think of all these and the story of his life may look like a failure. But Edwards saw it very differently. 'I acted', he could say, 'against all influence of worldly interest, because I greatly feared to offend God.'[70] In other words, he acted on the principle expressed in Calvin's words, 'We shall never be fit for the service of God if we look not beyond this fleeting life.'

3. *The life and teaching of Edwards impresses the truth that Calvinistic orthodoxy cannot advance the gospel and the salvation of men unless it has the power of the Holy Spirit.*

The danger for the churches in the early eighteenth century was that orthodoxy had ceased to be accompanied by effective evangelism. Edwards saw the necessity of a reconnection between the two. How he made that reconnection has been the subject of much discussion. The common idea in many modern writers is that Edwards discovered what they call 'a technique of revival behaviour for pulpit and pew'.[71] He was

[68] *Works*, vol. 2, pp. 244–5.
[69] *Works* (Yale), vol. 16, p. 699.
[70] Ibid., p. 647.
[71] Winslow, *Edwards*, p. 172.

the pioneer 'revivalist', the prototype for the evangelistic campaigns of a hundred years later.

But an older school of writers on the Great Awakening period saw the whole thing very differently. Thomas Murphy, for example, who wrote in the 1880s, explained the Great Awakening, not in terms of personalities or techniques but as 'a wonderful baptism of the Holy Ghost'.[72] 'The Church', he observed, 'was orthodox before; she now became imbued with a life and energy that were irresistible'. The common characteristic of the preachers of the revival was that 'they believed in refreshings from on high, felt some of them in their own souls, and were ready for still more'.[73]

This is the true key to understanding Edwards. There could be no greater mistake than to suppose that what we need today is simply Edwards' sermons in more modern dress. The truth alone is not enough. In preaching, God makes men a part of the message. They need to come from him. Their heart and spirit has to be in harmony with what they say and this can only be as they are 'filled with the Spirit'. Edwards concurred exactly with David Brainerd who wrote in the closing pages of his diary:

> *Lord, let Thy kingdom come.* I longed for a spirit of preaching to descend and rest on ministers, that they might address the consciences of men with closeness and power. I saw that God *had the residue of the Spirit;* and my soul longed it should be *poured from on high.*[74]

[72] Thomas Murphy, *The Presbytery of the Log College* (Philadelphia: Presbyterian Board, 1889), p. 445.

[73] Ibid., pp. 150–1.

[74] A. Smellie, ed., *Diary & Journal of David Brainerd,* 2 vols in 1 (Edinburgh: Banner of Truth, 2007), vol. 1, p. 359

4. *Edwards' great lesson is the call to cease looking to men and to live to honour God alone.*

Ask Edwards what he considered is ever the first need of the church, and his answer is very definite. It is 'humility', for pride is the peril ever nearest to us. It was pride that brought down the Northampton church. It was pride that led the eighteenth century to glory in the delusion of its supposed 'Enlightenment'. And in the way it can turn even the best of things to its use, pride is the most subtle of temptations. Orthodox faith, good scholarship, able preachers, successful congregations—these are all desirable things, but pride can ruin them all.

We want revival, but revival where pride is not mortified will quench the Holy Spirit. Joseph Tracy says perceptively of Whitefield's second visit to Boston that while there were conversions, there was not the profound impression of 1740–1: 'Nor ought any thing else to have been expected. Both ministers and preachers were thinking too much about the man, to profit by his preaching.'[75]

Pride is the cause of the idolatry that is hateful to God. Congregations can idolize preachers, preachers can idolize congregations. In Edwards' life we are taught not only by his words but by his history, that we are to 'cease from man'. The praise of man one day may turn to opposition the next. We are not to depend on human nature. 'Beware of men', is the injunction of Christ. And the warning is most needed when it seems least necessary.

To the Bible's question, 'What is man?' Edwards knew the right answer: man is 'a leaf driven of the wind, poor dust, a shadow, a nothing'. And of himself he says that he was

[75] *The Great Awakening*, p. 369.

empty, 'a helpless creature', of small account, and needing 'God's help in everything'.[76]

There is *one text* more than any other to which the life of Jonathan Edwards leads us back. It is at the heart of the Resolutions he wrote as a young Christian; he preached it in Boston at the age of twenty-seven when he said, 'the creature is nothing, and God is all'; and he delighted in it the longer he lived. The text is 1 Corinthians 10:31: 'Whatsoever ye do, do all to the glory of God.' To exalt man is to disown the purpose of God that 'no flesh should glory in his presence'. All good is given to believers—all grace, all revival, all redemption, all eternity—that we might be abased and find our all in God. Whatever the hardships, the persecution or the disappointments in things temporal, the church's brightest and happiest days are those in which she is learning to sing, 'Not unto us, O Lord, not unto us, but unto thy name give glory' (*Psa.* 115:1), for this is God's preparation for the world where all will say,

> Blessing, and glory, and wisdom, and thanksgiving, and honour, and power, and might, be unto our God for ever and ever. Amen (*Rev.* 7:12).

[76] *Works* (Yale), vol. 16, p. 110. 'What a vain, and vile helpless creature I am.' The words 'vain' and 'vile' had not then hardened into our contemporary meanings.

2

GEORGE WHITEFIELD AND CHRISTIAN UNITY

George Whitefield (1714–70)

When we confine the Spirit of God to this or that particular church; and are not willing to converse with any but those of the same communion; this is to be righteous over-much with a witness . . . The Spirit of God is the centre of unity; and wherever I see the image of my Master, I never enquire of them their opinions; I ask them not what they are, so they love Jesus Christ in sincerity and truth, but embrace him as my brother, my sister, and my spouse: and this is the spirit of Christianity. Many persons, who are bigots to this or that opinion, when one of a different way of thinking hath come where they were, have left the room or place on that account: this is the spirit of the devil. Christianity will never flourish till we are all of one heart and one mind.

This may be esteemed as enthusiasm and madness, and a design to undermine the established church: No, God is my judge, I should rejoice to see all the world adhere to her Articles. I am a friend to her Articles, I am a friend to her Homilies, I am a friend to her Liturgy; and if they did not thrust me out of their churches, I would read them every day; but I do not confine the Spirit of God there; for I say again, I love all that love the Lord Jesus Christ . . . To be righteous over-much is to be uncharitable, censorious, and to persecute persons for differing from us in religion.

GEORGE WHITEFIELD, 'The Folly and Danger of Being Not Righteous Enough' (*Eccles*. 7:16), (*Works*, vol. 5, pp. 130–2).

There can be no understanding Whitefield's testimony to Christian unity without remembering something of the history that went before him, and what followed after. Living from 1714 to 1770, he stands between the churches of the seventeenth and the nineteenth centuries – centuries that contrast sharply on the subject before us.

The churches of the English-speaking world in the seventeenth century were often strong and rich in biblical truth, but in one area a wide difference grew up among them. They parted company over the question of how churches were to be organized, and out of that disagreement several denominations came to be established.

The most critical division came in 1662 when, on the Restoration of the Stuart monarchy, the Act of Uniformity permanently divided the Church of England from all the other Protestants who were thereafter to be known as 'Dissenters'. John Wesley's father typifies the strength of feeling between the two sides at the beginning of the eighteenth century. He wrote so furiously against the Dissenters that he was actually imprisoned for it.

By that date the Dissenters themselves were settling into Presbyterian, Congregationalist (Independent), and Baptist communions. Thus separated, they did their own work and, in the course of time, there was often little or no coming and going between them. As far as we know, such contemporaries as Richard Baxter and John Bunyan never met.

But to move on to the nineteenth century is to discover a significant change. While the denominations and their differences remain, a new, broader unity and fellowship has come into being; for evangelicals the old boundaries have been transcended. On both sides of the Atlantic, Christians now commonly work together; they aid one another in Missionary Societies; they share in evangelistic outreach; they support the same Bible and Tract Societies; they sing the same hymns. An age of evangelical unity had dawned, and it gave strength to the advance of the gospel across the world. How is this contrast with the seventeenth century to be explained? Whence came the change?

In part the explanation lies in the better recognition of a truth which Calvin had argued long before. He wrote:

> Not all the articles of true doctrines are of the same sort. Some are so necessary to know that they should be certain and unquestioned by all men as the proper principles of religion. Such are: God is one; Christ is God and the Son of God; our salvation rests in God's mercy, and the like. Among the churches are other articles of doctrine disputed which still do not break the unity of faith . . . Does this not sufficiently indicate that a difference of opinion over these non-essential matters should in no way be the basis of schism among Christians?[1]

[1] Calvin, *Institutes of the Christian Religion*, IV, 1:12, F. L. Battles trans., vol. 2 (Philadelphia: Westminster Press, 1960), p. 1026.

Yet what led to the new situation in the nineteenth century was not the writing of Calvin, nor the influence of any other author; it was a consequence of the Evangelical Revival. At the heart of the awakening that began on both sides of the Atlantic in the 1730s and 1740s was the renewed evidence that all who believe in the fundamental gospel truths, necessary for salvation, are one. So a new title came into general use: believers in these truths were 'evangelicals'.[2]

This brings us to our subject. If we ask whether any one person was especially responsible for this renewal of unity in the eighteenth century, the answer would have to be George Whitefield. Before proceeding, however, a note on terminology is necessary, for Whitefield commonly uses a word that has been hijacked and devalued today. For centuries Protestants, in the words of the Apostles' Creed, confessed their faith in 'the holy catholic church'. They did so without apology. For them 'catholic' was an honoured word, taken directly from the Greek and Latin and meaning 'universal', 'embracing all'. The Roman church, far from being catholic, was in schism from the true. She denied that wherever there is saving faith, there is a person who belongs to the body of Christ and to the family of God. 'Catholicity' is the feeling generated in every true believer; it is seen in a readiness to love and embrace all who belong to Jesus Christ. So the stronger the catholicity, the more evident will be the unity. Few Christians in modern times have understood this, and demonstrated its attractiveness, as much as Whitefield. It was his teaching and example that prepared the way for the great era of evangelical co-operation after his death.

[2] It is true that the name, and its equivalent 'gospellers', was used in the sixteenth century, but it did not then become established as a descriptive term.

Whitefield's Life

Born in Gloucester, in the west of England, Whitefield went up to Oxford in 1732 at the age of seventeen. There, helped by fellow students Charles and John Wesley, he experienced conviction of sin and came to a saving knowledge of Christ. Ordained to the ministry of the Church of England, at the age of twenty-two he astonished churches in London by preaching on the new birth.

The parish churches generally at this date were sunk in nominal formal religion. The only regeneration of which churchgoers had heard was the one they supposed they had received at their baptism. Two years later, when Whitefield fully understood all the main doctrines of the Protestant Faith, opposition to his condemnation of works as a means of our justification became so intense that churches of his own denomination were shut against him and he was forced to preach in the open air. It was then, in 1739, that an awakening began that affected all kinds of people.

Division and controversy followed. There were many opponents within the Church of England who took the view that what was happening could all be explained on the natural level: it was no revival of true Christianity but merely the result of Whitefield's personality and eccentricities. The same explanation is offered today.[3] But the problem with it is that Whitefield's preaching was accompanied by effects similar to those produced by the preaching of the apostolic age. Can personality and oratory produce conviction of sin and

[3] Basically the same explanation can be found today in books such as Harry S. Stout's *The Divine Dramatist: George Whitefield and the Rise of Modern Evangelicalism* (Grand Rapids: Eerdmans, 1991) and Frank Lambert's *Inventing the Great Awakening* (Princeton University Press, 1999), where the viewpoint is essentially that of Whitefield's opponents.

bring moral change to the lives of thousands? Can it reverse the priorities that control human nature? This is precisely what happened to multitudes, from Lady Betty Hastings and Selina, Countess of Huntingdon, among the aristocracy in England, to the hundreds of unnamed Bristol coal miners whose tears moved the grime on their faces. The only explanation that fits the facts is the same one that explains the preaching of the apostle Peter on the day of Pentecost: God intervenes in history. Christ is risen from the dead! 'God has made that same Jesus, whom you crucified, both Lord and Christ.'

Two things stand out as evidence of the supernatural in the life of Whitefield. First, the manner in which events unfolded so unexpectedly in the course of his career. They were not the results of his own planning. He set out to be a missionary in the new colony of Georgia. When there the destitution among children appalled him and he became burdened with the need for an orphanage. That led to the necessity of raising funds and, as there was no money available in the youngest of Britain's American colonies, he came back to England for help; then to Pennsylvania, New Jersey and New England for the same reason in 1740. His purpose was to raise aid for an orphanage, but God had a greater purpose in view. The gospel was to be recovered for nations and God had prepared Whitefield to preach it. While the orphanage was built, it fell into the background as the Evangelical Revival dawned. Thus Whitefield was constrained to become an itinerant evangelist on both sides of the Atlantic. He came to have the oversight of two churches in London, but the wider needs led him to labour for a much larger harvest. He preached in all parts of the British Isles, and thirteen times crossed the Atlantic, preaching through America, from Boston to Georgia. His life was another demonstration of the truth of Jeremiah's words, 'O LORD, I know that the way of man is not in himself: it is not in man that walketh to direct his steps' (*Jer.* 10:23).

There is a second evidence that Whitefield was sent by God. Personality and natural gifts might account for a temporary excitement; but such things cannot explain how his whole life saw a continuance of what began in 1738–9.

I cannot sketch that life here, but let us go on to the year 1770, when he was aged fifty-five. Although dying of asthma, his motto was still, 'No nestling, no flagging, this side of eternity', and he was still practising it. From New York on July 29, 1770, he writes to Robert Keen, a friend in London:

> Since my last, and during this month, I have been above a five hundred miles circuit, and have been enabled to preach and travel through the heat of the day. The congregations have been very large, attentive and affected . . . O what a scene of usefulness is opening in various parts of this new world! All fresh work where I have been. The divine influence hath been as at the first.[4]

On September 23, 1770, he is in Portsmouth, New England and writes his last known letter. Again it is to Keen. He had been ill, he tells him, but 'by riding sixty miles, I am better, and hope to preach here tomorrow. I trust my blessed Master will accept of these poor efforts to serve him. O for a warm heart; O to stand fast in the faith!'[5]

[4] *Works of George Whitefield* (London: Dilly, 1771–2), vol. 3, pp. 424–5.

[5] Ibid, p. 427.

A few days later Whitefield preached at Exeter. Although church buildings were open for his use they could not begin to accommodate the immense multitudes and for the last time the evangelist stood on top of a barrel in the open air. The text was, 'Examine yourselves, whether ye be in the faith.' It was the old message. 'Works! works!' he cried, 'a man get to heaven by works! I would as soon think of climbing to the moon on a rope of sand!' As he drew to a conclusion there were words long to be remembered:

> I go to a rest prepared; my sun has arisen . . . It is now about to set for – no, it is about to rise to the zenith of immortal glory. I shall soon be in a world where time, age, pain, and sorrow are unknown. My body fails, my spirit expands. How willingly would I live for ever to preach Christ! But I die to be *with* him.

To universal mourning the man whom Toplady described as 'the apostle of the English empire' died the next morning, Sunday, September 30, at 6 o'clock. When the news spread, funeral sermons were preached on both sides of the Atlantic.

Dr Ebenezer Pemberton of New York said of him, 'Perhaps no man, since the apostolic age, preached oftener, or with greater success.'[6] John Newton, who heard Whitefield often, declared: 'If anyone were to ask me who was the second preacher I ever heard, I should be at some loss to answer; but, in regard to the first, Mr Whitefield exceeded so far every other man of my time, that I should be at none.'[7]

[6] L. Tyerman, *Life of George Whitefield*, vol. 2 (London: Hodder and Stoughton, 1877), p. 623.

[7] A. C. H. Seymour, *Life and Times of the Countess of Huntingdon* (London: Painter, 1844), vol. 1. p. 92.

Perhaps the finest funeral testimony came from John Wesley who asked, 'Have we read or heard of any person since the Apostles, who testified the gospel of the grace of God through so widely extended a space, through so large a part of the habitable world? Above all, have we read or heard of any, who has been a blessed instrument in his hand of bringing so many sinners from "darkness to light, and from the power of Satan unto God"?'[8]

Identifying True Catholicity

If catholicity is an idea that tends to have near universal approval, it is, in part, because people attach different meanings to the word. There is such a thing as a false, anti-biblical catholicity. What then did Whitefield regard as the marks of true catholicity? First the negatives:

1. *Catholicity does not mean treating Christian doctrine as a matter of indifference, or as something altogether secondary.* There have been many who have believed this. They say that Christian unity is a matter of life and experience, not belief. If the heart is right, if there is devotion to Christ, then they think there need be no disputing over doctrinal questions. That is not what Whitefield meant by catholicity. He believed that the Holy Spirit glorifies Christ by giving sinners 'the love of the truth, that they might be saved' (2 *Thess.* 2:10). Abiding in, and confessing, the teaching of Christ is a necessary part of salvation (*Mark* 8:38, 2 *John* 9). Just as there is one Lord, so there is 'one faith'. Believers are people who have been taught by the Spirit of truth, and together they embrace those foundational truths that are necessary to

[8] 'On the Death of George Whitefield', John Wesley, *Sermons on Several Occasions* (London: Kershaw, 1825), vol. 1, p. 676.

salvation. Accordingly Whitefield, preaching on the conversion of Zacchæus from the text, 'Zacchæus stood, and said . . . Behold, Lord . . .', could say:

> It is remarkable, how readily people in Scripture have owned the deity of Christ immediately upon their conversion. Thus the woman at Jacob's well; 'Is not this the Christ?' Thus the man born blind; 'Lord, I believe; and worshipped him.' Thus Zacchæus, 'Behold, Lord.' An incontestable proof this to me, that those who deny our Lord's divinity, never effectually felt his power.[9]

There are truths which are a question of life or death, and for these Whitefield believed that every Christian has a duty to contend. The statement of a recent writer about Whitefield who said, 'Throughout, he showed no interest in theology', is absurd.[10] If catholicity meant indifference to doctrine there would never have been the Evangelical Revival and the Great Awakening. It was definite beliefs that turned the world upside down in the apostolic age and it was when these beliefs were recovered in the eighteenth century that something similar occurred. 'Many of the clergy', Whitefield said, 'deny us the use of the pulpits, for no other reason but because we preach the doctrine of justification in the sight of God *by faith alone.*'[11]

But something more must be said on this point. Because Whitefield, like Calvin, believed that fundamental truths can be distinguished from other truths, he did not think that therefore catholicity requires that there should never be controversy among Christians on those other truths. Though

[9] Whitefield, *Sermons on Important Subjects* (London: Baynes, 1825), p. 363.

[10] Stout, *Divine Dramatist*, p. 39.

[11] Whitefield, *Six Sermons* (London: Strahan, 1750), p. 52.

there will be differences in the understanding of non-fundamental truths, they are not to be treated as mere 'opinions'. Christians must have a conscientious regard for *all* that Scripture reveals.[12] So while Whitefield had no doubt at all that John Wesley was an eminent Christian, when his friend began to defend Arminian teaching on 'free will' and universal redemption, Whitefield opposed it. Though the friendship was not ended, the disagreement was so definite that the two men were not often able to work together after 1740. The same is true of Whitefield and Moravianism. Moravians were often earnest Christians, but when their leader, Count Zinzendorf, erred and truth was in danger, Whitefield publicly wrote to defend it.

2. *Catholicity does not mean that we must treat everyone who professes to be a Christian as a real Christian.* Too often that idea has held sway. It is said that love requires us to accept people for what they say they are, and that it is narrow and uncharitable to do anything else. Just at this point lay the fundamental difference between Whitefield, Wesley and other evangelicals on the one hand, and most of the clergy on the other. It was an age when most people nominally belonged to the Church of England, and yet the influence of the church upon moral and social life was very feeble. How was this to be explained? The popular diagnosis was very different from that of Whitefield and Wesley. It was that the churchgoers were weak, deficient Christians. The evangelical leaders, on the contrary, preached that great numbers

[12] C. H. Spurgeon was following this principle when he was accused of disturbing the unity of the Evangelical Alliance by his sermon against Baptismal Regeneration. See *C. H. Spurgeon: Autobiography*, vol. 2, *The Full Harvest* (Edinburgh: Banner of Truth, 1973), p. 57.

of these churchgoers were not Christians at all. More than that, the fault lay with many of the clergy themselves. They did not preach the gospel, and if congregations were not hearing the gospel it was no wonder there should be so many unbelievers in the churches: 'Many deceivers are gone abroad into the world. Mere heathen morality, and not Jesus Christ is preached in most of our churches.'[13] Whitefield swept aside any idea that baptism made a person a Christian, and his sermons are full of discriminating marks of what constitutes a real Christian. The first work of an evangelist, he believed, was to speak like John the Baptist and to shake the refuge of lies in which the nominal Christian tries to hide.

In speaking in this way, in the zeal of youth, Whitefield may have gone too far at times, but his basic principle was sound: a Christian is someone who has recognized what he is by nature, who has repented, and whose life gives evidence that he belongs to Christ and lives for Christ. The truth, he used to say, is that 'Christ is all, or he is worth nothing'.

3. *Catholicity does not mean that church/denominational attachments can be held very loosely.* Whitefield has been accused of this. It has been said that he was indifferent to matters of church government,[14] or that he had an 'individualistic understanding' of Christianity. I do not believe the accusations are true. Certainly he attacked 'churchianity', but that was not because he was against the Church of England, or any other Protestant Church; it was because, too often, the existing state of these Churches was not what their creed

[13] *Sermons on Important Subjects*, p. 243.

[14] 'Whitefield had no patience with ecclesiastical polity,' J. B. Wakeley, *Anecdotes of George Whitefield* (London: Hodder and Stoughton, 1879), p. 46. The statement, often repeated, is only true of times when church order came into collision with the gospel.

professed. Bishop Ryle's statement that Whitefield loved the Church of England is true. There was much in her constitution and history that he praised, and he spoke similarly about the Presbyterian Church of Scotland. It is true he said very little about such things as church order and government. The reason was not, however, that he belittled the subject. It was because he believed that the primary need of the hour was much more serious. That brings me to the positive side of the definition of catholicity.

1. *Catholicity lies in a spirit focused on Christ and the gospel.* God has given only one message by which we may come to peace with him – one way only from condemnation to life – and it all centres in Jesus Christ. In the apostolic age it is Christ who is constantly uppermost in the lives of the disciples. If they are persecuted, it is their joy that they are 'counted worthy to suffer shame for his name'. If they are at liberty, we read, 'Daily in the temple, and in every house, they ceased not to teach and preach Jesus Christ' (*Acts* 5:42). The gospel is the message of how God, in incomparable love, offers sinners everything they need in his Son. Through Jesus, men and women under condemnation who receive him are declared righteous and begin to be conformed to his likeness. Nothing else can be of equal importance. No other truths have this saving power. And as Christ is exalted we may expect the message to be attested by larger measures of the Holy Spirit's power. That, Whitefield constantly asserted, is where the great need lies:

> It is a want of more of this, that now at present disunites us. I despair therefore of a greater union, till a greater measure of the Spirit be poured from on high. Hence, therefore, I

am resolved simply to preach the gospel of Christ, and leave others to quarrel by and with themselves.[15]

Whitefield used the word 'methodist', not in any denominational sense, but to describe persons we would today call 'evangelicals'. They are marked, he says, by one common purpose:

> To awaken a drowsy world . . . and put them upon seeking after a present and great salvation, to point out to them a glorious rest, which not only remains for the people of God hereafter, but which, by living faith, the very chief of sinners may enter into even here, and without which the most blazing profession is nothing worth, is, as far as I know, the *one thing*, the grand and common point, in which all the Methodists endeavour to centre.[16]

To be a real Christian is incomparably more important than any mere denominational difference or distinction. It means a present deliverance, condemnation ended, the indwelling of God in our hearts, the prospect of full likeness to Jesus Christ. Wherever this is believed, and kept uppermost, a catholic spirit is going to be found.

2. *Catholicity means that loyalty to the gospel will always take precedence over loyalty to my denomination.* As I have already said, this does not mean that loyalty to one's denomination is a little thing. It is not, and Whitefield did not think it was. But he believed that for many professing Christians denominations held too high a place: 'Most talk of a catholic spirit; but it is only till they have brought people into the pale of their own church. This is downright sectarianism, not

[15] *Works,* vol. 1, p. 376.

[16] John Gillies, *Memoirs of George Whitefield*, revised by John Jones (London: Williams, 1811), p. lx.

catholicism.'[17] He believed that there may well be times when the peace and unity of a denomination have to give way to a prior loyalty to the gospel. This was the challenge he and others faced in the eighteenth century. Evangelicals were often confronted with a painful choice. They were told that to be loyal to their denomination they must accept the *status quo* and not disagree with tradition, with their superiors, or with church courts. Had they agreed, there would have been no Evangelical Revival.

How Whitefield Learned Catholicity

1. *It was the result of his rebirth.*

In one of his earliest sermons Whitefield quotes the apostle John to prove that a mark of the new birth is the special love that a believer has for all believers: 'We know that we have passed from death unto life, because we love the brethren.' 'Where a person is truly in Christ, all narrowness of spirit decreases in him daily.' This, he says, 'the primitive Christians were so renowned for, that it became a proverb, "See how these Christians love one another." . . . Further, this love is not confined to any particular set of men, but is impartial and catholic: A love that embraces God's image wherever it beholds it, and delights in nothing so much as to see Christ's kingdom come.'[18]

Even so, the recovery of Christian catholicity was far from easy in the eighteenth century. As I have said, the divide between the Church of England and the 'Dissenters', was a great one. 'The Jews had no dealings with the Samaritans' , and neither did the people of 'the Church' with the

[17] *Works*, vol. 1, p. 372.

[18] *Works*, vol. 6, p. 168.

chapel-goers. As a youth Whitefield had never worshipped in a Dissenting church; at Oxford none of his friends was a Dissenter, for by law none was allowed into the university. His upbringing and education were all against catholicity. There was prejudice on the Dissenting side also. The first reference to Dissenters in Whitefield's *Journals* occurs after the publication in 1737 (when he was twenty-two) of his sermon on *The Nature and Necessity of Our Regeneration or New Birth*. He notes: 'The Dissenters, I found, were surprised to see a sermon on such a subject from a clergyman of the Church of England; and finding the author came from Oxford, were ready to say, "Can any good thing come out of Nazareth?"' Whitefield would soon be criticized by Church of England men for having conversations with Dissenters. When he reached Gibraltar on his way to Georgia later that year, he found a 'Society of the Scotch Church' – all Presbyterians, who had no dealings with the Church of England. At first, he says, 'I did not think it agreeable to visit them,' but as he had contact with individuals from among them he was impressed:

> I exhorted them to love and unity, and not to let a little difference about a few externals occasion any narrow-spiritedness to arise in their hearts. I advised them to come and hear me expound in the church, which they did; and providentially the Lesson was on the 4th of Ephesians, from whence I took occasion to urge on them the necessity of loving one another with a catholic disinterested love, to be of one heart and one mind.

The outcome was that 'God gave blessing to what was said,' for the Scotch Society joined harmoniously with another Society of evangelical Englishmen.

When this experience of Whitefield's at Gibraltar was published in his *Journal*, a Welshman wrote to thank him for his ministry and said: 'I observed that your affections clave to the Scotch Society at Gibraltar, though of different sentiments in religion with those of the Established [Church].' It was, he went on, 'a *rara avis* [rare bird] indeed that can be in love with the divine stamp in whomsoever he beholds it . . . whose faith breaks forth and worketh in love to all the saints, though of different denominations.'[19] Whitefield's first biographer, John Gillies, says that he was 'early convinced of the great hurt that was being done to Christianity by a bigoted spirit'.[20] In 1739, when he was only twenty-four years of age, we find him writing, 'I long to see a catholic spirit over-spread the world; may God vouchsafe to make me an instrument in promoting it.'[21]

2. *The evidence of his reading strengthened Whitefield in catholicity.*

The first evangelical book that Whitefield ever read was by the Scotsman, Henry Scougal, who had lived in the previous century. Scougal, who was probably Episcopalian in his sympathies, was therefore acceptable in Oxford. But other books soon came into his hands that were not by Episcopalians or Church of England men. Chief among these books were the commentaries of the Puritan and Dissenter Matthew Henry (who died in the year of Whitefield's birth), and the *Life of Thomas Halyburton*, a Scottish Presbyterian. White-

[19] Thomas Jones to Whitefield, 25 April 1739, in *George Whitefield and Friends: The Correspondence of Some Early Methodists*, ed. Graham C. G. Thomas, *The National Library of Wales Journal*, 1991–2, pp. 296–7.

[20] John Gillies, *Memoirs of George Whitefield* (London: Dilly, 1772), p. 286. Herafter cited as 'Gillies'.

[21] *Works*, vol. 1, p. 66.

field was soon committed to the value of the whole school of Puritan authors. To appreciate the significance of this one has to understand the odium in which Puritan authors were commonly held at this date. Even John Wesley shared in the dislike in which they were held and did not start to read them seriously until several years later. Proof of this comes to light in the correspondence between Wesley and Whitefield over the doctrines of grace in 1740. Wesley believed that his younger friend was being misled by the Dissenters, and told him that 'no Baptist or Presbyterian writer' he had read, 'knew anything of the liberties of Christ'. The fact was that Wesley did not know these authors and Whitefield was right to reply: 'What! neither Bunyan, Henry, Flavel, Halyburton, not any of the New England and Scots divines. See, dear Sir, what narrow spiritedness and want of charity arise from your principles, and then do not cry out against election any more on account of its being "destructive of meekness and love".'[22]

3. *An unhappy division in Scotland increased Whitefield's commitment to catholicity.*

I must take more time on this point as it illustrates the whole subject in a memorable way. In the 1730s, when the Evangelical Revival began in England, something significant was also happening in Scotland. A group of evangelical ministers, protesting against abuses in the Church of Scotland,

[22] *George Whitefield's Journals*, (repr. Banner of Truth: London, 1960), p. 583. Long after this, Whitefield was still being blamed by Thomas Olivers, Wesley's assistant, for being 'strongly prejudiced in favour of the Dissenters . . . I myself have heard him speak, perhaps on forty occasions, with great partiality, of our English Dissenters in general – particularly of the Puritans of old, and also of our modern Presbyterians, Independents, and Baptists' (*Rod for a Reviler*, 1777, p. 22), quoted in L. Tyerman, *George Whitefield*, vol. 1, p. 395.

were deposed by that denomination, and so they continued their preaching apart, under the name of the 'Associate Presbytery'. This was the beginning of a new Presbyterian denomination later to be known as the Secession Church. Two brothers, Ralph and Ebenezer Erskine, were the main leaders. Ralph Erskine invited Whitefield to Scotland, and when he came in 1741 there was much discussion in the Associate Presbytery on what should be required of him. Their motive was honourable. Speaking of Ralph Erskine, the historian of the Secession Church wrote: 'He conceived that he, and those who were associated with him in the [Associate] Presbytery, were engaged in carrying forward a great public cause, – a cause which, in their estimation, deeply involved in it the glory of God, and the best interests of the human race. In giving support to this cause, they had, by an unrighteous sentence, been deprived of their livings; had been branded as trouble-makers of the peace of Zion; and had encountered no small reproach.'[23]

Whitefield met with the Erskines and other ministers of the Associate Presbytery at Stirling on the first Wednesday of August, 1741. They welcomed him, but then discussion turned to controversial matters. First, he was asked whether he accepted that Presbyterian church government was the scriptural pattern, and that it 'excluded a toleration of those who might not have the same views, such as independents, Anabaptists, and Episcopalians, among whom there are good men'.[24] When Whitefield replied that he did not have light to receive this, he was asked, he said, 'to preach only for them until I had further light'. Reporting this, Whitefield wrote:

[23] John McKerrow, *History of the Secession Church* (Edinburgh: Fullarton, 1848), pp. 153–4.

[24] Ibid., p. 157.

'I asked, why only for them? Mr Ralph Erskine said, "They were the Lord's people." I then asked, whether there were no other Lord's people but themselves; and supposing all others were the devil's people, they certainly had more need to be preached to.'[25] Writing later of this episode, Whitefield said of their discussion:

> I thought their foundation too narrow for any high house to be built upon . . . At the same time they knew very well, I was not against all church government, (for how can a church subsist without it?) I only urged, as I do now, that, since holy men differ so much about the outward form, we should bear with and forbear one another, though in this respect we are not of one mind. I have often declared, in the most public manner, that I believe the Church of Scotland to be the best constituted national church in the world. At the same time I would bear with, and converse freely with all others, who do not err in fundamentals, and who give evidence that they are lovers of the Lord Jesus. That is what I mean by a Catholic spirit.[26]

The consequence was that, after that meeting in Stirling, Whitefield never preached for the Seceders. But worse was to follow. The next year saw, in the opinion of John Gillies, 'such a time for the revival of religion as had never before been seen in Scotland'.[27] At Cambuslang and many other places there were large numbers of well-documented conversions. These were connected with pulpits of the Church

[25] *Works*, vol. 1, p. 308. Preaching in August 1740, when this controversy was not in the air, Ralph Erskine had said, 'We are far from thinking that all are Christ's friends that join with us, and that all are his enemies that do not. No, indeed!' Quoted in Arthur Fawcett, *The Cambuslang Revival: The Scottish Evangelical Revival of the Eighteenth Century* (London: Banner of Truth, 1971), p. 184.

[26] Gillies, p. 121.

[27] Ibid., p. 118.

of Scotland, and commonly with the preaching of George Whitefield who returned to Scotland in 1742. The Associate Presbytery denounced the whole revival as a work of the devil. In Whitefield's words:

> Taking it for granted, that all converted persons must take the Covenant, and that God had left the Scotch established churches long ago, and that he would never work by the hands of a curate of the church of *England*, they condemned the whole work as the work of the devil; and kept a fast throughout *Scotland*, to humble themselves, because the devil was come down in great wrath, and to pray that the Lord would rebuke the destroyer (for that was my title).[28]

This was a sad mistake made by good men. They missed blessing that others received. It weakened their cause for a number of years to come, and it was not until a different spirit began to prevail in the Secession churches that their influence for good multiplied. At that later date none justified what had been said in 1741–2. The biographer of Ebenezer Erskine, writing in 1831, said that the former criticisms of Whitefield were now 'almost universally regarded with feelings of sincere regret'.[29] Similarly the historian of the Secession Church goes as far as writing of Whitefield in 1848, 'Few men have ever appeared in any church that were more honoured of God in the conversion of sinners than he was.'[30] Long before these

[28] Ibid., p. 121. 'The Covenant' here means the Solemn League and Covenant of 1643, a religious and political agreement between England and Scotland which some Presbyterians considered binding on later generations.

[29] Donald Fraser, *Life and Diary of Ebenezer Erskine* (Edinburgh: Oliphant, 1831), p. 429.

[30] *History of the Secession Church*, p. 169. There is some difference in the accounts given of the disagreement at Stirling by McKerrow and Whitefield, and the former disputes the latter's accuracy. But Whitefield's letters, in which he reports the conversations, were written at the time, whereas McKerrow's account was compiled many years later. Yet there is an overall agreement in the two accounts. By way of

dates Whitefield had himself buried the controversy and in one of his last sermons in London he quoted as an example of Christian dying, the last words of Ralph Erskine, 'Victory, victory, victory!'[31]

4. *The providence of God in Whitefield's widespread travels played an important part in his learning of catholicity.*

Whitefield was one of the most widely travelled men of the eighteenth century. He was in almost all parts of the British Isles and he journeyed through all thirteen American colonies on horseback. Such journeys in his day were no matter of pleasure. His motive was to pursue evangelistic opportunities; but we can surely see that God also had another purpose. Repeatedly, far and wide, Whitefield saw the evidence that true Christian experience transcends lesser differences among believers. Catholicity for him, far from being a matter of theory, was as real as his everyday life. He was at home with Dissenters in Wales; he preached in Baptist chapels and praised John Bunyan's writings; he valued the fellowship of Congregationalists in America as much as he did that of the Presbyterians in Virginia.

Wherever he preached, no one suspected him of wanting to strengthen denominational distinctions. 'I will preach,' he would say, 'wherever God gives me opportunity, but you will never find me disputing about the outward appendages

apology for the Associate Presbytery, McKerrow says: 'Their conduct, in refusing to hold Christian or ministerial communion with Mr Whitefield, on the ground of a diversity of opinion about church government, was quite consistent with their avowed principles' (Ibid., p. 159). In other words church government took priority over catholicity, indeed over what the Westminster Confession (Chapter 27) teaches, 'Of Communion of Saints'.

[31] *Sermons on Important Subjects*, p. 711.

of religion; do not tell me you are a Baptist, an Independent, a Presbyterian, a Dissenter, tell me you are a Christian: this is the religion of heaven and must be ours upon earth.'[32]

How is the Failure of Catholicity Among Christians to Be Explained?

Whitefield gave much thought to this, and we need his help here.

1. *Catholicity fails because fallen human nature is universally prone to prejudice, ignorance and the adoption of wrong principles.*

From this tendency no Christian is yet perfectly delivered. We have noted an illustration of this in the action of the seceding Scots Presbyterians in 1741–2 but the mistake was by no means unique to them. From Maryland, Whitefield wrote in 1740, 'Here is a close opposition from some of the Presbyterian clergy.'[33] And on the same grounds there were numbers in the Church of England who could not believe that the Holy Spirit could bless a ministry that did not follow all the traditions of their denomination. Whitefield refers to those who would confine 'the power and Spirit of God within the bounds of *human establishments*'. He adds, 'But blessed be God, there are some few amongst us that are men of greater latitude, who can think, and dare speak, more worthily of God's sovereignty, and acknowledge a work to be his, though it be not according to the exact measure of *canonical fitness*.'[34]

[32] 'Spiritual Baptism', in *Sermons on Important Subjects*, p. 684.

[33] *Works*, vol. 1, p. 225.

[34] *Works*, vol. 4, pp. 248–9.

All Christians are prone to mistakes about their party, and 'offences and divisions about some *non-essentials*' will always be liable to arise. 'It must needs be, that such offences come, whilst good men carry about with them the remainders of indwelling sin, prejudices of education, blindness in their understandings. . . . The blessed Jesus wisely permits such things, to cure us of spiritual pride, to remind us of the necessity of looking to himself, to teach us to cease from man, by convincing us, that the best of men are men at best, to inure us to longsuffering and forbearance towards another, to excite us for a more eager desire for heaven, where these disorders will be at an end.'[35]

2. *Catholicity fails because 'church' in the sense of denominational organization is identified with the body of Christ.*

This is an old error. It was because of this belief that the Roman Catholic Church, at the time of the Reformation, accused Protestants of schism. In the New Testament it is real Christians who are the 'church'. External association with others did not make them so, but union with Christ and the indwelling of the Holy Spirit. If that is true, then differences over the outward form of a congregation's life are not differences that break the reality of Christian unity. Listen to Whitefield debating this point with the Rev. Dr Timothy Cutler, Rector of Christ Church, Boston and the Church of England Commissary in that city. Cutler approved of John Wesley's position when he had visited Boston, saying, 'He was very strenuous for the Church [of England], and rigorously against all other forms of government.'

'I answered,' said Whitefield, 'He was then a great bigot, but God has since enlarged his heart . . . I then urged that

[35] Ibid., pp. 247–8.

a catholic spirit was best, and that a Baptist minister had communicated lately with me at Savannah [the reference, of course, being to their sharing in the Lord's Supper]. "I suppose," said another, "you would do him as good a turn, and would communicate with him." I answered, "Yes," and urged "that it was best to preach the new birth, and the power of godliness, and not to insist so much on the form: for people would never be brought to one mind as to that; nor did Jesus Christ ever intend it."

'"Yes, but He did," said Dr Cutler. "How do you prove it?" "Because Christ prayed, 'That all might be one, even as Thou, Father, and I are One." I replied, "That was spoken of the inward union of the souls of believers with Jesus Christ, and not of the outward Church." "That cannot be," said Dr Cutler, "for how then could it be said, 'that the world might know that Thou hast sent Me?'" He . . . taking it for granted that the Church of England was the only true apostolical Church.'[36]

For Whitefield this was the great divide. Was Christ praying in John 17 for an outward, organizational unity of his disciples, and therefore one that must still be considered to lie in the future? Or, is this union *already* a spiritual reality? An evangelical, Whitefield believed, must assert the latter. Christ's prayer has not failed. Every repentant, believing individual belongs to the church. There is a present union with Christ and it is Christ's indwelling in his people that constitutes the unity that speaks to the world. So external organization is no part of the essence of the church. Often in history the true church has survived and multiplied without it.

[36] *Journals*, pp. 457–8.

Where this is not understood narrowness and bigotry are almost bound to prevail. It was a better understanding of the true nature of the church that prepared the way for the strong catholicity of nineteenth-century evangelicalism. When the Sixth General Conference of the Evangelical Alliance was held in New York in 1873 much time was given to demonstrating the same view of the church as Whitefield had sought to see recovered.[37] It was Bishop Ryle's testimony in Britain. All believers in Christ, he wrote, are

> the only Church which possesses true *unity*. Its members are entirely agreed on all the weightier matters of religion, for they are all taught by one Spirit. About God, and Christ, and the Spirit, and sin, and their own hearts, and faith, and repentance, and the necessity of holiness, and the value of the Bible, and the importance of prayer, and the resurrection, and judgment to come, – about all these points they see eye to eye. Take three or four of them, strangers to one another, from the remotest corners of the earth. Examine them separately on these points. You will find them all of one mind.[38]

3. *Catholicity fails because it encounters constant opposition from the powers of darkness.*

For Whitefield one of the greatest proofs of the importance of love between Christians is the manner in which the devil works against it. He does this by intruding unbelievers into the churches to create division. Speaking of opposition from professing Christians, Whitefield writes, 'The seed of

[37] See the addresses on 'Christian Union' in *History, Essays, Orations, and Other Documents of the Sixth General Conference of the Evangelical Alliance*, eds. Philip Schaff and S. I. Prime (New York, Harper, 1874).

[38] J. C. Ryle, *Knots Untied* (London: Hunt, 1874), p. 261.

the serpent is the same in all, of whatever communion.'[39] But true believers can themselves become unwittingly involved in doing the devil's work. If our indwelling sin is not mortified it will certainly be used by him as fuel to weaken catholicity among brethren; pride will lead us to exaggerate the faults of others; selfishness will make us party-minded; cold orthodoxy will make us contentious. 'If ye have bitter envying and strife in your hearts, glory not, and lie not against the truth. This wisdom descendeth not from above, but is earthly, sensual, devilish' (*James* 3:14–15). If we have such an adversary, Whitefield urged, we have need to be constantly on our guard against his devices. 'Good men,' he writes, 'have an artful enemy always near at hand, and always ready to blow up the coals of contention, in order to raise a smoke, whereby he may blacken or blemish the work of God.'[40] 'What infinite mischief have needless divisions occasioned in the Christian world! *Divide et impera* [divide and rule], is the Devil's motto.'[41] He would quote as a prayer the verse

> O may we find the ancient way
> Our wond'ring foes to move,
> And force the heathen world to say,
> See how these Christians love!

Evidence of Catholicity in Whitefield

It is possible for us all to teach with our words what we may deny by our example. In Whitefield's case, I believe it can be said, it was the catholicity of his example that did such immense good.

[39] *Works*, vol. 1, p. 225.
[40] *Works*, vol. 4, pp. 247–8.
[41] *Journals*, p. 133.

He showed it first by humility. What he criticized in others he condemned in himself. He never thought of himself as a model for others. There were occasions when he was criticized when he publicly acknowledged his fault. Referring to what he once wrote about Archbishop Tillotson, he said, 'I condemn myself most heartily, and ask pardon for it.' There was an element of the head-strong and of wild-fire in his early Journals for which he similarly expressed regret. Whitefield's life was one of deepening humility. On his fortieth birthday he wrote: 'I am now forty years of age, and would business permit, I would gladly spend the day in retirement and humiliation before that Jesus for whom I have done so little.'[42] Twelve years later, and just four years before his death, he wrote after another birthday: 'Fy upon me, fy upon me, fifty-two years old last Saturday; and yet, O loving, ever-loving, altogether lovely Jesus, how little, yea how very little have I done and suffered for thee! Tomorrow, God willing, I intend to take the sacrament upon it, that I will begin to begin to be a Christian.'[43]

Whitefield's attitude to John Wesley was a true example of catholicity. I have already said that they were seldom able to work together after 1740 on account of the older man's Arminian convictions. Yet Whitefield esteemed him, publicly acknowledged him as better than himself, and sought to maintain a personal friendship. Had he ever met a later generation of Calvinists who doubted whether Wesley was a regenerate man, he would have been deeply shocked. To a Calvinist Presbyterian whom Whitefield believed 'breathed much of a sectarian spirit', he wrote in 1742:

[42] *Works*, vol. 3, p. 111.

[43] Ibid, p. 343.

> Though I am a strenuous defender of the righteousness of Christ, and utterly detest Arminian principles, yet I know that God gave me the Holy Ghost, before I was clear in either, as to head-knowledge: and therefore, dear Sir, I am the more moderate to people who are not clear, supposing I see the divine image stamped upon their hearts. Mr Wesley, Mr Law, etc, I take to be holy men of God, though they think far widely from me. . . . I desire to act as God acts. I shall approve and join with all who are good in every sect, and cast a mantle of love over all that are bad, so far as is consistent with a good conscience. This I can do without temporising; nay, I should defile my conscience if I did otherwise.[44]

When there was a report that Wesley was dying in 1753, Whitefield wrote to him, with tears, 'I pity myself, and the church, but not you. A radiant throne awaits you, and ere long you will enter into your Master's joy.'[45] But Wesley did not die then and it was John Wesley, at Whitefield's request, who preached his funeral sermon. The last paragraph in Whitefield's will reads like this:

> I also leave a mourning ring to my honoured and dear friends and disinterested fellow-labourers, the Rev. Messrs. John and Charles Wesley, in token of my indissoluble union with them, in heart and Christian affection, notwithstanding our differences in judgment about some particular points of doctrine. – Grace be with all them, of whatever denomination, that love our Lord Jesus, our common Lord, in sincerity.[46]

In one of the last sermons Whitefield ever preached in London there is a final example of humility. He was about

[44] *Works*, vol. 1, p. 406.

[45] *Works*, vol. 3, p. 44.

[46] Whitefield's will is printed in John Jones' edition of Gillies, *Memoirs of Whitefield* (London: Williams, 1811), pp. lxi –lxiv.

to go back to Georgia and his heart was set on making the orphanage a college for students. To make such a change a great advantage would have been to have a charter, approved by the Archbishop of Canterbury. But, Whitefield told his hearers, the Archbishop would only give his sanction 'if I should confine it totally to the Church of England'. 'I would sooner cut my head off than betray my trust, by confining it to a narrow bottom', Whitefield declared. 'I always meant it should be kept upon a broad bottom, for people of all denominations, that their children might be brought up in the fear of God.'[47]

How Catholicity Is to Be Increased

1. *Let us see other believers first as Christians.*

A real conversion is not a conversion to a party, or to a church, but to Christ. And as Christ indwells all his people, we are to treat fellow Christians as we would treat Him. This is the rule that will apply in the day of judgment: 'Inasmuch as ye have done it unto one of the least of these my brethren, ye have done it unto me' (*Matt.* 25:40). Brotherly love is not something additional to love for Christ; it is the evidence of our being in Christ: 'If we love one another, God dwelleth in us' (*1 John* 4:12); 'Love one another as I have loved you' (*John* 13:34). Bigotry and narrowness find an entrance among us as Christians when we forget how much fellow believers mean to our Saviour. 'The blessed Jesus cares for his people of all denominations, He is gathering his elect out of all. Happy they, who, with a disinterested view, take in the whole church militant.'[48] 'A catholic spirit is the plague

[47] 'Jacob's Ladder, A Farewell Sermon,' *Sermons on Important Subjects*, p. 724.

[48] *Works*, vol. 2, p. 226.

of bigots,' was one of Whitefield's favourite sayings. Again: 'I wish all names among the saints of God were swallowed up in that one word *Christian.* I long for professors to leave off placing religion in saying, "I am a church man," "I am a dissenter." My language to such is, "Are you of Christ? If so, I love you with all my heart."'[49]

An example of how this should affect our language is that it is better not to designate fellow Christians by words which carry a derogatory sense, such as, 'He is an Arminian'. If it is necessary, let a man's opinions be described by such labels and not the man himself.[50]

2. *Let us desist as far as possible from controversies on secondary issues.*

It is not to be denied that such controversy is sometimes necessary, for the Bible does not reveal only truths essential for salvation. But who can doubt the need today for Whitefield's example? Our first business surely is to lead people to heaven, not to contend with brethren whose fundamental work is the same as our own.

There is no doubt that in the eighteenth century the devil threw controversies into the work of the gospel to distract the leaders from the inroads that were being made into his kingdom.

History would have been different if Whitefield had not been given the wisdom expressed in the following words when he was still a young man:

> Mr Wesley I think is wrong in some things, and Mr Law is

[49] Robert Philip, *The Life and Times of George Whitefield* (1837; repr. Edinburgh: Banner of Truth, 2007), p. 383.

[50] C. H. Spurgeon's practice changed in this regard between his early and later ministry. Pejorative labels, attached to persons, often engender more heat than light.

> wrong also; yet I believe that both Mr Law and Mr Wesley, and others, with whom we do not agree in all things, will shine bright in glory. It is best therefore for a gospel minister, simply and powerfully to preach those truths he has been taught of God, and to meddle as little as possible with those who are the children of God, though they should differ in many things. . . . I have not given way to the Moravian brethren, or Mr Wesley, or to any, whom I thought in an error, no not for an hour. But I think it best not to dispute, when there is no probability of convincing.[51]

The last sentence was a settled principle with Whitefield: 'To contend, where there is no probability of convincing, only feeds and adds fuel to an unhallowed fire.'[52] Is it not our danger to fall into this mistake? When faithful ministers come to die, they never regret that they gave too much time to prayer and to making Christ known, but they do often grieve over the amount of time given to lesser things. Controversies commonly distract us and rob us of greater achievements.

3. *Let us be sure to recognize our own failures in this grace.*

John Newton, who emulated Whitefield in this as in other respects, found reason to write: 'I find great cause to pray to the Lord for a candid spirit. Though I am apt sometimes to think highly of my Catholicism, I cannot but confess to much bigotry and spiritual pride remaining in me. Oh that my censures might be more directed to my own faults!'[53]

[51] *Works*, vol. 1, pp. 438–9.

[52] Ibid., p. 376.

[53] Josiah Bull, *The Life of John Newton* (1868; repr. Edinburgh: Banner of Truth, 2007), p. 72.

4. *Let us seek to keep the unity of heaven before us.*

It was common in the eighteenth century for men to have a seal with which to seal their letters, and these seals would often carry a short motto. On Whitefield's seal the inscription was, *Astra petamus,* 'Let us seek heaven.' He was profoundly influenced by the consciousness of the brevity of this present pilgrimage. Only the narrow stream of death separates every generation of Christians from the church in glory.

Ought we not then to be in preparation for glory, and aim to live in love like those who are already there? If we regard heaven as a world of universal love ought that belief not be more in evidence in our practice here? Should not what was said once of the Puritan Richard Sibbes be said of all Christians, 'Heaven was in him before he was in heaven'? It was on this note that Whitefield made one of his last appeals to his people in London before leaving them for the last time: 'If we be all going to one place, God, of his infinite mercy, keep us from falling out by the way.'[54]

Many years earlier, preaching from the balcony of the Court House in Philadelphia, he had stopped in a sermon and suddenly directed this question heavenwards:

> Father Abraham, whom have you in heaven? Any Episcopalians there? 'No.' Any Presbyterians? 'No.' Have you any Independents or Seceders? 'No.' Have you any Methodists there? 'No, no, no.' Whom have you there? 'We don't know those names here. All who are here are Christians – believers

[54] *Sermons on Important Subjects*, p. 705. When a woman in New England asked Whitefield whether he supported the position of Cotton Mather in what he had taught on qualifications for coming to the Lord's Table, or that of another equally eminent deceased minister, he replied: 'Good woman, I believe they have never talked about it since, for they will no more talk about such things.'

in Christ – men who have overcome by the blood of the Lamb and the word of his testimony.'[55]

5. *Let us seek closer fellowship with our Saviour, Jesus Christ.*

Without any doubt this was the first thing for Whitefield. For him catholicity was not a kind of duty that a Christian ought to add to his or her life; it was the inevitable consequence of being in the presence of Christ. The closer the attachment to Christ, the more his love is known, the more will be the overflow of catholicity. Above all else, Whitefield taught that Christianity is attachment to a Person.

It was said of him, 'He had such a sense of the incomparable excellence of the person of Christ.' An enlarged heart is what makes all the difference.[56] This is what made Whitefield the man and the preacher as attractive as he was. In his funeral sermon on Whitefield, John Wesley asked, 'What was the foundation of his life?' He answered: 'It was "the love of God shed abroad in his heart by the Holy Ghost that was given unto him," filling his soul with tender, disinterested love for every child of man. From this source arose that torrent of eloquence, which frequently bore down all before it; from this, that astonishing force of persuasion, which the most hardened sinners could not resist . . . Can anything but love beget love? This shone in his very countenance, and

[55] Wakeley, *Anecdotes of Whitefield*, p. 135.

[56] 'Disputing with bigots and narrow-spirited people will not do. I intend henceforth to say less to them and pray more and more to our Lord for them, "Lord, enlarge their hearts".' Philip, *Whitefield*, p. 386. Elsewhere he refers to the possibility of just being converted to principles, and speaks of 'many sour and severe professors [of orthodoxy]. I knew a rigid man that would beat Christianity into his wife; and so many beat people with their Bibles, that they are likely by their bitter proceedings, to hinder them attending the means God has designed for conversion.' *Sermons on Important Subjects*, p. 613.

continually breathed in all his words, whether in public or private.'[57]

It was the appeal of this feature that once made a dying child, after hearing Whitefield, say, 'I will go to Mr Whitefield's God.'[58]

There can be an attachment to principles, an attachment to orthodox belief, and yet coldness, narrowness and sectarianism be prevalent. But only let us know more of fellowship with Christ and catholicity will invariably follow. Let the Spirit of Christ and his love fill our hearts and at once we shall find ourselves in a deeper relationship with 'all saints'. So we must take up Paul's prayer for the Ephesians for ourselves:

> that he would grant you, according to the riches of his glory, to be strengthened with might by his Spirit in the inner man; that Christ may dwell in your hearts by faith; that ye, being rooted and grounded in love, may be able to comprehend with all saints what is the breadth, and length, and depth, and height; And to know the love of Christ that passeth knowledge, that ye might be filled with all the fulness of God (*Eph.* 3:16–19).

In conclusion, there is perhaps no better testimony to Whitefield's influence on catholicity than the words of Rowland Hill:

> It pleased God to give him a most enlarged mind, and liberated him from all the trammels of education. He knew no party; his glory was to preach the gospel to every creature. Bigotry his soul abhorred; and like a second Samson, he had so made her main supporting pillars to totter, that we may

[57] 'Death of Mr Whitefield,' *Sermons on Several Occasions* (1825), pp. 675–6.

[58] *Journals*, p. 469.

rejoice she trembles to the very foundation, and daily live in hope that her entire destruction shall complete our joy. Now, though I cannot thank the Devil for any thing, yet I will say I thank God for that permissive providence, whereby that great man, being turned out of churches, esteemed it his duty to preach at large.[59]

[59] Quoted in John Morrison, *The Fathers and Founders of the London Missionary Society* (London: Fisher, n.d.), vol. 2, p. 150.

3

JOHN NEWTON: 'A WONDER TO MYSELF'

John Newton (1725–1807)

Strange and mysterious is my life;
What opposites I feel within!
A stable peace, a constant strife;
The rule of grace, the power of sin;
Too often I am captive led,
Yet daily triumph in my Head.

John Newton

As an outward-looking, seafaring nation, it is not surprising that eighteenth-century Britain saw a spate of books on foreign travel. Some authors wrote factual narratives; others, headed by Daniel Defoe with *Robinson Crusoe* (1719–20), turned travel into fiction; and even satire was dressed up as travel when Jonathan Swift took the readers of *Gulliver's Travels* (1727) to the imaginary island of Lilliput. Then in 1764 a travel book of yet another kind was published in London, *An Authentic Narrative of Some Remarkable and Interesting Particulars in the Life of ——, Communicated, in a Series of Letters, to the Rev. T. Haweis.* Despite the disadvantage of the author's anonymity, attention to this title was immediate. A reprint was at once necessary; a third printing came out the next year; nine came out in England alone before the end of the eighteenth century.

Unlike Defoe or Swift, the work had the appeal of not being fiction. While it concerned subjects familiar enough in those times – ships, romance, slaves, the West Coast of Africa – the story line was by no means commonplace. Here was a man who was himself, for a time, virtually a slave; yet he became a sea captain, set to make (as he hoped) a small fortune. But in the outcome he became the opposite of what he had once been, and ready to tell the world that Jesus Christ is the pearl of great price, whom it is worth leaving all to gain.

The Life

As we all now know, the author of the *Authentic Narrative* was John Newton. It is not our purpose here to retell his life but we need to have the main facts before us. Born in Wapping, London, in 1725, he was the only child of a devout Christian mother and a father whom he describes as 'a man of remarkable good sense'.[1] This family circle was broken by his mother's death before he was seven. From the age of eight to ten years John went to school; when he was eleven he made the first of five voyages with his father who was a sea captain trading with the Mediterranean. At the age of seventeen, and ready to start a career, his father arranged a post for him in Jamaica which would keep him overseas for several years.

Before his ship left for that destination there were a few days when he was free to undertake an errand for his father in Kent. This business required no more than three days, yet it was three weeks before he returned home, long past the sailing date to Jamaica. Impetuosity was a characteristic of Newton's youth; thus after fulfilling the duty given him, he had decided to make a visit to another Kent address, the house of George and Elizabeth Catlett in Chatham. This was the home where his mother had died ten years earlier. It was Newton's first visit and he found it captivating. After what must have been a rather lonely childhood, here was a warm family circle

[1] I am inclined to believe that some of Newton's biographers are too unsympathetic to his father, who, even after all his son's later waywardness, 'was willing to contribute all in his power to my satisfaction'. 'I loved and revered him,' Newton wrote after his father's death while swimming in Canada.

with young people closer to his own age. They included two Catlett sons and a fourteen-year-old daughter, Mary, known to everyone as 'Polly'. Newton was never the same from the time he first met vivacious Polly Catlett: 'I was impressed with an affection for her, which never abated or lost its influence a single moment in my heart from that hour.'

The first practical effect of losing his heart to Mary was his deliberate decision to miss the boat that would have taken him to Jamaica. Instead, much of the next year (1743) was taken up with another voyage to the Mediterranean. Then, in February 1744, when John in sailor's dress was walking in the port of London, he fell victim to one of the navy's notorious press-gangs. The Royal Navy at this time had the strange privilege of being able to impress any able-bodied man for service irrespective of his willingness. At this date war with France was imminent; invasion was threatening, and the navy needed far more men than the number willing to volunteer.[2]

Thus on February 6, 1744, Newton found himself crowded into the common sailor's fo'c'sle on HMS *Harwich*, a ship which carried 350 men. He knew ships well enough but never in such conditions, nor under such strict discipline. Within a few weeks an appeal from his father to the captain of the *Harwich* made a difference as he was taken up to the quarter deck as a midshipman.

In June of 1744, when the *Harwich* was moored off the Kent coast, Newton was twice late in returning from shore leave; in both instances Polly was the explanation. He was rebuked by the captain and lost his favour, but in November 1744 far worse was to follow. At that point his ship was part of a convoy of 116 ships, warships and merchantmen, assem-

[2] The number of men in the Navy rose from 23,000 in 1734 to 53,000 in 1744.

bling in the English Channel. Some of this fleet were bound for North America, others for Africa, and Newton's ship was among those destined for India to combat the French in that region. When he learned that the absence from England could be as long as five years, the anticipation of such a separation from Polly was too much for him to bear. So when a great storm delayed the convoy, and took the *Harwich* into Plymouth for repairs, he deserted.

While the action was foolhardy, it was not without an element of reason. One of the men responsible for preparing some of the merchantmen before their departure was his own father, a role that put him in close touch with the Admiralty. Captain Newton at this point was in Torquay, little more than thirty miles from Plymouth. Resting his hopes on his father's influence, John had almost covered the distance on foot, expecting 'to have been with my father in about two hours', when he was arrested on the road by suspicious soldiers. He was brought back to his ship as a deserter, stripped of his rank and flogged before the assembled crew: 'Though I had well deserved all I met with, and the captain might have been justified if he had carried his resentment still further; yet my pride at that time suggested I had been grossly injured, and this so far wrought upon my wicked heart, that I actually formed designs against his life.' As he considered how he could both kill the captain and accomplish his own suicide, one thought restrained him – his love to Polly, 'I could not bear that *she* should think meanly of me when I was dead.'

When the fleet, heading south through the Atlantic, reached the island of Madeira, Newton was one morning lying in his hammock when a midshipman came in and cut the hammock down. Disgruntled, Newton arrived on the deck to find a fellow sailor about to be transferred from the *Harwich* to a merchant ship. The naval escorts, he discovered, required two trained seamen and were taking them from a merchantman. Two of the crew of the *Harwich* were to be given in exchange, but only one man had been selected for that purpose when Newton saw what was happening. At once he pleaded that he should be allowed to join the sailor about to leave, and, probably thankful to be rid of him, the captain gave him leave to go. Barely a few minutes intervened between his being asleep in his hammock, and his hasty departure, with only a few clothes and one book.

This was the event that pitched Newton into the slave trade. The ship he joined was en route to the Guinea Coast where it was to collect a human cargo. It was but one of many such ships that together carried up to 6,000 Africans a year from their homeland to the West Indies and America. These vessels then completed their work by returning to Britain with holds full of cotton, rum and sugar. On board this ship Newton met a passenger who had made himself wealthy by a shore business on the African coast. Imagining he could repeat the man's success, Newton sought employment from him. His discharge from the merchantman was obtained and so at the age of nineteen Newton began his life in Africa.

Dreams of wealth and prosperity were soon dispelled. He was often alone; cruelly treated by his employer's black mistress; sometimes near to starvation and close to death; and, at times, knowing what it was to be chained like the slaves themselves. Newton found himself in the depths of loneliness and isolation. In after years he attributed this condition to the providence of God: his moral condition was so bad that God had put him in a place where he could no longer tempt and drag others down:

> I have seen frequent cause since to admire the mercy of God in banishing me to those distant parts, and almost excluding me from all society, at a time when I was big with mischief, and, like one infected with a pestilence, was capable of spreading a taint wherever I went. But the Lord wisely placed me where I could do little harm . . . I was too low to have any influence. I was rather shunned and despised than imitated; there being few, even of the Negroes themselves, during the first year of my residence, but thought themselves too good to speak to me.[3]

How Newton got into this condition is spelt out in the *Authentic Narrative.* After a religious period in his childhood, he came across the literature of unbelief which worked in him like poison. By the time he was on board the *Harwich* his rejection of Christianity was complete and swearing and blasphemies were part of his everyday language.

But God had not given him up, and neither had his earthly father. Having many friends who were captains of ships, his father had urged those trading on the African coast to appeal for information about his son. Eventually in February 1747 the captain of the *Greyhound* found him and took him on board. The ship did not live up to its name and a year later, with the coast of Ireland almost in sight, mountainous seas almost took the leaking vessel to the bottom. On March 10, 1748, with the sails 'mostly blown away', and one of his companions washed overboard, Newton manned the ship's pumps for nine hours until he was exhausted. After an hour's

[3] *The Works of John* Newton (repr. Edinburgh: Banner of Truth, 1988), vol. 1, p. 14. The quotation is from the 'Memoirs' of Newton by Richard Cecil, contained in this volume, and was taken by him from Newton's *Authentic Narrative.* The full text of the latter will be found in the one volume edition of the *Works of John Newton* (Edinburgh, 1838), and reprinted in many other places. In the following footnotes *Works* refers to the current 6-volume edition.

rest, he was put to the helm of the ship for eleven hours. Afflictions of themselves do not produce repentance, as his life had already proved, but it was now that new words were heard on his lips, 'The Lord have mercy upon us.' 'I began to pray: I could not utter the prayer of faith; I could not draw near to a reconciled God, and call him *Father:* my prayer was like the cry of the ravens, which yet the Lord did not disdain to hear. I now began to think of that Jesus that I had so long derided.'

Newton's return to England in 1748, after more than three years away, was as joyful to his father and friends as it was surprising. But how would Polly take his return? In the five years since they had first met, he had only received a total of six lines from her. Perhaps in his long absence she was already married. In fact she was still single and Captain Newton had even visited the Catletts and consented to Mary's marriage to his son if that should be their wish. So Newton's homecoming brought their engagement, and later (1 Feb. 1750) their marriage.

His life and his language changed, Newton was now a different prospect for an employer and he found a patron in his father's friend, Joseph Manesty, a Liverpool ship-owner. Between 1749, when he was twenty-four, until 1754, Newton sailed four times on Manesty's slave ships, as captain on the last three voyages. His long experience of the sea had equipped him for such commands.

Then a sudden illness – that proved temporary – ended his seafaring in 1754, and for the next ten years he lived in Liverpool where Manesty had obtained the office of Tide Surveyor for him. This employment, largely concerned with the detection of ships avoiding customs duties, he began at the age of thirty on August 18, 1754.

After his conversion Newton's concern was to undo, as far as he could, the destructive effects of the unbelief into which he had fallen and which he had encouraged in others. He had serious desires for the Christian ministry but the way seemed blocked during his years at Liverpool. Two archbishops and one bishop all denied him ordination. Unable to preach, he turned to writing as a means of usefulness. A few items from his pen were published and others circulated in manuscript form; among the latter were eight letters describing, as he wrote in his diary, 'the Lord's gracious dealings with me from my infancy'.[4]

These letters, privately circulated, had a repercussion that was entirely unexpected. They came into the hands of a young evangelical nobleman, Lord Dartmouth who, when informed of the author's identity, proceeded to ensure that Newton was ordained by the Bishop of Lincoln for ministry in the Church of England. In addition, Lord Dartmouth presented him with the curacy of Olney in Buckinghamshire. So it was that in 1764, at the age of 39, Newton began his work as a minister of the gospel. In the same year the eight letters, revised and expanded to fourteen, were published with the title *An Authentic Narrative.*

Olney was a small market town, largely only one street three quarters of a mile long, and lined with thatched cottages in which the majority of the people earned what they could from such things as lace making and weaving.[5] Newton was

[4] Entry of September 28, 1762. See Josiah Bull, *The Life of John Newton* (1868; repr. Edinburgh: Banner of Truth, 2007), p. 95.

[5] In the *Parliamentary Gazetteer* of 1840–3, Olney still had only 529 houses. That there was a wild and godless element in the town is also evident from several contemporary sources. Newton's income as curate was a mere thirty pounds a month and it would have been impossible for him to have done what he was to do without the patronage of John Thornton (1720–90, a Christian banker in London), who

correct in his impression that the people were poor, and the district, at first, seemed to him 'low and dirty'. But he believed he could be happy in this obscure part of Buckinghamshire 'if the Lord made me useful to the people there, though neither they nor I should be spoken of beyond the bounds of the parish'.[6] On the Sunday he preached his first sermons in the Olney church (May 27, 1764), he wrote in his diary: 'I find a cordial reception amongst those who know the truth, but many are far otherwise minded.' The majority of his congregation were nominal Christians, and there were numbers in the population of some 2,500 who were never in church at all. He sought to reach the latter by printing *An Address to the Inhabitants of Olney*. In this he wrote:

> Jesus Christ in his providence has placed me among you, that if I only pass you on the street, you may have a proof before your eyes of his gracious declaration, 'All manner of sin and blasphemy shall be forgiven to men for the Son of man's sake.'[7]

Those he describes as the 'praying people' became the nucleus of his future work. 'To be interested in the simple, affectionate, and earnest prayers of such a people is a privilege of more value than the wealth of kings.' They would meet informally with the Newtons in the vicarage on Sunday evenings and again on Tuesday nights for prayer and teaching. Slowly their numbers were to grow. In 1772 he could speak of 'a good number of lambs added to the fold of late'. In 1776, while commenting that 'most of our old experienced believers have finished their course', he goes on, 'others have

permitted him to draw two hundred pounds a year, or more, for hospitality and other purposes.

[6] *Works*, vol. 5, p. 536.

[7] Ibid., vol. 6, p. 561.

been added. Many miracles he has wrought among us in the twelve years I have been here.'[8]

For three of those twelve years Newton had great help and companionship from William Cowper. Cowper shared in the preparation of hymns to be sung in the Tuesday night meetings and in much else.[9] Newton loved Olney yet, after sixteen years, he believed it right to accept an appointment to the parish of St Mary Woolnoth, in the heart of London. In Olney, while the air was not salt as in his younger days, it was at least fresh. 'London,' he wrote, 'is such a noisy, hurrying place.' But at the age of fifty-four, London was where he was meant to be, and, at the age of eighty, although almost blind and unable to read his text, he was still to be found in the pulpit of St Mary's. His last sermon was in October 1806 at a service to raise support for those who suffered as a result of the Battle of Trafalgar. 'How are you today, sir?' he would be asked; and the invariable reply was, 'I am just as God would have me.' He died on December 21, 1807, his wife of his youth having preceded him by seventeen years. 'More light, more love, more liberty,' were the petitions in one of his last prayers.

The Man

A casual look at Newton's writings might suggest that he was a homespun individual, without the depth associated with men better trained for the ministry, and thus necessarily confined to simplicities. This would be a considerable mistake. Newton was capable of compiling a Greek lexicon, and

[8] Ibid., p.54.

[9] I have written on Cowper in *The Banner of Truth* magazine, Issue 96 (1971), pp. 12–32.

of making close exegetical comment on the Hebrew text of the Old Testament. He was well read in theologies and in church histories. Not without reason, Princeton wished him to receive a doctorate in 1779, which he declined.[10] It was probably Newton's deliberate concentration on the simplicities and fundamentals of the faith that have sometimes led a subsequent generation to misjudge him; those who knew him personally knew differently.

Two students, fresh from Oxford, spent the summer of 1777 as guests in the vicarage at Olney, and expressed delight at the instruction they received.[11] Ministers also went to him for advice and one of them, Thomas Jones of Creaton, said of Thomas Robinson (of Leicester) and John Newton, 'I look upon them both to be the first casuists in Britain, especially Mr Newton.'[12]

Newton was a social being and a lively conversationalist – in today's language, a 'people person'. Few have been more given to hospitality. The invited and the uninvited were all welcomed to his door. Richard Cecil, his first biographer, says, 'His house was an asylum for the perplexed or afflicted.' When William Cowper fell into serious depression in 1773, Newton and his wife cared for him at the vicarage in Olney for a year. One of the features that made Newton's company appealing to others was his cheerfulness and humour. These features were with him to the end when he could describe himself, before death, as 'packed and sealed and waiting for the post'. Yet this was not frivolity. He believed that grav-

[10] 'The dreary coast of Africa was the university to which the Lord was pleased to send me, and I dare not acknowledge a relation to any other.'

[11] One of them was Thomas Charles of Bala (see the following chapter).

[12] John Owen, *Memoir of the Rev. Thomas Jones* (London: Seeleys, 1851), p. 86n. 'Casuist' = 'One who studies and resolves cases of conscience.' A 'counsellor' would be the nearest modern equivalent.

ity, arising from 'a fixed persuasion of the presence of God', should be the mark of every gospel minister.

The leading feature of his character was pinpointed by Richard Cecil who knew him well: 'He possessed so much affection for his people . . . Mr. Newton could *live* no longer than he could *love*.'[13] In his own eyes, Newton was nothing more than an 'old weather-beaten Christian'. He believed that the words he ordered for his gravestone said all that was important:

JOHN NEWTON, CLERK
ONCE AN INFIDEL AND LIBERTINE,
A SERVANT OF SLAVES IN AFRICA,
WAS, BY THE RICH MERCY
OF OUR LORD AND SAVIOUR
JESUS CHRIST,
PRESERVED, RESTORED, PARDONED,
AND APPOINTED TO PREACH THE FAITH
HE HAD LONG LABOURED TO DESTROY.

The reading of John Newton has been of great encouragement to many Christians. One group of readers, however, is especially likely to be helped. While in his lifetime he was the counsellor of all comers, 'Young ministers were peculiarly the objects of his attention: he instructed them; he encouraged them; he warned them; and might truly be said to be a father in Christ.'[14] For him the gospel ministry was more important than any earthly office; more important than being 'a first Lord of the Treasury or a mere Archbishop.' I turn, then, to some of the lessons that he believed to be of abiding importance for the Christian ministry.

[13] *Works*, vol. 1, pp. 92, 95.
[14] Ibid., p. 95.

Experience and Understanding Are Gradual

Newton regarded it as of first importance for ministers to understand that *grace matures slowly*. Few lessons were repeated more often to fellow ministers than this one. It comes up repeatedly:

'God works powerfully, but for the most part gently and gradually.'[15]

'He does not teach all at once, but by degrees.'[16]

'A Christian is not of hasty growth, like a mushroom, but rather like the oak, the progress of which is hardly perceptible, but in time becomes a great deep-rooted tree.'[17]

One of his fullest treatments of this principle is in his three letters based on Christ's words on the manner in which the kingdom of God grows: 'First the blade, then the ear, and after that the full corn in the ear' (*Mark* 4:28). On this parable Newton based what he saw as three stages in the life of a Christian, from its beginning to its maturity, and he describes each stage under the heads, 'A, B, and C'.[18]

Underlying this teaching was Newton's own experience. When was he converted? Was it at the age of twenty-two, the day of the great storm of March 10, 1748, when he began

[15] Quoted in Bernard Martin, *John Newton* (London: Heinemann, 1950), p. 282.

[16] *Letters by John* Newton, ed. Josiah Bull (1869; reprint ed., Edinburgh: Banner of Truth, 2007), p. 124.

[17] Ibid., p. 285

[18] *Works*, vol. 1, pp. 197–217. Also in *Letters of John Newton* (London; Banner of Truth, 1990). The letters published by Newton in his lifetime were entitled *Omicron* (1774; mistakenly dated 1762 by Richard Cecil); *Cardiphonia* (1780), and *Letters to a Wife*. Subsequently some of his correspondents published others, e.g. John Campbell (1809) and William Barlass (1818). *Omicron*, as his *Authentic Narrative*, was published anonymously but when John Berridge obtained a dozen copies he soon recognized the author: 'I suppose by the matter and style that the shame-faced Omicron is Mr Newton. He wears a mask, but cannot hide his face. Pithiness and candour will betray the Curate of Olney, notwithstanding his veil of a Greek signature.' *Works of John Berridge* (London: Simpkin, Marshall, 1838), p. 395.

to pray? Certainly he commemorated that day for the rest of his life. Yet writing of that storm experience in his *Authentic Narrative,* he said, 'I cannot consider myself to have been a believer (in the full sense of the word) till a considerable time afterwards.' And speaking of his spiritual condition in 1749 – the year *after* his deliverance at sea – he wrote:

> My first beginnings in a religious course were as faint as can well be imagined. Who would not expect to hear after such a wonderful, un-hoped for deliverance, as I had received, and, after my eyes were in some measure enlightened to see things aright, I should immediately cleave to the Lord and his ways, with full purpose of heart . . . But, alas, it was otherwise with me.

In 1750, after his marriage, he described himself as at best a babe: 'If I had any spiritual light, it was but the first faint streaks of the early dawn.'[19]

In another place, after speaking of the year 1754, he said, 'My believing in Christ was (I trust) of three or four years longer standing.' That would be to make 1750 or 1751 the time of his 'believing' – two or three years after the storm deliverance.

Newton believed that regeneration – the point when a sinner is savingly and secretly renewed by the Holy Spirit – is instantaneous, and in a letter of 1753 he says of himself, 'In one day I became diametrically opposite to what I was the day before.'[20] That being so, we may question why dating the

[19] *Works*, vol. 6. pp. 307; also 322n. Of the same period he could also say: 'I had, for the most part, peace of conscience, and my strongest desires were towards the things of God.' Had he married Mary Catlett earlier than 1750, 'a year or two sooner, before the Lord was pleased to change my heart, we must have been mutually unhappy.'

[20] *Letters*, ed. Bull, p. 23. He does not give the date, but a reference in the *Authentic Narrative* would appear to place the change as taking place on the coast

beginnings of his Christian life is so uncertain. His answer would be that although regeneration is instantaneous: 'It is by no means necessary that it should be just *in the like manner* instantaneous in its discovery.'[21]

So it is not the settling of a date that matters, but the progressive evidence of the new life that shows itself in faith, repentance and holy living.[22] While regeneration is instantaneous, the process of conversion is commonly gradual. A babe has life but little understanding; and so it was with Newton. Spiritual truths, he writes, 'the Lord was pleased to discover to me gradually. I learnt them here a little and there a little.' He tells us that it was only after his first voyage as a captain that he gained 'a fuller view of the pearl of great price', and this led him to read books that 'gave me further views of Christian doctrine and experience'. On his third and last voyage as a captain he learned much from the conversation and example of another captain whom he met, and by 1754 his assurance was deepened as he came to understand that salvation rests upon the immutable grace of God.

Newton's slow development was in part the result of his seafaring life.[23] For six years after his storm deliverance in 1748, he was without church connection, or the hearing of evangelical preaching. Only after he settled at Liverpool in 1754 did he become publicly identified with Christians, and begin to pray regularly with others. Even so, he believed that

---

of Africa in 1749: 'From that time, I trust, I have been delivered from the power and dominion of sin; though, as to the effects and conflicts of sin dwelling in me, I still "groan, being burdened".'

[21] *Works* 6, p. 220 where he enforces the lesson for a minister.

[22] The idea of conversion as the decision of a moment was unknown to Newton. His experience was close to the teaching of the Puritans, but he was careful to point out that there is no norm to which all true Christian experience must correspond.

[23] At the same time he regarded the relative isolation of his voyages as ordained of God that he might give much time to study.

the gradual nature of Christian growth is a universal truth. Newton's wife's passage from darkness to light was even more indefinite than her husband's, and it taught him the same lesson. At the time of their marriage he says,

> I believe it was not yet daybreak with my dear wife. She was not wanting in that decent religion which is compatible with the supposed innocent gaieties of a worldly life; and which disposes people to be equally ready and punctual (in their respective seasons) at church and at cards, at the assembly or theatre, and at the sacrament. Farther than this she knew not, nor was I qualified to teach her.[24]

By 1755 Newton thought he saw marks of a true believer in Mary, but thereafter there were still many ups and downs in the progress of her Christian experience and understanding, as there are with all believers.

For Newton, God's great patience in his people's slow progress in grace and truth was a lesson that ministers must ever remember. Preachers are to teach, but they do not control the pace at which grace develops in their hearers. They cannot give the experience that prepares a Christian for fuller light. He concluded that it is a dangerous thing to hurry young believers into an acceptance of teaching they are not ready to receive. Our Lord himself taught the people 'as they were able to hear it' (*Mark* 4:33). Newton regarded this as very relevant to 'the doctrines which are now stigmatized by the name of Calvinism'. On the presentation of those doctrines he writes:

> I am an avowed Calvinist: the points that are usually comprised in that term, seem to me so consonant with Scripture, reason (when enlightened), and experience, that I have not the shadow of a doubt about them. But I cannot dispute, I

[24] *Works*, vol. 5, p. 307.

> dare not speculate. What is called by some, high Calvinism, I dread. I feel much more union of spirit with some Arminians, than I could with some Calvinists; and, if I thought a person feared sin, loved the word of God, and was seeking after Jesus, I would not walk the length of my study to proselyte him to the Calvinistic doctrines. Not that I think them mere opinions, or of little importance to a believer, – I think the contrary; but because I think these doctrines will do no one any good till he is taught them of God. I believe a too hasty assent to Calvinistic principles, before a person is duly acquainted with the plague of his own heart, is one principal cause of that lightness of profession which so lamentably abounds in this day, a chief reason why many professors are rash, heady, high-minded, contentious about words . . . I believe that most persons who are truly alive to God, sooner or later meet with some pinches in their experience which constrain them to flee to these doctrines for relief, which perhaps they had formerly dreaded . . . In this way I was made a Calvinist myself; and I am content to let the Lord take his own way, and his own time, with others.[25]

If pastors do not observe this principle and lack wisdom and gentleness in presenting the truth, they ought not to be surprised at bringing trouble into their churches. The preacher ought to have a higher aim than to make people Calvinists; and if people are only made Calvinists in their heads they invariably become a blot on the unity and catholicity that ought to mark every true Christian. To the Scot, John Campbell, who lived in a situation where this was too little remembered, he wrote in 1801:

> If a man be not born again, it signifies little, whether he be called a Calvinist or Arminian, whether he belongs to Church

[25] Ibid., vol. 6, pp. 278–9.

> or Kirk, Relief, Circus, or Tabernacle.[26] He may have a name to live among his party, but he is dead, and incapable, as to spirituals, as the stones in the street. On the other hand, if he be born from on high, he is a new creature, and though he may be for a season, under many incidental mistakes, the grace which has called him will prevail over all, and will teach him, in due time, all that the Lord sees needful for him to know. His children will all see eye to eye in heaven, but they have not all equal light upon earth. Who teacheth like him? He taught his disciples gradually, as they were able to bear it: but we are apt to be too hasty tutors . . . Calvinists should be the meekest and most patient of all men, if consistent with their own principle, 'That a man can receive nothing unless, and until it is given him from above.'[27]

Newton is not here advocating any holding back of the gospel necessary for salvation, but he knew that the gospel could be savingly received by those who, as yet, understand no difference between Arminianism and Calvinism. In other words, granting the importance of what are called Calvinistic truths – as he certainly did – they are not to be understood as marking the boundaries of the body of Christ.[28]

[26] The names refer to different branches of the Scottish church and their meeting places in Edinburgh.

[27] *Letters and Occasional Remarks by John Newton*, ed. John Campbell (London, 1809). In another letter to Campbell he wrote: 'If the heart be upright, we usually grow wiser by years and experience. Thus some who set out as Arminians, in the Lord's time become Calvinists; and many who were once speculative and positive are ripened by age, and become less assuming and dogmatical, learn to bear and forbear, and though they have not changed their sentiments, are strongly suspected by some, because they can love even an Arminian.' *Letters*, Bull, p. 373,

[28] It would be a serious mistake to doubt the reality of Newton's Calvinistic beliefs. He believed there was 'no medium between holding them and not holding them' (*Works*, vol. 6, pp. 245–6); and in the Preface to the *Olney Hymns* he wrote: 'The views I have received of the doctrines of grace are essential to my peace; I could not live comfortably a day, or an hour, without them' (vol. 3, p. 303). Preaching on the atonement, he is unambiguous on its extent (vol. 4, pp. 190–1). But he believed an unwise preaching of Calvinistic doctrines had done much harm in the later eight-

His warnings were clearly necessary; and some painful alienations between Christians in the eighteenth century would have been prevented had they been more widely heard. Josiah Bull quotes another minister who was of the same mind, and who wrote to Newton about John Fletcher, the defender of evangelical Arminianism:

> I fear those on our side have often delivered truths in a raw, unguarded manner. I think he is sincere in his concern for the interests of holiness; but I wish he was more sensible than I fear he is of our obligations to grace; yet this, I think, he has a real regard for too.[29]

Before leaving this point on the gradualness of Christian growth there are two things to be briefly added.

First, *this truth throws light on how Newton as a Christian could engage in the slave trade for some four years.* 'My religious views were not very clear', he writes of that time. 'Custom, example, and interest, had blinded my eyes. I did it ignorantly.' Yet it would be wrong to imply, as some have done, that his conversion made no difference to his treatment of slaves. It clearly did: 'I thought myself bound to treat the slaves under my care with gentleness, and to consult their ease and convenience, as far as it was consistent with the whole family of whites and blacks on board my ship.'[30]

eenth century. Replying to a minister in 1780 he wrote: 'I pity such wise-headed Calvinists as you speak of . . . They are wise in their own eyes; they trust in themselves and despise others. One modest, inquiring Arminian is worth a thousand such Calvinists in my esteem' (*Works*, vol. 6, p. 197). This background must be taken into account in understanding some of Newton's emphases.

[29] *Newton*, Bull, p. 209. The writer was 'a Rev. Mr Woodman of Thorn'.

[30] *Works*, vol. 5, pp. 406–7n. It should be remembered that while the British did not start the slave trade, they were to be the first to end it, following the spread of Christian truth in the national consciousness.

Second, it may be asked *whether Newton's emphasis on the slow growth of the kingdom of God does not ignore the powerful and sudden work of God in revival.* The answer is to be found in a letter he wrote to a correspondent in Scotland in 1792. That was the year of a remarkable work of God in North Wales under the preaching of his friend Thomas Charles and others:

> The revival at Bala demands thankfulness. The Lord, according to his sovereign pleasure, now and then vouchsafes such seasons of *refreshment* to draw the attention of many. But hitherto they have usually been local and temporary. I remember one in Scotland, almost fifty years ago. The most extensive, I think, took place in America about the same time, and was first observed under Dr Edwards's ministry at Northampton.

Newton's thinking was that such revivals are extraordinary. They are not to be seen as the normal way in which the grace of God is at work in the world. When this is forgotten Christians may too easily give way to discouragement. Commenting in 1804 on the little success attending the entrance of the gospel into Sierra Leone, he advised a friend: 'Wait an hundred years first. God is often not so quick with his works as men would have him to be. I once heard of a gardener who boasted that he could sow salad when the meat was put to the fire, and have it ready for eating before the meat was roasted. This is seldom God's way.'

The Place of Books in the Advance of Christianity

One of the first evangelical books Newton read had an enduring influence on his life. It was the biography of a recently deceased army colonel, written by Philip Doddridge, with the title, *Remarkable Passages in the Life of Colonel James Gardiner* (1747). Gardiner was a Scottish aristocrat who, after a Christian upbringing, commenced an army career in which he cast off Christian belief and behaviour. One evening in July 1719, while in Paris, he had enjoyed a party with friends that finished at 11 pm. This left him with an hour to fill before a planned meeting with a married woman at midnight. Carelessly he picked up a book, which a Christian relative had slipped into his baggage. It was Thomas Watson's *The Christian Soldier, or Heaven Taken by Storm* and, while it was still in his hands, he had 'an astonishing sight of my blessed Lord'. Confronted by Christ, says Doddridge, 'he immediately gave judgment against himself, that he was most justly deserving of eternal damnation.'[31] Newton read the book in 1752 and two years later he was still referring to it as affecting him 'more frequently and sensibly than all the books I ever read'. He saw in its pages the same grace that had changed his own life, and it may be that Gardiner's testimony pointed the way to his own later *Narrative*. What is more, the book helped to turn his thoughts favourably to other Puritan authors besides Thomas Watson, and we know he read John Owen, John Flavel, and Richard Baxter, as well as his contemporary, Jonathan Edwards.[32]

It was the help Newton had from Edwards that led him, in 1776, to give a small book to a young Baptist pastor, John Ryland, Jr. The gift had great consequences. Ryland was at first a 'high Calvinist' who struggled with the question how

[31] Philip Doddridge, *Some Remarkable Passages in the Life of Colonel James Gardiner* (London: Seeley, 1825), p. 51.

[32] In 1762 Newton spoke of Edwards as 'my favourite author'. In later years he would be critical of Edwards' more metaphysical writings.

it is possible to be both a Calvinist and a true evangelical preacher. The book, by a disciple of Edwards, spoke to his problem, and Ryland's change of understanding, with that of others that followed, led to the beginning of the missionary movement that took William Carey to India in 1792.[33]

Newton's own books were to influence millions. His unique contribution to the literature of his century was his publication of letters written to friends and enquirers, which appeared under the titles of *Omicron* and *Cardiphonia*. These were books that would in turn affect the lives of other leading writers. Thomas Scott the commentator, for instance, was at first a hostile neighbour of Newton's and cared nothing for his company. But he received a copy of *Omicron*; a friendship slowly developed, and Scott was to go into print on how the truths he learned from Newton led him to submit to Christ and Scripture.

John Aikman was a Congregational minister of strong evangelical persuasion in Edinburgh in the early nineteenth century. In earlier life his interests had been far different, until he met *Cardiphonia*. In his own words:

> I was returning to Jamaica, where I was engaged upon one of the plantations, and wishing to take some books for the use of the people there, amongst others I selected Newton's *Cardiphonia*. Its title struck me and I supposed it was a novel. Looking over the books on the voyage I took up this, and soon found it something very different from what I had thought; and *that book* was, in God's providence, the means of my conversion.[34]

[33] The book was John Smalley's *The Consistency of the Sinner's Inability to Comply with the Gospel with His Inexcusable Guilt in Not Complying with It* (1769). See further in D. Bruce Hindmarsh, *John Newton and the Evangelical Tradition* (Grand Rapids: Eerdmans, 2000), p. 153.

[34] Newton's *Letters*, ed. Bull, p. 375n.

Hannah More (1745–1833) was one of the best-known female writers of her age, writing a first drama at the age of seventeen. By the 1770s she was fêted in the most fashionable set in London, admired both for her published verse and for her dramas. Speaking of her place among the famous in that circle, William Wilberforce would later say, she 'was so courted by them all'.[35] ' But in the 1780s, when the emptiness of her life was dawning on her, *Cardiphonia* came into her hands and this led to correspondence and then friendship with Newton. Her life changed, she used her writing gifts in evangelical tracts and small books;[36] these were extensively read and played a decided part in the way the gospel changed the tone of society in early nineteenth-century England.

Wilberforce was one of Hannah More's friends after his own conversion. He, too, acknowledged his benefit from Newton's writings, noting how the *Authentic Narrative* gave him light on his own danger.[37] He also enjoyed Newton's personal counsel on many occasions, as well as hearing him preach. In his diary for Sunday, December 11, 1785, he wrote: 'Heard Newton on the "*addiction*" of the soul to God. "They that observe lying vanities shall forsake their own mercy." – Excellent. He shows his whole heart is engaged.'[38]

In 1787 Wilberforce was the leader in the formation of a Society for the Abolition of Slavery. The slavery industry at this date remained at its height. It is said that between 1783

[35] R. I. and S. Wilberforce, *Life of William Wilberforce* (London: Murray, 1838), vol. 1, p. 238.

[36] More's *Thoughts on the Importance of the Manners of the Great in General Society* went through seven printings in the year of its publication (1790). Martin, *Newton*, p. 319.

[37] The danger to which he referred was that of relapsing, as Newton had done after his deliverance in the storm.

[38] *Life of Wilberforce*,vol. 1, p. 99.

and 1795 more than three-quarters of a million Africans were carried from Africa to the plantations of the New World and mostly by British ships. Thankful for the endeavour of Wilberforce and the abolitionists, Newton wrote a lengthy pamphlet entitled, *Thoughts upon the African Slave Trade* (1787). The abolitionists immediately took three thousand copies 'to be dispersed about the Kingdom'. Hannah More thought it was a 'sensible, judicious, well-timed, and well-tempered pamphlet'.

The most influential of all Newton's works is yet to be mentioned. During the time of William Cowper's good health at Olney, the two men had composed hymns on Christian belief and experience to aid the understanding of the congregation. The main motive, said Newton, was to promote 'the faith and comfort of sincere Christians'. Often they composed a hymn to confirm a passage or text of Scripture that was then being taught. Thus 'Amazing Grace' was written by Newton in December 1772, to accompany a sermon he was to preach on David's amazement over God's promises in 1 Chronicles 17:16–17, 'And David the king came and sat before the LORD, and said, Who am I, O LORD God, and what is mine house, that thou hast brought me hitherto . . .'

On Cowper's serious illness their joint work did not continue, but Newton persisted, and in 1779 he published *Olney Hymns*. There were nearly 350 in all, with 281 by Newton. As an historian of hymnody writes, 'Their appeal was immediate, and to an unusual degree permanent . . . it became a manual of evangelical doctrine and an instrument of spiritual discipline.'[39] In Britain the book was in a ninth edition by

[39] Louis F. Benton, *The English Hymn: Its Development and Use in Worship* (New York: Doran, 1915), p. 338.

1810. In America there were New York editions as early as 1787 and 1790, and it was printed in Philadelphia in 1792. Without exaggeration another writer could say, 'The collection has become a standard book among devout readers of every evangelical denomination.'[40]

A great deal more could be said on the role of books and the manner in which God has used them to change lives. There is only one proviso that Newton would wish to add. Let us be careful, he would say, not to give too much credit to human authors. Books come into our lives by the providence of God, and at the time we need them, but we have to be careful not to allow human authority to stand alongside the Word of God. In 1773 he advises a fellow minister: 'Christ alone is Lord of conscience; and no *ipse dixit* is to be regarded but his. Men are to be followed so far as we can see they speak by his authority; the best are defective; the wisest may be mistaken.'[41] Nearly thirty years later he is making the same point in writing to John Campbell: 'Study the *text* of the good word of God. Beware of leaning too hard on human authority, even the best; you may get useful hints from sound divines, but call no man *master*. There are mixtures of infirmity, and the prejudices of education or party, in the best writers. What is good in them they obtained from the fountain of truth, the scriptures; and you have as good a right to go to the fountain head yourself.'[42]

[40] Quoted in Bull, *Life of Newton*, p. 201. It was, however, not the *Olney Hymns* as such that attained world-wide fame and use, but rather the twenty or so hymns that were its best. Many of the compositions are better thought of as didactic poems, based on Scripture, rather than as hymns for regular public worship. For a full modern discussion of Newton as a hymn writer, see D. Bruce Hindmarsh, *John Newton*.

[41] *Works*, vol. 6, p. 229.

[42] Campbell, *Letters*, p. 148

Wisdom in Pastoral Counselling

Newton was an outstanding pastor in the sense that he studied people and understood them as individuals. He had no general formulas that he applied to all and sundry. This is apparent, for example, in the varied way in which he counselled those troubled by lack of assurance.

First, he would seek to ascertain whether the person had ever truly known Christ. He would want to know whether he clearly understood the difference between the gospel and the covenant of works, and whether he had a right understanding of true Christian experience. The holiness of a regenerate person, he would insist, 'seems principally to consist in self-abasement, and in admiring views of Jesus as a complete Saviour'. Where that exists, fruit will follow, but, 'If you will look for a holiness that shall leave no room for the workings of corruption and temptation; you look for what God has nowhere promised.'[43]

He was alive to the possibility that the reason for lack of comfort in a Christian may be constitutional, in his physical condition. 'Have you no friend in Cornwall or the north of Scotland you could visit?' he might ask such a person. 'I thought a ride to Land's End, or John o' Groats, might do them more good than all the counsel I could give them.' Such advice he certainly would not offer to those (such as his dear friend Cowper) whom he recognized as clinically depressed. To yet others he could say, 'Spend more time in company with others, avoid musing by yourself, and reasoning.'

There was in this way wise variation in his counsel. What is consistent throughout is his affection for those he is seeking to help.

[43] *Works*, vol. 6, p. 177

This same wisdom appears in the manner in which he describes a mature Christian – the believer who has reached stage three, 'C', or 'the full corn' (see p. 99 above). A first characteristic of such a person is humility. When a reader of Newton's letters wrote to tell him that he had arrived at 'C', Newton replied that he had forgotten to say that it is true of all in stage three that they do not know they are there! This humility shows a greater union of heart with God's will and glory: the young Christian is more taken up with his own interests. Towards others, humility shows itself in patience, and a loving spirit. Holiness of life, he was always insisting, does not consist of 'great attainments', nor 'extraordinary experiences'; at no stage does the Christian have 'a stock of grace' or experience on which to depend. The mature Christian is the one who knows more dependence on Christ alone; Christ in him is his only strength. They that have most grace, he writes, are those who are conscious that 'they, in and of themselves, are nothing, have nothing, can do nothing, and see daily cause for abhorring themselves'.[44]

The mature Christian is one who knows he is a poor, weak sinner still. This is a pervasive note in Newton, as it was with Paul (*Rom.* 7:18–25; *1 Tim.* 1:15). He kept before him what he was without Christ, and looked daily at the words painted above the fireplace in his study, 'And thou shalt remember that thou wast a bondman in Egypt, and the LORD thy God redeemed thee' (*Deut.* 15:15).

This was nothing more than the consequence that Scripture says will follow the gospel blessings of the gift of 'a new heart and a new spirit': 'Then shall ye remember your own evil ways, and your doings that were not good, and shall

[44] *Letters of Newton*, p. 176

loathe yourselves in your own sight for your iniquities and for your abominations' (*Ezek.* 36:31).

A consideration of this penitential note in Newton's hymnody must lead one to reflect on what is too commonly absent from numbers of the songs substituted for hymns in worship today. It is not simply that certain words are omitted; the whole ethos is different. Too often the emphasis is on the worshipper's devotion, 'I will praise'; 'I will exalt'; 'I will love', etc. While the language is good, the old saying needs to be remembered, 'He loves little who tells how much he loves.' And when the language is used in the absence of expressions of poverty of spirit, mourning, hungering and thirsting for what is not yet attained, it may be akin to the ignorance that led Simon Peter to assert, 'I will lay down my life for thy sake.'[45] Professing Christian worship that omits humility and self-abasement would have been incomprehensible to Newton. His best hymns are always striking a note that is the opposite of self-confidence or self-satisfaction;[46] rather it is:

Weak is the effort of my heart,
And cold my warmest thought.

Newton points us to the need for a reversal of features that have entered into Christian worship today.

The most important example of Newton's pastoral wisdom has still to be stated. It is the prominence he always gives to the basis upon which a sinner is accepted before God.

[45] 'No man feels so acutely how far he falls below the full measure of holy duties, pious zeal, and heavenly love, as he who is growing up nearest to the stature of a perfect one in Christ.' George Burrowes, *Commentary on Song of Solomon* (London: Banner of Truth, 1960), p. 107.

[46] Consider, for instance, the words of 'Come, my soul, thy suit prepare,' or 'Approach, my soul, the mercy seat'.

This is the lesson that runs through his letters, his preaching and his hymns. Peace with God comes through the believing recognition of the death of Christ as our Substitute, and the continued enjoyment of that peace is only in looking to what the Saviour has done. It is true that those who so trust in Christ will show evidence of it in their lives, but that evidence, he was careful to say, must never be confused with the basis upon which God accepts them. The work of grace in the soul is too weak to sustain assurance of glory at any stage in the Christian's life. He writes to his wife when she was still only a young Christian:

> Our comfort is that the blood of Christ cleanseth from all sin. What a great word is that little word ALL! Not only from sins of one kind, or of one degree, but of all kinds, and of all degrees, when we apply to it in a truly humble and repenting spirit.[47]

Nearly twenty years later he is still writing to Mary on the same truth:

> What arithmetic can compute the whole that is included in the word *all*! One transgression would be sufficient to sink the soul into ruin. But the blood of Jesus Christ frees those who believe in him from the guilt of all.[48]

It is possible for preachers to speak of sin and the deficiencies of believers in such a manner that it confirms depression and morbidity. In Newton's case, the way he dealt with sin in the light of the cross had a very different effect. Listen to him writing to encourage another minister from his own experience:

[47] *Works,* vol. 5, p. 514.
[48] Ibid., p. 579.

I seem to groan under darkness, coldness, and confusion, as much as ever. And I believe I must go out of the world with the same language upon my lips which I used when I first ventured to a throne of grace, – Have mercy upon me, O Lord, a poor worthless sinner. My feelings are faint; my services feeble and defiled; my defects, mistakes, and omissions innumerable; my imaginations are wild as the clouds in a storm: yea, too often foul as a common sewer. What can I set against this mournful confession? Only this, – That Christ hath died and risen again . . . Upon his person, worth, and promise, rests all my hope; but this is a foundation able to bear the greatest weight.[49]

Oh, wondrous love! To bleed and die;
To bear the cross and shame;
That guilty sinners, such as I,
Might plead thy gracious name.[50]

We best remember John Newton by admiring the grace of God. What a strange life – a man who left school at the age of ten; press-ganged at eighteen; delivered from his own slavery when he was about twenty-four; slow in understanding his new faith; failing at first in efforts to preach; then, at the age of thirty-nine, becoming the curate of an obscure town; yet, ultimately, dying a much-loved teacher of the whole Christian world! Our lives may be very different but, in Christ, every life is for 'the praise of the glory of his grace'. With Newton every believer may sing,

'Tis grace has brought me safe thus far,
And grace will lead me home

[49] Ibid., vol. 6, p. 286.

[50] *Works*, vol. 3, pp. 583–4, and in most hymn books with the first line, 'Approach, my soul, the mercy seat.'

4

THOMAS CHARLES OF BALA

Thomas Charles (1755–1814)

Jesus, Jesus, all-sufficient,
   Beyond telling is Thy worth;
In Thy Name lie greater treasures
   Than the richest found on earth.
      Such abundance
Is my portion with my God.

In Thy gracious face there's beauty
   Far surpassing every thing
Found in all the earth's great wonders
   Mortal eye hath ever seen.
      Rose of Sharon,
Thou Thyself art heaven's delight.

WILLIAM WILLIAMS
tr. by BOBI JONES

Although the Principality of Wales is a comparatively small region, the spiritual conditions in the North and the South of that country in the mid-eighteenth century presented a striking contrast. From the 1730s the South and the West experienced a spiritual awakening which had begun to make the population a Bible-loving people. Clergymen of the Church of England, led by Daniel Rowland and William Williams, together with unordained exhorters such as Howell Harris, drew hundreds and thousands from the world and set them on a joyful course for heaven. Given the name of 'Methodists' (to which was soon added 'Calvinistic'[1] to distinguish them from the Wesleyan movement in England), these people nevertheless remained a part of the Church of England though their fellowship and organization in 'societies' existed apart from the parish system.

In the North it was entirely different. Not a single clergyman favoured the preaching which had brought such change elsewhere; on the contrary, most were like Dr Edwards, the Vicar of Machynlleth, who would refer to Rowland and his

[1] James Hutton, reporting something of the spiritual conditions in England to Count Zinzendorf in March 1740, wrote: 'In Wales some thousands are stirred up. They are an exceedingly simple and honest people, but they are taught the Calvinistic scheme.'

brethren as 'those wicked Methodists'. Edward Morgan, himself an Anglican clergyman, could speak of his colleagues in North Wales as 'rich, self-indulgent and idle'. Those outside the Established Church – the Nonconformist successors of the Puritans – had ceased to provide any challenge to this situation and in 1736 they could number only six chapels in the whole area, including one at Bala, a wool-manufacturing village in the heart of North Wales. When Howell Harris preached in a private house in Bala in 1741 the service was disrupted and he was nearly killed by a mob. In later years an older citizen of that town recalled the conditions which then prevailed: 'Bibles were very scarce; hardly any of the lower ranks could read at all . . . Gluttony, drunkenness, and licentiousness like a torrent overran the land . . . From the pulpit the name of the Redeemer was hardly ever heard; nor was there much mention made of the natural sinfulness of man, nor of the influence of the Holy Spirit.'[2]

But Harris' fearless preaching in Bala was not without fruit and one who passed from death to life under its influence was Jane Jones who, with the husband she married in 1737, became one of the leading shop-keepers of the town. David and Jane Jones would have remained unknown to posterity if it had not been for their one child, Sarah, who was born in 1753, sixteen years after their wedding. Twenty-five years later 'Sally' Jones, still unmarried, was famed in Merionethshire for her personality, her looks and her earnestness in religion. It seems that news of her played a part in drawing a student at Oxford by the name of Thomas Charles to accept the invitation of a fellow Welsh student to visit North Wales

[2] *Trysorfa Ysprydol* (Spiritual Treasury), 1799, pp. 30–1. Quoted in *Life of Howell Harris*, J. Hughes, Newport and London, 1892, p. 75.

in the summer of 1778. Upon just such seemingly small issues great matters often turn.

The Preparation for Usefulness

Thomas Charles was born near Carmarthen two years after his future wife. He was a stranger to the North. Until 1773 he was also a stranger to the experience which made Sally different from so many of her contemporaries. On January 20 of that year, as a 17-year-old Carmarthen schoolboy, he heard Daniel Rowland preach. His 'mind was overwhelmed and overpowered with amazement' at the truth. He said, 'The change a blind man who receives his sight experiences doth not exceed the change I at that time experienced.' So, with the Christian ministry in view, Charles settled into a course of study at Jesus College, Oxford, in February 1776. The summer vacation of the following year he spent with John Newton at Olney. He wrote to a friend:

> Having a Newton to be instructed by, both by edifying discourses in the pulpit, and by conversation in the closet, what place or situation can I be in, more pleasing and delightful? I had formed in my mind great expectations of him, but really he has exceeded my most sanguine expectations . . . Had I the strongest constitution and the best advantages of human literature, yes, of all learning, both sacred and profane, yet I am perfectly convinced that all this would be much too little to make me a gospel preacher. One may speak a great deal, and that very orthodox; but unless he has a little of the unction of the Holy Spirit, he might, for aught I know, as well be silent. That is what I want in my prayers, studies and meditations.'[3]

[3] *The Life of Thomas Charles of Bala*, D. E. Jenkins, Denbigh, 1910, vol. 1, pp. 50–1. Further references to this title will be given as '*Thomas Charles*'.

In 1778, the year he first saw Sally Jones at Bala, Charles was ordained in the Church of England and settled in a curacy at Shepton Beauchamp in Somerset. No one could then have anticipated that these facts were going to collide with each other, nor did they at the outset. Sally remained on his mind, he even refers to her in a letter, to the former student friend who had introduced them, as 'My Dear Sally', but he had no further contact with her until a first letter was posted on December 28, 1779. It began:

> My Very Dear Friend – Such an unexpected address from a person who never saw you but once, and that at such a long interval of time, will I suppose at first not a little surprise you.

Such was the beginning of a courtship which ended in their wedding at the parish church of Llanycil, Bala, on August 20, 1783. For Charles that period seemed a great deal longer than three-and-a-half years. Sarah's letters, often written from the shop counter in Bala, show that she had been slow to reciprocate the feelings he expressed, and when at last she did, and marriage was discussed, it was only to encounter a new problem. The thought of Sally being as remote from home as Somerset was more than her parents could bear or allow. John Newton entered into the problem and obtained a curacy for Charles in South Wales, but even that location was unthinkable to David and Jane Jones. Sorrowfully, Charles explained in a letter to a friend: 'She is an only child of tender and affectionate parents . . . It would be worse than death for her to be removed, whilst they live, to a considerable distance . . . I would not for the world be the means of bringing their grey hairs with sorrow to the grave. Everything, therefore, must remain as it is, till I meet with a situation within a convenient distance of the place where they live in North Wales.'

Such was the background to the momentous decision that Charles finally reached. The reception his preaching of evangelical Christianity had received in Somerset was far from encouraging; all the indications were that it would be far worse if he found himself settled in a parish in Merionethshire where Bala was situated. Even so, he tried without success to find an appointment in North Wales.

'Is it not the easiest and safest way to put an end to our acquaintance than to be perplexed with it?' Sally asked in a letter of February 1781. After further disappointments in the way of finding a curacy (and therefore a source of support) near her home, Charles gave up Somerset, where he had recently been offered a 'perpetual curacy', and married Sally, and it might be said, Bala, in the summer of 1783; he was without any sure source of future income. The many letters of their courtship show the foundation on which their marriage was to be based. Two months before that event, he wrote in a letter to Sally:

> O let us not forget Him who for our sakes became poor . . . See him laying aside his riches and taking our poverty, leaving his throne, and entering our dungeon! Behold Him in *all* things made like unto his brethren, having become in every thing the same with us! He came to the same poverty, wore the same garment, spoke the same language of misery, endured our curse, and will not leave us till we are taken to the same place and to the same glory, till we are filled with all the fulness of God. He was not, he is not, ashamed of us. He was, he is, he ever will be, in every thing like to his brethren. He will wear the same nature, when he cometh with His holy angels in the last day. He will appear as 'the firstborn among many brethren' in the height of his glory in heaven. We cannot think too much, or too well of Him. May it ever be your

and my only ambition to be in every thing like Him, and in every thing to live to Him.[4]

In 1783, the year of their wedding, Charles had still not given up hope of finding a place among his clerical colleagues in North Wales, and soon after his marriage we find him with an opening at Llangynog, a parish twelve miles from Bala. This lasted for only two Sundays. The nearest evangelical ministerial friend was probably John Major of Shawbury, Shropshire, and as he was in poor health, Charles left Sally at Bala and gave help in Major's two churches in the autumn of 1783. In one of Major's pulpits two Sundays were again the limit of what the people would receive: 'Last Sunday, the whole parish, with two or three of the principal inhabitants at their head, came and accosted me in a rougher strain than I have ever been used to before. They insisted on my preaching no more in their church; for they added, "You have cursed us enough already." I took care that nothing but the plain simple truth should give offence.'

Back in Bala, where Sally's mother said he would 'make an excellent shop-keeper', Charles found another invitation, to the curacy at Llanymawddwy, fourteen miles from Bala, and over a wild mountainous track. From January 25, 1784, Charles made that journey on foot in all weather; but in March, and for the third time, he was given a dismissal. It was his last curacy.

John Newton, for one, was apprehensive about Charles' course of action, and his likely inaction, as far as his future in the Established Church was concerned. Probably word had

[4] *Thomas Charles' Spiritual Counsels*, ed. Edward Morgan (Edinburgh: Banner of Truth, 1993), pp. 284–5. First published in 1836 as *Essays, Letters and Interesting Papers* (London: Seeley) this is an inspiring book. So also is Edward Morgan's, *John Elias: Life, Letters and Essays* (Edinburgh: Banner of Truth, 1973, repr. 2004).

reached him that Charles was 'at times nearly resolved to lay aside all thoughts of the Church'. 'For aught I can tell,' Newton wrote to him, 'the reason why the Lord has permitted you to be silenced in Wales, may be, that he has a work for you to do in Yorkshire or Northumberland.' Was it right, he went on to ask, to leave the Church of England 'entirely on considerations of a temporal nature, and your own personal apparent interest?' (that is, Charles' wish that their home should be in Bala). Commenting on these words, D. E. Jenkins, Charles' biographer, writes: 'Mr Charles was as convinced as his good and distinguished friend of God's leading and blessing; the point now was, Why had God led him to Bala? and why did the surrounding mountains refuse to lower their heads in order to expand his horizon? The Church offered him nothing, and God offered him (1) Bala (2) Merionethshire, and (3) North Wales.' But Jenkins writes with all the advantages of hindsight. That was certainly not the choice as Charles saw it in 1784. The most he could say in the summer of that difficult year was, 'I feel myself much inclined to take Wales, as I did my wife, "for better, for worse, till death do us part".'[5]

Judged by the appearance of things, Sally and her parents were the reason why he was unemployed and to be found at times behind a shop counter. But behind the appearance there was in Charles the constraint of a prayerful faith. Uncertain of the future though he was, he had learned more necessary things in all the sore trials of the years following his ordination. His disappointments in Somerset and elsewhere, the long wait for Sally, and, worst of all, his conscious incapacity and the small influence for good which seemed to attend

[5] Despite taking steps that would remove him from ministry in the Church of England, Charles remained a life-long friend of Newton's, visiting him every summer he was in London in later years.

his work, had all worked for good. It is significant that the first chapters in *Spiritual Counsels* are on 'Spiritual Pride' and 'Humility'. He was brought low. In the words of D. E. Jenkins, 'God had appointed him to plough a field of virgin soil, as far as Evangelicalism was concerned, and was sharpening his ploughshare with the hone of tribulations and the grit of tested faith.'[6] And, more fully, Edward Morgan comments:

> When God intends a person for some great work, he prepares him for it. He makes him know and feel what he is in himself, sinful, depraved, weak, devoid of every spiritual good, and full of every evil . . . Mr Charles was destined by heaven for great and glorious services. He was now undergoing a course of hard discipline, to fit him for his work. The success he met with in after life, and the honour to which he attained, would have found in the pride of the heart too ready a combustible, and might have proved his ruin, had not that pride been previously mortified . . . The foundation of his humility was deeply laid: and it was laid, no doubt, during the first years of his ministry, by the realizing views he had of his own sin and unworthiness.[7]

The course of action which Charles finally took to end his enforced silence, unsurprising though it sounds to us, was one which for some time, he tells us, he 'never thought of'. In spite of the connection of his parents-in-law with the despised Methodists (Sally's father preached among them), Charles never seems to have been at their small meetings in Bala. He

[6] *Thomas Charles*, vol. 1, pp. 415–6.

[7] *A Brief Memoir of the Life and Labours of the Rev. Thomas Charles*, Edward Morgan, 2nd edition, London, 1831, pp. 198–200. This same lesson Charles urged on others. While writing to the Countess of Huntingdon in 1791 about the need of London he says, 'Let us go in humble, humble faithfulness, we shall certainly sow if not reap the harvest'.

certainly never preached among them, yet here, unlike the congregations as dead as 'so many stocks or stones' which he had faced elsewhere, were people eager to hear the Word of God. With the local clergy declining to use even his unpaid services, Charles went to the Society meeting in Bala in July 1784. Soon he began to preach among them and within a few months he was to be found as an itinerant preacher among the Calvinistic Methodists in North Wales – the first clergyman in the North ever to cast his lot among them.

Entering on His Life Work

At twenty-nine years of age Charles was now a comparative youngster among older believers. John Evans, one of the Calvinistic Methodists in Bala, recalled the coming of Charles into their midst in a conversation which occurred many years later when Charles was questioning a woman seeking church membership. Evans was present but, being elderly and deaf, was unable to follow the conversation. At length Charles turned to his old friend with the words, 'I find her very uninformed, John Evans, what do you think ought to be done with her?' 'Well,' replied the Christian of long experience, 'you were uninformed yourself when you came to us.'[8]

A new chapter had opened in Charles' life and experience. In April 1785 we find him writing: 'I am just this moment come home from three weeks' tour through Caernarvonshire and Anglesey. The fields here all over the country are white for the harvest. Fresh ground is daily gained. Whole neighbourhoods where the Word has been heretofore opposed call aloud for the gospel. Thousands flock to hear and many in

[8] *Thomas Charles*, vol. 3, p. 607.

different parts of the country, we have good reason to believe, are effectually called.' When the aged Daniel Rowland heard Charles at Llangeitho later that summer he was in no doubt why the young man had been shut up to Bala: 'Charles is the Lord's gift to North Wales.'

In this same eventful year, 1784–5, another form of service had opened for Charles. Impressed by the utter ignorance of the children and youth of the town he began to invite some of them to the home he and Sally shared with her parents above and behind the shop. Whether this was done on a Sunday or weekday is not clear, but the numbers grew, so that before long the gathering had to be moved to the building used by the Methodists. As Charles began to travel about the North he was soon convinced that the need of children could not be met without a much wider effort. Charity Schools had been instituted in the South many years earlier and had become valuable spiritual agencies. His initial experiment in Bala now led to a parallel development in the North. In a letter of March 24, 1787, he writes:

> When I came a little acquainted with the country, I was surprised and grieved to find so many totally illiterate and not able to read a word in the Bible in their Mother's tongue. I have attempted and succeeded far beyond my expectations in setting up charity schools, with a view only to teaching poor children and young people to read the Bible in a language they understand, and teach them the principles of the Christian religion by catechising them. We had seven schoolmasters last year in employ, and we think of increasing the number to twelve this ensuing summer . . . . I visit all the schools myself as often as I can. The money is raised by voluntary subscriptions among our societies . . . I have been often, in my journeys through different parts of the country,

questioned, whether I knew if a Welsh Bible could be bought for a small price? and it has hurt my mind much to be obliged to answer in the negative.

These were circulating schools, that is to say, schools set up in a district for about nine months (which Charles believed was the time needed to teach young people to read the Scriptures), and then the schoolmasters moved on to other places. By 1789 there were fifteen such teachers and by 1794 the number had reached twenty. Simultaneously the Calvinistic Methodist Societies, under Charles' leadership, were developing Sunday Schools. There can be no question that he had an unusual aptitude for this work, coupled with much affection for children. In his own home their first child, a son, was born in June 1785, to be followed by a daughter two years later who was only to live for twelve months in this world: 'How free was the grace which saved her and took her to glory! It came to her unthought of, unsought for, and undesired.'[9] In the instruction of children supreme attention was given to the memorization of Scripture and Charles found that, with the right help, children of only five years old were capable of memorizing many chapters of the Bible.

Remarkable effects sometimes followed this practice. Edward Morgan speaks, for instance, of one area where it seemed as though no spiritual impression could be made upon the low moral standards of a particular neighbourhood. Sexual promiscuity, associated with dancing and drunkenness, was widespread. Wakes arranged to watch over a corpse before burial often became occasions for this kind of behaviour and an 'annual wake' had long assumed the character of a revel. One year, about two months before the annual wake, Charles

[9] *Spiritual Counsels*, p. 364.

sent word to the teachers of Sunday Schools in this district,

> requesting them to get the children to search the Bible for texts which prohibit directly or indirectly such evil practices as dancing, drunkenness, fornication etc., and to commit them to memory, saying that they might expect him there at the feast to catechise the children. The young people set to work and there was a great deal of talk in the town and neighbourhood about the subject. When the time arrived, Mr Charles went there, and most of the people of the place, led by curiosity perhaps in a great measure, went to hear what the children had to say on these subjects. The meeting began as usual with singing and prayer. Then Mr Charles began to ask some questions on the points given them to learn. 'Is dancing, my dear children, a sin?' 'Yes,' said one emphatically, 'it was owing to dancing that the head of John the Baptist was cut off.' 'Is drunkenness set forth as bad and sinful in the Scriptures?' 'Yes,' answered another, and repeated these words: 'Woe unto them that follow strong drink, that continue till night till the wine inflame them, and the harp and the viol, the tabret and the pipe are in their feasts; but they regard not the work of the Lord, neither consider the operations of his hands.' Isaiah 5:11, 12. In this way he proceeded with them concerning the other sins and the answers were given with great propriety and seriousness. The people began to hold down their heads, and appeared to be much affected. Observing this, he addressed them in the kindest manner and exhorted them by all means to leave off their sinful practices, and to learn the Word of God after the example of the children, and to try to seek superior pleasures and a better world. The effect was so great that all went home and the houses of revelling were completely forsaken.

This anecdote is a reminder that the spread of the gospel in North Wales was not without much hard work and organization but the main emphasis was always upon prayerful dependence upon God. When he was among Major's indifferent hearers at Shawbury in January 1784, Charles wrote to his wife: 'Help me, my dear, with your fervent prayers . . . I long to see past times of the outpouring of the Spirit returning again, when the voice of God by his ministers was terrible, powerful and full of majesty.' Three years later, in March 1787, after speaking about a new chapel at Dolgellau, he could report:

> In the mountainous country surrounding that little town the gospel spreads powerfully, and those who never heard the sound of the gospel till within these few years are brought by its power under the yoke of Christ. Indeed, it is wonderful to see and pleasing to think of the amazing change effected in different parts of this hitherto dark country, by its power alone. The outpouring of the Spirit has been and still continues at times so abundant and powerful among those who made the utmost opposition to it, that we see with our eyes an evident fulfilment of the promise of the Father to the Son – 'The Lord shall send the rod of his strength out of Zion: rule thou in the midst of thine enemies' (*Psa.* 110:2).[10]

Revival at Bala and Beyond

Four years after this, Bala itself saw a great awakening. Charles wrote to a minister in London on December 7, 1791:

> Here, in our town of Bala, for some time back, we have had a very great, powerful, and glorious outpouring of the Spirit of our God on the people in general, especially young people. The state and welfare of the soul is become the general concern of the country. Scores of the wildest, and

[10] *Thomas Charles*, vol. 1, pp. 565–6.

most inconsiderate of the people, have been awakened . . . This glorious work began on a Sunday afternoon, in the chapel, where I preached twice that day, and cannot say that there was anything particular in the ministry of that day, more than what I had often experienced among our dear people here. But, towards the close of the evening service, the Spirit of God seemed to work in a very powerful manner on the minds of great numbers present who never appeared before to seek the Lord's face; but now, there was a general and loud crying, 'What must I do to be saved?', and, 'God be merciful to me a sinner'. And, about nine or ten o'clock at night, there was nothing to be heard from one end of the town to the other but the cries and groans of people in distress of soul. And the very same night, a spirit of deep conviction and serious concern fell upon whole congregations, in this neighbourhood, when calling upon the name of the Lord.

In the course of the following week we had nothing but prayer meetings, and general concern about eternal things swallowed up all other concerns. And the spirit of conviction spread so rapidly that there was hardly a young person in the neighbourhood but began to enquire, What will become of me? The work has continued to go on with unabated power and glory, spreading from one town to another, all around this part of the country. New conquests are gained every week and new captives brought in. A dispensation so glorious, I never beheld, nor indeed expected to see in my day . . . Whilst it stirs up the dormant enmity and rage of some, who continue the determined enemies of our Lord; yet the coming of the Lord amongst us has been with such majesty, glory, and irresistible power, that even his avowed enemies would be glad to hide themselves somewhere from the brightness of his coming . . . It is an easy and delightful work to preach the glorious gospel here in these days; for many are the fervent

> prayers put up by the people for the preacher; and they hear the word for eternity. Divine truths have their own infinite weight and importance in the minds of the people. Beams of divine light, together with irresistible energy, accompany every truth delivered . . . I bless God for these days, and would not have been without seeing what I now see in the land – No; not for the world.[11]

This year 1791 proved to be of the greatest importance in many respects. It marked the beginning of revivals which continued in several districts of North Wales over the three following years and, more occasionally, similar scenes were to be seen there repeatedly over the next forty years. The moral change was immense and permanent for several generations to come. In 1795 the Calvinistic Methodist Association at Bala (which brought together the leaders from many Societies) could record that while family worship had been virtually unknown sixty years earlier, 'now, by the grace of heaven, there are hundreds of families worshipping God in every county'.[12] In 1811 we find Charles writing: 'The whole country is in a manner emerging from a state of great ignorance and barbarity, to civilization and piety . . . Bibles without end are called for, are read diligently, learned by heart, and searched into with unwearied diligence and care. Instead of vain amusements, dancing, card-playing, interludes, quarrelling, and barbarous and most cruel fightings; we have now prayer meetings, our congregations are crowded, and public catechising is become pleasant, familiar and profitable.'[13]

The year 1791 also marked the beginning of a passing of spiritual leadership to the North and to Charles.

[11] *Thomas Charles*, vol. 2, pp. 88–91.
[12] *Thomas Charles' Spiritual Counsels*, p. 459.
[13] *A Brief Memoir*, Morgan, p. 368.

Daniel Rowland had died in 1790, to be followed by his close associate, William Williams, best remembered for his hymn, 'Guide me, O Thou great Jehovah', on January 11, 1791.[14]

In 1790, Williams wrote a long letter to Charles on the importance of purity of doctrine and of maintaining the credal statements of the Reformed churches. Another long letter from his hand followed, written only a few days before his death.[15] He told the younger man that though he had 'travelled nearly three thousand miles every year for over fifty years' he could now only move between his fireside and his bed. More than anyone else, Williams had been the penman among the preachers of the Awakening in Wales, and perhaps he correctly surmised that Charles would be his successor in this respect as in others. What was needed at this later date was a work of preservation and consolidation. Charles was prepared by God for that role. A lesser leader in his position might have supposed that, given the expanding evangelistic opportunity in the country, this was no time to think of anything else. That was not Charles' view. Only a few months after Williams' death, we find him involved in examining errors alleged in the teaching of one of the best-known men among the Calvinistic Methodists, the Rev. Peter Williams, and it was at an Association meeting at Bala that the expulsion of Peter Williams from the connexion was confirmed.

Few men have held the objective contents of the faith – for which we are to contend – in better balance with experimental Christianity than did Charles. He knew that knowledge and piety belong together and understood the danger of

[14] Williams's hymns (over 800 in Welsh and 100 in English), in the words of Elvet Lewis, 'both stirred and soothed a whole nation for more than a hundred years'.

[15] See *Spiritual Counsels*, pp. 368–9, where extracts of Williams' letters of May 28, 1790 and of January 1, 1791 are conflated.

making emotion and excitement the primary characteristics of Christianity – a danger which is too easily forgotten in times of revival. Much though he loved itinerant preaching, from about this date he gave increasing time to putting the means of acquiring clearer biblical knowledge into the hands of the people. With this in view he published a catechism in 1789 which immediately established his theological reputation. A second edition was called for in 1791. In 1799 he originated an influential quarterly magazine, *Trysorfa Ysprydol* ('The Spiritual Treasury'), and early in the 1800s he began work on what became his *magnum opus*, *Y Geiriadur Ysgrythyrol* ('Scriptural Dictionary') which occupied him over many years. In January 1809 he could at last write to a friend: 'I have finished the *Geiriadur*. It really had well nigh finished me.' Edward Morgan believed that, next to the Bible, the *Scriptural Dictionary* was 'by far the best book in the Welsh language'. Besides his own literary work, Charles superintended the reprinting of older books. In 1803 he established a printing press – 'the Lord's Press' – at Bala and became responsible for supervision and proof-reading. In the next eleven years the Bala press issued fifty-five editions of elementary school books.

All these and other efforts, however, were subsidiary to an overriding consideration – the giving of the Bible itself to the people. As already noted, the primary purpose of the circulating schools was to enable people to read the Bible. But the very success of these schools only underlined a more basic problem, namely, where were cheap copies of the Scriptures in Welsh to be obtained? Charles was concerned with that question as early as 1787. Through the 1790s his chief hope of a supply lay in the 'Society for Promoting Christian Knowledge' in London. In 1792 Charles urged the Society to print ten thousand copies of the Welsh Bible, and promised to pay for five thousand copies as soon as they were printed. The board of the SPCK was so hesitant and desultory that the asked-for edition of ten thousand did not appear until 1799. This supply had scarcely reached Wales before it was sold out. In the opinion of one observer, 'Not one fourth part of the country was supplied.' Back in 1787, writing of the Bible, Charles had supposed he could put 'one thousand or two thousand to very good use'. Twelve years later, such had been the success of the gospel that ten thousand copies were not enough for a quarter of the country! The meaning of the statistics was perhaps best embodied in the story of sixteen-year-old Mary Jones who, after careful saving, walked barefoot the thirty miles to Charles' home in Bala to buy a Bible in the year 1800. She succeeded, though others who followed must have found the stocks entirely gone.

Despite such demand, astonishingly, the SPCK relapsed into its former inaction and so, convinced that other steps were necessary if the need of Wales was to be met, Charles gave a lead which set in motion events that secured the formation of the British and Foreign Bible Society. The impression made by Charles' pleas for Wales, accompanied by news of what was happening there, played a major part in bringing evangelical leaders in London and elsewhere to see what a flow of cheap Bibles might do for the whole world. Thus, in 1804, one of the most important agencies of the nineteenth century was born.

When the first Welsh New Testament from the Society was published in 1806, and the whole Bible the following year, the expectations of further large sales in Wales were more than fulfilled. In the words of one report: 'The young people were to be seen consuming the whole night in reading it. Labourers carried it with them to the fields, that they might enjoy it during the intervals of their labour and lose no opportunity of becoming acquainted with its sacred truths.' One testimony to the truth of this quotation comes from the one-time notorious English atheist, William Hone. Travelling in Wales, Hone was surprised to see a girl at a cottage door reading a Bible. 'Oh! the Bible!' he said to her as he stopped. 'Yes,' answered the girl, 'It is the Bible.' 'I suppose you are performing your task?' the Englishman enquired. 'Task?' responded the girl, 'What do you mean "task"?' 'I suppose your mother has set you so much to read,' Hone said confidently. 'Surely you would not otherwise read the Bible?' 'Not at all,' was the answer, 'I only wish I could read it all day long.'

Where there is true love of Christ and Scripture there will always be a wide catholicity of interest and concern. Charles was never preoccupied with his own work. He had valuable correspondence with Christians in Scotland and America; he visited Ireland and was often in London. He longed for the Bible to go to 'all the inhabitants of our globe'.[16] It was in that same spirit that the generally poor Christians of North Wales were among the most generous supporters of the Bible Society. Commenting on that point, Charles wrote: 'There are none of our poor people willing to live and die without contributing their mites towards forwarding so glorious a design. Their zeal and eagerness in the good cause surpass everything I have ever before witnessed. On several occasions we have been obliged to check their liberality, and take half of what they offered, being what we thought they ought to give. Great joy prevails universally at the thought that poor heathens are likely soon to be in possession of the Bible; and you never

[16] *Spiritual Counsels*, p. 310.

hear prayer put up without petition for the Bible Society and the heathen nations.'

Considering the extent of Charles' labours and travels, one is inclined to think that he was a man of unusually strong physique. That was not the case, as his letters show. In 1800 his health was particularly low and a thumb had to be amputated on account of frostbite which he had suffered on an urgent winter journey in the mountains of Snowdonia. It was long remembered in Bala how, when his illness looked most serious, an old man named Richard Owen thrilled a prayer meeting with the earnestness of his petition, 'Fifteen, Lord; wilt Thou not give him to us for fifteen years? for my brethren's sake, this prayer is made, and for my neighbours too.'

Charles lived to within six weeks of the time asked for in 1800. According to a long-expressed desire, he was active until within a month of his death: 'There is nothing worth living for but to advance the Lord's work. I can sincerely say that I would far sooner die than live to serve myself.' He died at his home in Bala on October 5, 1814, in his fifty-ninth year, and his beloved Sally (of whom he said, 'I bless the Lord that I have had a praying wife') followed him just nineteen days later. [17]

A Life and Faith Too Little Remembered

Edward Morgan concludes his *Brief Memoir* with comments on what he saw as the four outstanding characteristics of his subject. They were his love and benevolence; his spirituality

[17] There is much in Charles' life and writings on the centrality of prayer in the life of the believer, including the caution: 'To see God by faith in prayer will cause our words to be few. Our distance from him, and losing sight of him, is what makes us talkative.'

of mind; his great popularity despite the fact that he did not have 'popular talents' as a preacher; and his humility. 'The year before his death Charles wrote: 'I feel ashamed when I think how little I have done, compared with what I ought to have done – with what was wanted to be done. "O God, be merciful to me a sinner," is the language of my heart daily.'[18]

Today Charles' statue stands silent outside the large Calvinistic Methodist Chapel in Bala and his old home, converted into a branch of Barclay's Bank, deals in lesser riches than it did two hundred years ago. Perhaps no man was the means of bringing more blessing to his native land, and yet no books on his life have been available for a long time.[19] Too often, if he has been thought about at all, his life and writings have been adjudged to have little significance for modern times.

The records of revival are considered as examples of primitive emotionalism, and the impact of the Bible is explained in terms of a simple, uneducated people. But if, on the contrary, we believe that Christ is risen and that in history he has been pleased to show his power and presence through the preaching of the gospel, then the times when Charles lived both raise serious questions and give us great encouragement. To know 'the Holy Ghost sent down from heaven' is not the prerogative of any one century. Our contemporary poverty is the poverty of ignorance and unbelief. We have lost truth and in so doing we have lost experience. The writings of Thomas Charles reveal nothing original but they can renew in us clearer convictions about the extent of man's fall and

[18] *Spiritual Counsels*, p. 392.

[19] In addition to *Thomas Charles' Spiritual Counsels* (see note 4 above), there is much valuable material on Charles in vol. 2 of *The Calvinistic Methodist Fathers of Wales*, translated by John Aaron (Edinburgh: Banner of Truth, 2008).

rebellion against God, and the amazing plan of redemption. This alone is the message which has changed and can change the world.

Charles was no party man and it was only slowly and reluctantly that the connexion to which he belonged became a separate denomination. But he believed the truths commonly designated 'Calvinistic' to be bound up with the very life and existence of the church. The supreme reason why there is any salvation at all is that there might be a people 'to the praise of the glory of his grace' (*Eph.* 1:6). He did not preach 'Calvinism', but he and his associates preached the gospel in a way that unashamedly upheld those truths that humble man and display the sovereignty of divine grace. Far from thinking that such preaching inhibits evangelism, he believed it was the very means in the hands of God for conviction of sin and that wherever such conviction is found the truths called 'Calvinistic' are instantly relevant to man's condition:

> Everything in the councils of heaven favours a *returning sinner* – election, particular redemption, vocation, justification, etc. – all, all are in his favour.[20]

These same truths, joyfully believed, were at the heart of his daily living. In one of his early letters, he writes:

> I find it daily indispensably necessary to have a clear apprehension of the eternity, unchangeableness, freeness and independency of God's love, to enable me to walk forward with any degree of confidence and comfort. God's love depends upon nothing outside of himself, but upon his sovereign will and pleasure only. Christ did not die for us to cause God to love, but God's love alone was the cause of Christ's

[20] *Spiritual Counsels*, p. 388.

> propitiation . . . I want nothing but to know more experimentally the power of this love, more effectually influencing my heart and life.[21]

When Charles drew near his end, like William Williams before him, he urged the maintenance of these truths upon the rising generation of ministers. Fine examples of this will be found in his *Spiritual Counsels*. John Elias, and other leaders in North Wales, continued this witness for several decades until a gradual change took place that was to affect both evangelism and spirituality. Valuable insight into why this happened will be found in Morgan's *Life of John Elias*.

As I have said, there is currently no biography of Charles in print. The two biographers he has had inclined to opposite directions. Edward Morgan (1783–1869) was the first, with his *Brief Memoir of the Life and Labours of the Rev. Thomas Charles* in 1828. It is a fine spiritual book but follows too closely the Christian custom of those times in its omission of almost all personal details. In his use, for instance, of any of Charles' letters to Sally Jones in the years of their courtship, Morgan could never bring himself to include such words as 'reams of paper could not tell you how much I love you'. D. E. Jenkins, the second biographer in 1910, says that Charles had a 'supramundane notion of what an autobiography ought to be,'[22] and he thought that Morgan erred still more in that respect as a biographer and editor. Unabridged copies of Charles' letters can be found in Jenkins' *Life of Thomas Charles*. But Jenkins fell into a fault of a very different kind (and magnitude!) in the near-two-thousand pages which make up the three volumes of his biography. Had he

[21] *Thomas Charles*, vol. 1, p. 264.

[22] Ibid., p. 85.

been briefer, his work might have made the best starting point for the rediscovery of Charles today. Instead, it is loaded with magnificent detail which operates with the weight of a tombstone. Further, though Morgan has the faults already mentioned, he has one supreme factor in his favour in his handling of Charles and his materials: he was in thorough sympathy with the whole outlook and doctrinal commitment of the Welsh leader. 'Supramundane' he may be, but, like Charles, he speaks to our souls and speaks for eternity.

In 1788 the Rev. Thomas Jones (of Creaton, Northamptonshire) wrote to Charles:

> O! highly favoured country! I believe that you have more of the spirit and simplicity of the primitive Christians, among the rocks of Wales, than there is anywhere else at this day throughout the whole world.[23]

The statement was probably too strong but we rise from reading the life and writings of Thomas Charles understanding, at least, why it could be made.

[23] Ibid, p. 597.

5

TWO MEN AND AN ISLAND

William Hepburn Hewitson (1812–50)

Robert Reid Kalley (1809–88)

Lord, thou knowest all my weakness, my folly, my sin, my utter insufficiency. But here I am. Oh, do thou take me, make me what thou wilt, send me where thou pleasest, do with me what thou seest fit, only let me feel thou art with me.

ROBERT KALLEY, on his conversion, 1834.

It comes to us as a surprise to find two men, and a small island, identified by Andrew Bonar as seeing 'the greatest happening in modern missions'. The statement is unexpected because the island to which he referred is scarcely mentioned in the annals of Christian history, and the names of the two men are almost unknown today.[1] But Bonar was speaking in 1846, and this is not the only example of great events that have not survived in the memory of the following generations. At the last day there will be a resurrection of reputations as well as of bodies, as the Puritans used to say.

The two men who are our subject were both born in the west of Scotland in the early part of the nineteenth century. They might never have known one another had they not met in Lisbon, Portugal, in January 1845. It was that meeting that joined them in the enterprise which Andrew Bonar described in the words already quoted.

[1] A welcome step to remedy this was taken by William B. Forsyth, in his biography, *The Wolf from Scotland: The Story of Robert Kalley – Pioneer Missionary* (Darlington: Evangelical Press, 1988). Mr Forsyth, himself a missionary in Brazil, lived to be over 100 and 'knew intimately' some of Kalley's contemporaries. For all that follows I am very largely dependent upon his book, and on the larger work, *Memoir of the Rev. W. H. Hewitson*, John Baillie (London: Nisbet, 1874, 11th edition).

Hewitson

William Hepburn Hewitson, the younger of the two men, was born in a country district of Ayrshire, near Maybole, on September 16, 1812. Little is known of his parents, save that his father sought to earn a living as a school master. This was no remunerative career in rural Scotland and it may have been financial need which took the family to Newcastle-on-Tyne when William was a boy of eight years. When he was thirteen they returned to Ayrshire, to Dalmellington, where his father was appointed parish teacher.

The father certainly taught his own son well. By the time he was seventeen, William was familiar with Latin and Greek, and learning Hebrew. His great and persisting disability was poor health, and it was on that account that he was not able to take up a university place in Edinburgh until November 1833 when he was 21 years old. His linguistic ability was quickly recognized. He bypassed the Junior Humanities Class, and went straight into the Senior. Before the end of his first year he entered the annual university competition for the prestigious gold-medal prize awarded to the best writer in Latin. He was competing with 139 others, who came, says his biographer, from 'the two great Edinburgh schools' as well as from other parts of Scotland and England. Hewitson tied first place with another student, and then lost by a slip in the play-off. The next year he was easily first, and the coveted gold medal was hung round his neck at a ceremony on March 31, 1835.

Hewitson's distinction was not limited to languages. He was first in his class in logic, and in his last year won the prize for an essay open to all students on the subject, 'The Nature, Causes and Effects of National Character'. Winners of this prize had to read their words to an assembly of the students and this was the occasion when several future colleagues heard him speak in public for the first time. One of these was Robert M'Cheyne's friend, James Hamilton, who commented, 'What a fine sense he has of the sublime!'

His Arts course ended in 1837. Hewitson then enrolled at the Divinity Hall in Edinburgh. Under the leadership of Thomas Chalmers and David Welsh, the Hall was now approximating to a 'school of the prophets'. Yet Hewitson did not enter the Hall at this date, but went instead to act as a tutor at Leamington in England. Part of the explanation for this course of action is significant. From the age of three he had thought of the Christian ministry as his life work, but one thing hindered him; he knew that to become a minister of Christ presupposes first being a Christian, and in 1837, at the age of 25, he was still unconverted. He had not previously allowed his consciousness of this fact to disturb his ambition to achieve fame in the university: 'I thought life without fame not worth having.' But when the ambition was fulfilled it did not bring the pleasure he had anticipated; instead there was misery and the discovery that pride was his master. 'Ambition', he would later write, 'is a devil – and public praise is a syren, which soothes while it destroys.'

It was this sense of inner failure that now held him and took him south to Warwickshire. Forty years earlier, Leamington was a mere village. When medicinal springs were found there in 1797 everything changed and the *Parliamentary Gazetteer* for 1840–3 could report that 'the principal street is scarcely excelled in any town throughout the whole kingdom'. The new spa town was 'a resort of the votaries of health or pleasure'. In this unlikely place Hewitson was to meet an example of what it means to be converted that he could not forget. One November day in 1837, soon after his arrival, he visited the baths and pump-room where the smart and well-dressed 'took the water' for their health. As he watched, he noticed a young man of very different appearance – emaciated, walking feebly and dressed in a coarse linen smock. While others drank from tumblers, this invalid used an earthenware cup, and then quietly withdrew. Meeting him later, Hewitson opened a conversation which led to a visit to his cottage home, shared with his parents. Here the youth spoke with joy of Christ's obedience unto death and his love for sinners, and, pointing to his clothes, said to his father, 'These will be no more needed: I wish you to sell them; the price of them will be enough to pay for my coffin.' Not long after, this unnamed friend fell asleep in Jesus.

Hewitson's struggle for real faith now increased, and the answer did not come at once. He was in the process of learning the difference between being religious and being a Christian. Religious he certainly was, but the religious man still lives for self; only the Christian for Christ. Now more serious, he entered the Divinity Hall in November 1838, although still feeling he was in darkness. 'I cried to *the unknown God* with my voice, and often cried in despair. The cry seemed never to reach his ears.' In a reference to how Hewitson appeared at this time, a fellow student said he would make 'an admirable professor of biblical criticism'. He certainly would not have made an evangelist. Yet it was not for lack of evangelical preaching that he remained in this condition. Among those he heard was Robert M'Cheyne at St Peter's, Dundee. After a visit to that congregation, about December 1839, Hewitson returned with more prayers and resolutions. In a 'covenant' dated December 29, 1839, he committed himself to crucify and subdue 'pride, vanity, revenge and worldly-mindedness'. But what he needed was personal knowledge of Christ and this was given to him in the Spring of the next year, 1840. Now he experienced what Chalmers meant when he said: 'The cross of Christ by the same mighty stroke wherewith it moved the curse of sin away from us, also surely moves away the power and love of it from over us.'

No longer was there any trust in resolutions. To his father he wrote:

> I am now convinced that, after hearing it preached a thousand times over, we still remain ignorant of the gospel, unless we see clearly, and feel joyfully, that Christ is offered to us, wretched, lost sinners, in all His fulness, as the free gift of God. I am sure of this, that for a long, long time I have been deceiving myself, and making myself miserable every day, through ignorance of a free, glorious gospel, while I imagined I clearly understood its gracious nature . . . While Satan thus blinded my eyes, I found myself unable to do the good works that I would. Now I see that the gospel is quite different – that it is free, and full, and wholly of grace.

On one of his first testimonies of this truth to others, he had the joy of seeing the heart of an old woman, 'an aged formalist', opened as he preached Christ to her. When he returned to Dalmellington in May 1840 the change in him was apparent to all. Laying his hand on the family Bible, he said, 'That shall henceforth be my daily study; I desire to converse through it daily with God.' After this he had only one more year at the Divinity Hall, where he was now among the foremost in house visitation and in the work of the College Missionary Association. 'We should be missionaries', he told his fellow students, not because we may be ministers but 'because we are Christians. "I am a missionary," is a thought which we should frequently – every day that passes – entertain in our minds.' John Braidwood, one of his friends who would become a veteran Free Church missionary in India, said this of the change that he saw:

> We knew him in the heyday of his intellectual vigour, and remember well how he read his prize essay, in the University of Edinburgh, to the admiring assembly of his fellow students. We knew him also after the love of Christ had touched his heart, and given a purer and more divine direction to all his powers. His fine genius was turned to the cross, and he became a little child.

When Hewitson finished at the Divinity Hall in March 1841, Dr Chalmers spoke of him as one of the most accomplished students who had ever passed through the Hall. The attention of others was also drawn to him, among them M'Cheyne, who later that year invited him to become his assistant. 'Glad would I have been to accept,' Hewitson said, but it was not to be. The state of his health had become a concern to many and an Edinburgh medical doctor had forbidden him to preach for a year. Not only had he weakened his whole constitution by the near-incredible amount of time he had given to study, but the state of his lungs was now in doubt. His biographer says, 'Again and again Mr M'Cheyne had applied to him in the hope of securing him as his assistant, but Mr Hewitson was still detained.'

His 'detention' was in fact to last for some two years. Unable to preach, he spent the summer of 1842 in Germany with friends and meeting with Christians. The spiritual scene there grieved him. 'Philosophy is the Dagon of many here', he wrote home. 'The mildew of rationalism has long been the religion of Germany . . . Even among the best Protestants, religion is in a very backward and dull condition.' He connected these conditions with the disregard for the fourth commandment, and observed, 'Germany tells me, that if Scotland lose her Sabbaths, she will lose along with them her religion and her God.' Before the end of 1842 he was back in Scotland and spent more than a year as an invalid, forbidden to leave the house in winter. He was suffering from inflammation of the throat and lungs. He could only observe from afar the events of the Disruption year, 1843, but his hope was still set on future usefulness, believing, 'The Lord has given me a long time for the cultivation of personal godliness, before it has pleased him to call me to the work of "planting and watering" in His fields.'

There was some improvement in Hewitson's health in 1844. He preached a first sermon in May and was ordained by the Free Church Presbytery of Edinburgh in November. By that date the Foreign and Missionary Committee of the Free Church had come up with a proposal. Unable to take on parish work, could he not go to the Mediterranean area, both for the discovery of missionary opportunities and for the sake of his health? A little later, the spiritual darkness of the island of Madeira was especially drawn to his attention, and it was proposed he go to Lisbon, Portugal, to learn Portuguese for a year, with the possibility of Madeira in view. Thus in December 1844 he arrived in Lisbon, where he found a few nervous Protestants, their homes watched by the Roman Catholic authorities. He set about learning Portuguese, helped by his Latin, and made rapid progress. The future still uncertain, he noted in his diary for January 27, 1845: 'Prayed that the Lord would direct my way to Madeira, or whithersoever he saw fit to send me.' The next day a visitor came to his door with news that was to change his life: 'Mr A— called this evening to tell me that Dr Kalley had arrived from Madeira.' Before the significance of this can be understood we must retrace our steps to Scotland to explain who this Dr Kalley was.

Kalley

Robert Reid Kalley, three years older than Hewitson, was born in Glasgow on September 8, 1809. His father, a wealthy and prosperous merchant, died when he was only a year old, and he lost his mother five years later. He was brought up by his stepfather. It seems that family wealth came down to him, for throughout later life he often acted as a man of independent means. The family background was Presbyterian, and his stepfather, he tells us, 'was a true father, giving me a moral and spiritual education by his example and precepts – together with much prayer'.

Kalley's thoughts turned early to the Christian ministry; perhaps with the inducement that his grandfather was the patron of a parish with an annual stipend of £350, a considerable sum in those days. So the young Kalley, after finishing at Glasgow Grammar School, proceeded to the Arts course at the University at the age of sixteen. Some come to faith in their student years. For Kalley it was the opposite. His nominal Christianity was not enough to withstand the clever unbelief he heard and he broke off his plans for the Christian ministry. He would later write: 'I could not bear the thought of being obliged to preach that which I considered a pack of lies. I therefore gave up all idea of becoming a clergyman and studied medicine.' Years of study in pharmacy and surgery followed, and his medical career started as a ship's doctor in 1829. In 1832 he settled as a medical practitioner in

Kilmarnock, Ayrshire. The fact that he was now a declared atheist did not hinder his popularity. He soon achieved a reputation both for his medical ability and for his socializing at sports and parties. 'The dancing doctor of Kilmarnock', was his nickname.

Confident in his superior education, Kalley was, at first, little troubled by what he regarded as the superstitious beliefs of some of his Christian patients. But the words with which one humble Christian man spoke to him about Christ were hard to shake off. Then he was confronted by something beyond his explanation, the end of a woman dying in poverty from painful cancer. As she lay there, with a peace stronger than her disease, and knowing the unbelief of her doctor, she urged him, 'Read the Book! It's all in the Book!' This direction he now began to follow. A stepsister guided him to evangelical literature and Alexander Keith on *Fulfilled Prophecy* was especially helpful to him. Years later, addressing the Free Church General Assembly, he was to say:

> I was an infidel, and revelled in the coldness, the darkness, the thrill of openly declaring my unbelief. When I discovered, be it said to my satisfaction, there is a God, and that this book [pointing to the Bible] is from God, I then felt that every Christian is called to enter that field of service in which he or she can use for God's glory the varied talents with which each has been endowed.

Kalley dated his conversion to the year 1834, by which time he was a member of the local Church of Scotland. When he started a class for boys on Sundays and Thursdays, in his dispensary, he did not have the support of some of the ministers, who condemned him for intruding on their work. Kalley was undeterred. It was another death that now influenced him further. On August 1, 1834, the Scots missionary and Bible translator, Robert Morrison, died in Canton. News of Morrison's passing drew his attention to China, and this, coupled with a magazine of the London Missionary Society calling for medical missionaries, led him to apply to that Society. He was accepted for China, with permission to stay longer in Scotland to further his medical and theological knowledge.

In the intervening period there was, however, an unexpected setback. Kalley became engaged to a Margareth Crawford of Paisley. She was a devout Christian and ready for missionary service; but unknown, it seems, to them both, the LMS rule was that no candidates for the mission field should be engaged without the approval and permission of the Board. The rule could not be bent, and so, with deep regret, Kalley had to resign as an LMS candidate and relinquish the hope of going to China. Even so, he was to have a part in the spread of the gospel in China, for it is said that as he pleaded the need of the Far East in a missionary meeting in January 1838, a Glasgow student named William Chalmers Burns was led to offer himself for missionary service.

MADEIRA

Scripture teaches us that 'the way of man is not in himself', and so it proved for Kalley at this point in his life. The happiness of marriage in February 1838 was soon overshadowed by his wife catching a cold that became pneumonia. Before she was fully recovered from this it became apparent that she had the beginnings of tuberculosis. This turned Dr Kalley's thoughts to the island he had once visited while at sea. Madeira – 'a floating garden', as some called it, on account of its seven hundred species of flowers and plants – had a warm climate, with temperatures rarely as low as 50°F., and seldom above 80°. It had won a reputation in Britain as an ideal resort for invalids. It was here that Kalley took his wife in October 1838 in the hope that a winter on the island would aid her recovery. He had no idea that he would be there, in all, for eight years.

Over one thousand miles from Britain, and nearly four hundred from the coast of north-west Africa, Madeira is 38 miles long and 12 to 15 miles wide. It has precipitous cliffs and mountains over 5,000 feet in height. At that time Funchal on the south coast was its only harbour. As a province of Portugal, the island's population of several thousand was ruled from Lisbon. At the same time its strategic position on trade routes had also made it a kind of commercial colony for Britain and Kalley found about three hundred Britishers there on his arrival. These fellow countrymen, he soon discovered, had no ready medical advice or treatment, and his help was soon called upon.

What concerned him still more was the absence of spiritual help. There were regular Church of England services taken by a clergyman, and also a Presbyterian chaplain, but neither of these men seem to have known what their calling was. So Kalley began Sunday services in a private house and quickly ran into the same opposition as he had faced from ministers in Kilmarnock. The Anglican chaplain warned the people against this unordained intruder. This resistance only deepened Kalley's concern, not only for the Britishers but also for the indigenous population who were all claimed by the Roman Catholic Church. He concluded that two steps were needed to enable him to break through existing barriers. To help the Britishers he needed to be ordained, and to reach the local populations he needed to get a Portuguese medical diploma in Lisbon. The natural place for ordination would have been the Church of Scotland but the urgency of the need made further years of study out of the question; he was convinced that 'Madeira was stretching forth her hands for the gospel'. So he went to London (in June 1839) where he was ordained by the Congregationalists. Then, calling at Lisbon, he gained the necessary qualification to practise medicine in Portuguese territories. Thus prepared, he returned to Funchal in October of the same year with his calling as a pioneer missionary to Madeira clearly before him.

Kalley had been shocked at the extent to which the Britishers remained exclusively apart from the Madeirans, who were a mixture of Portuguese, Moorish, and black African. With the exception of the owners of vineyards and a few others, the Madeirans were mostly servants and poor peasants. Lisbon prohibited the manufacture of any goods on the island. Illness and disease were common, and yet the people were largely without medical care. Their spiritual condition was still worse. All were baptized in the Roman Church and paid reverence to its cathedral and priests in Funchal, yet few had ever seen a Bible and none sat under its saving message.

Kalley's first attention was now directed to these people. He set up a medical clinic, offering free treatment and prescriptions, and there were twelve beds for those too ill simply to visit. With every patient it was his practice both to pray and to give them a written verse of Scripture. The Bible had been the principal means of his own conversion and he knew how the Holy Spirit could use it once in the hands of the people. But Madeira did not have what the Reformation had brought to Scotland – free schools where people could learn to read. He established the first before the end of 1839, and at his own expense began to spread a network of some twenty schools through the island where free education had previously been unknown. These were gatherings in cottages, usually in the evenings when adults could attend after work, and the text books were the Portuguese 'ABC' and the Portuguese Bible. The teachers were hired by Kalley. It is said that almost two and a half thousand attended these schools between 1839 and 1845, and that well over a thousand learned to read and study the Scriptures for themselves. Each one who gained the ability was held responsible to teach someone else. In a letter home Kalley reported:

> Hundreds of men, after heavy labours in the fields, went to school at night, and in almost every case they were motivated by the desire not merely to read the words of men, but the Word of God.

This degree of interest did not, of course, happen at once. But it grew steadily and was at its height in 1842, when, in addition to the schools, large numbers now gathered in the open air for Sunday worship. Kalley wrote:

> In 1842, especially in the summer and autumn, people came in large numbers to hear the Scriptures read and explained. Many walked ten or twelve hours, and climbed over mountains three thousand feet high, in coming and returning to their homes. The meetings were solemn – the hearers listened with unwearied attention – a hand was observed stealing up to remove a tear – and sometimes there was a general audible expression of wonder. This was especially the case when the subject of remark was the love of God in not sparing His own Son but giving Him up to die for the sins of the whole world, or the love of Christ in voluntarily taking upon Himself the wrath and curse which we deserved.

> For several months I believe that there were not fewer than one thousand persons present each Sabbath; generally they exceeded two thousand . . . We had a few simple hymns, expressive of adoration, gratitude, and praise. The tunes usually sung were the *Portuguese Hymn*, *Old Hundredth*, and *Martyrdom*; and there were few present who did not at least attempt to join in the singing.
>
> In some places the general topics of every-day conversation, in walking along the roads, or resting a little from labour in the fields, were the Word of God – the one sacrifice for sin – free salvation – the security of God's promises – the love of the Lord Jesus Christ – the peace of God – the hope of glory – the folly of image worship – the uselessness of penance. Often, too, the hymns of the Sabbath were heard through the week among the fields and vineyards; and there was much searching of the Scriptures, to know the Lord's declarations on the subjects brought before them.

Persecution

Such conditions could not last in a land dominated for centuries by Roman Catholicism. In 1841 a directive came from the government in Lisbon ordering the senior clergy to stop what was going on. This was, however, by no means easy to enforce, not least because the Bishop in Funchal himself admired what Kalley was doing. He had been one of Kalley's patients and had received the gift of a Bible from him. Some of the clergy were also sympathetic and tried to prepare a document in defence of Kalley, asserting (wrongly!) that he was only teaching what they taught. But enemies of Kalley outnumbered his friends, and when the Bishop was replaced by another man, hostility to the 'new sect' knew no restraint. The Canon of the cathedral, Carlos de Menezes, taught the people that Kalley was 'the wolf from Scotland'. A decree from Lisbon threatened imprisonment and fines on anyone holding public worship where any Portuguese were present, and on anyone propagating doctrines contrary to Catholic dogmas.

In January 1843 physical persecution began. That month a teacher, his wife and child were imprisoned for four months. Others were also condemned to prison for reading and teaching the Bible, among them a mother of seven children, Maria Alves. Two Madeirans who professed faith in Christ were at once excommunicated and compelled to hide in a cave for over a year. Kalley appealed against these proceedings to the supreme judge in Madeira and this man ruled that no law was being infringed by the Protestants. His finding was immediately appealed to the authorities in Lisbon who promptly annulled the judge's ruling (5 July 1843).

This seems to have been the signal for more widespread persecution. One thing especially seems to have incensed the church authorities in Funchal. Most of those who were turning to Christ were judged insignificant people but now a leading citizen of noble family, became a 'heretic'. Arsenio Nicos da Silva was drawn to Kalley on account of the serious illness of his daughter. When the local doctors had despaired of her life he appealed to the visitor. Kalley prayed with the patient, and successfully treated the girl. This prompted Da Silva to read the Bible that Kalley had given him, and there he found a message far different from the one he had long heard in the cathedral. Despite all the efforts of priests to prevent it, the man became a true believer.

Before the end of July 1843 Kalley himself was committed to prison, and he was refused bail on the grounds that his offence was punishable by the death sentence. One of his few privileges was the right to receive visitors, but only three at a time, which led to queues of his spiritual children waiting outside the prison for their turn to see him. After he had been five months in prison he had visitors all the way from Edinburgh; they were a deputation from the Free Church of Scotland and it was in his cell that together they constituted a Free Church congregation in Funchal. Meanwhile the British ambassador in Lisbon had been busy. It was determined that Kalley's imprisonment infringed a recent treaty that Britain had made with Portugal and he was released in January 1844.

But the attempts to stamp out his work continued. Twenty-six Madeirans remained in prison. The confinement did nothing to dim their testimony. The streets around the jail echoed the hymns sung by the happy prisoners until such singing was declared to be a violation of regulations. Obscene songs, apparently were allowed, but not hymns. Among the prisoners no testimony was brighter than that of Maria Alves and the authorities sought to make an example of her. After being in a cell for sixteen months she was charged with apostasy, heresy and blasphemy. The issue that finally condemned her was the judges' question, 'Do you believe the consecrated host to be the real body and real blood, and the human soul, and the divinity of Jesus Christ?' She firmly replied 'I do not believe it.' Upon which the judge pronounced,

> I condemn the accused, Maria Joaquina, to suffer death as provided in the law; the cost of the process, etc, to be paid out of her goods.[2]

Although Kalley was no longer in prison, he was no longer allowed to practise medicine in Funchal. The possibility of his assassination was publicly discussed, and the first six months

[2] The sentence was not carried out.

of 1844 he spent among the people in the mountainous district of Antonio da Serra. Here, in the summer months he would regularly address some 600 people in the open air and the district became one of the main centres of evangelical faith in the island.

Across the island there was no lessening of the persecution. Some Christians were beaten; some stoned; five families had their homes burned down. In several instances families were refused any place to bury their dead except on the public highway. For three days, Kalley reported, fifty soldiers were quartered among the people of Antonio da Serra, 'and allowed to plunder, and perpetrate every cruelty, as if in the land of a vanquished enemy. Twenty-two of the most peaceful and well-behaved men and women of the island were taken to Funchal in the *Diana* frigate and put in prison among criminals.'

There were now renewed attempts to prosecute Kalley himself and the British ambassador in Lisbon warned him that he would not be able to prevent his deportation from Madeira if he continued to teach the native people. Kalley was concerned not to be deported and in the hope that his temporary absence might reduce the level of persecution, he went with his wife to Lisbon in January 1845.

The Two Men in Partnership

The surprise that awaited Kalley in Lisbon was to meet his fellow-Scot, William Hewitson, and to discover the latter's intention of proceeding to Madeira. It may have been something of a surprise to Hewitson also to hear of the dangerous situation Kalley had just left. For years Hewitson had been eagerly looking forward to a field of service; now at the age of thirty-two, on the threshold of such service, the prospects were daunting. The persecuted Madeiran Christians on the island were not yet formed into a church; over twenty were in prison, and a woman remained under sentence of death. After hearing these things from Dr Kalley, Hewitson wrote in his Journal for January 30, 1845: 'Many circumstances of a trying kind to flesh and blood rose up before my view. But the Lord has made the way straight before my face, and I would not turn back. Had comfort in the prospect of going to Madeira.'

The two men took the five days' sail to Madeira in the middle of February. The warmth of their relationship was going to be essential in what lay ahead. The converts and the awakened on the island were all naturally attached to Kalley. Single-handed he had pioneered and led the work. But now, so well-known and watched by the authorities, and no longer allowed to practise as a pharmacist and a physician, Kalley saw that the best hope for the continuance of the work was for Hewitson to take up the lead role. He recognized that God had prepared the younger man for just this situation. The development at this stage resembled what is recorded in Acts chapter 11. When results of the awakening at Antioch were too much for Barnabas to handle, Saul came from Tarsus to his aid. In connection with Hewitson's coming to Funchal, Kalley wrote home to Scotland: 'Were there no one to enter on my labours, I should feel very much embarrassed; but I thank God we have here a better hand for polishing the stones than I could prove.'

The young disciples in Madeira quickly took to the new preacher, regarding his gift in their language as a gift of God. As Hewitson came to know them he could only admire what he saw of Christ in them. Their thirst for the Word of God reminded him of what had been seen in revivals in Scotland. As there was no question of holding public services in Funchal, the people gathered willingly in secret night meetings. At the end of one joyful service one Christian exclaimed, 'I should like if it had lasted for ever.' Hewitson emphasized to them the need to count the cost, yet the warning almost seemed unnecessary.

A woman, he says, whose heart overflowed with love to Christ, told him she would rather let them put her to death than hear them maligning the truth without defending it. Preaching one night on the man who found treasure hid in the field and was willing to part with all to obtain it, Hewitson asked one of his hearers if he understood. Only later did he see the man's bruises and learn that he had been beaten the previous evening for Christ's sake.

This man's name was Jeronymo. When he was seventeen he had suffered an illness that affected both his body and his mind. Thereafter he could not stop a tremor in his limbs, and in his mental state he was commonly regarded as an imbecile. The police ignored him as not worth their attention when he had begun to attend Kalley's meetings. He drank in the gospel; learned to read and instead of his former work at begging, became an earnest distributor of tracts and New Testaments. When Kalley was in prison, Jeronymo had been a regular visitor. On one of these occasions Kalley spoke to him about the resurrection of the body, but instead of being encouraged the Madeiran was grieved at the idea as he looked at his trembling hands and feet. The idea of their resurrection gave him no pleasure. But when Kalley went on to explain that the bodies of all those who die in Jesus will be raised in the likeness of His glorious body, the look on Jeronymo's face turned to wonder.

Hewitson held a first communion service the month after his arrival, and Jeronymo was among the thirty or forty Portuguese converts present. There appear to have been communions in successive months, all held in secret. In May 1845, he wrote home of fifty-nine or sixty Madeiran converts being present at a communion service, and added: 'No suspicion, I believe, exists as to our having had such a meeting. There are many applying, besides, for admission to the Lord's table. The work is going forward. No man can stay the hand of the Almighty Workman. There are many dear children of God in this place, whose sincerity is put to the test by many adversaries.'

It was impossible to organize a church on any regular basis, or for all those concerned to meet in one place in Funchal or to meet together at the Lord's table. Later in 1845 Hewitson speaks of eighty-seven Portuguese converts having received the Lord's Supper in the course of three weeks. 'Of almost all,' he writes, 'I may say that they afford good proofs of being born again. Besides these, there are more than one hundred who would gladly be admitted for examination with a view to communion. There are here, at this moment, hundreds – there are thousands – who would gladly listen to the preaching of the gospel, if the iron hoof of spiritual oppression did not keep them down. The work of the Lord is prospering.' Away from Funchal there was more freedom from the police and at Serra St Antonio, fifteen miles away, Hewitson was able to preach to nearly two hundred in the home of a merchant.

Two means are especially mentioned as causes for the advancement of the work. One was the distribution and reading of the Scriptures. The other was the personal witness of the believers. Numbers of them were notable in this regard.

One woman, Antonia da Corea, is described as overflowing with love; so influential was she that her enemies said she had 'an enchanted cup' and if any drank of it they were certain to become 'Calvinistas'. It is recorded of her that 'she was greatly honoured in bringing souls to Jesus'.

By the summer of 1845 Hewitson's work had the attention of the authorities and he was threatened with imprisonment. This did not disturb him unduly. The jailer in Funchal at this time had become a friend of his prisoners, and on occasions would allow them out on parole for an evening so that they could attend meetings. Roman priests were a different proposition, and were now doing all they could to stir mobs against the believers. It was evident to Hewitson that his comparative freedom could not last; in addition, a temporary breakdown in his health was a warning that he was stretched to the limit. Before the end of 1845 he was therefore intent on training future leaders and began a class of men he called 'catechists' with whom he met twice a week for a systematic study of doctrine. From these men came the first elders – foremost among them Arsenio da Silva – and deacons of the church who were ordained to their work in April 1846.

Meanwhile the persecution had steadily increased. Twenty-eight were in prison. Hewitson decided that it might lessen the fury if he were to leave the island for a short period and this he did in May 1846, intending to return. He had only been in Madeira for fifteen months, but in that time a church had been gathered and established, with many confirmed in the faith of Christ. For part of this time Dr Kalley had been absent in Scotland. After his return to Madeira he was to say, 'Mr Hewitson has been a source of incalculable good to Madeira. I feel myself to be very much a hewer of wood or a drawer of water' (5 February 1846).

Hewitson would never live in Madeira again. Soon after he left, the storm came to its height. The house of a British resident where a Portuguese service was being held on a Sunday morning was broken into by a mob. As Arsenio da Silva sought to leave he was confronted by the Canon of the cathedral who thrust an image into his face with the order, 'Kiss it', and, 'Adore your God!'

The British consul warned that he could offer the persecuted no protection, though he did take Mrs Kalley[3] and other women into the consulate building for their safety. It was none too soon. The next Sunday the mob broke into the Kalley's home. With the police standing by doing nothing, the house was ransacked as they looked for 'the wolf from Scotland'. Kalley had left the house a few hours earlier through a back entry, from which, disguised as an old sick woman, he was carried in a hammock to a British ship in Funchal harbour. This was Kalley's farewell to the island where he had settled as a benefactor. The Kalleys left behind them all their personal possessions. Worse was to happen to the Madeiran Christians across the island as mobs did what they pleased at the instigation of the Church. Homes were plundered and some destroyed. Hundreds took to hiding places in the mountains. One man was murdered; several women were beaten; one was assumed dead and dragged to a Protestant grave by a roadside where she was found to be alive. All known Bible readers were excommunicated, fined and left without food. A British naval officer reported, 'Every day we hear of new cases of violence and cruelty against believers. They are left with no other alternative than to flee for their lives.'

[3] Margareth Kalley is only a background figure in the story; it seems that her ill health persisted and prevented her sharing more largely in her husband's work. She died when with her husband in Beirut in 1851.

On August 22, 1846, two hundred of the persecuted were given space on a ship sailing for Trinidad. An English resident, describing the event, wrote to Hewitson: 'The sound of hymns is very sweet as it rises from the hold. It is a great privilege to be near them in this time of need, and to see that their faith does not fail. They never speak against their persecutors – they only mention them with pity. Sometimes I overhear them in prayer, praying for their enemies.'

Yet the sorrows of those forced to leave were great. Arsenio da Silva is an illustration. His life in danger and his home closely watched, he was not able to see his family again before he sailed. His wife and daughter, adhering to the Roman Church, refused to go with him. In response to a message, she sent him the money he requested and replied kindly but, as he said, 'with no faith in Jesus'. They would not meet again. Another ship was to take 350 more to Trinidad, until there was a church of some eight hundred gathered there. Others left Madeira for other destinations in the West Indies, making in all an estimated total of around two thousand.[4]

Lessons

1. *What happened in Madeira was the direct result of preaching and teaching*. The willingness of those who became Christians to suffer; the joyfulness of their words to others; their brotherly love; the tenderness of their feelings towards their persecutors – all these things were the consequence of the truths upon which they fed. Kalley and Hewitson had a high view of the power of the Word of God in the hand of the Holy Spirit. 'It is good to long to be filled with the Spirit,' Hewitson wrote, 'it is better to be filled. When we are,

[4] Figures given by Baillie and Forsyth differ somewhat.

the Spirit himself preaches by us, and the Word is in Divine demonstration and power.' The preacher must have faith in the indwelling presence of Jesus; it is not enough for him to repeat Christ's words; to speak as a witness, he must have Christ's heart. Effective preaching there cannot be without real communion with Christ. In Hewitson's words, 'A well-tuned violin is not more necessary to the musical performer, than a heart in unison with the heart of God is to the preacher of the gospel.' 'It was Bible preaching of Christ', says his biographer, 'which, in the hands of the Spirit, told with such marvellous effect on the consciences of the people.'

2. If it is asked whether there was *something particularly distinctive about Hewitson's preaching*, I believe the answer is that there was. He was persuaded that the greatest obstacle to the gospel lies in the wrong views of God in the human heart. Satan works to represent God as 'stern, pitiless, inexorable'. 'Oh, how Satan strives to make us believe that our Lord is "an austere man"! How he labours to give us false view and impressions of the character of our Lord!' Thus men come to think that self-inflicted suffering is a way to please God. 'Hence,' he says, 'the self-inflicted tortures of Hinduism. Hence the penances and mortifications of Popery', as if pain was in accordance with the divine nature. 'This is one of the depths of Satan. The effect is to make the poor sinner unable to realize any comfortable experience of the truth that "God is love", and to entangle him in vain endeavours to establish a righteousness of his own.'

In a citadel of Roman Catholicism it was given to Hewitson to attack with great power the legalism endemic in the heart of the natural man.[5] To people long bred in the idea

[5] The place of works as a ground of salvation continues to be confused in Roman

that God demands some satisfaction from us by way of works came the truth that salvation is a free gift, bestowed on the guilty wholly on account of divine love. This was the commending of God's love that brought awakening in Madeira, as it had in apostolic times and at the Reformation in Europe. In the first confession of faith to be translated in Scotland in the sixteenth century, George Wishart, the martyr, wrote:

> The principal intent of all the Scripture canonical is, to declare that God is benevolent and friendly minded to mankind; and that he hath declared that kindness in and through Jesus Christ his only Son; which kindness is received by faith.[6]

To those who had long believed that God was against them, Hewitson preached: 'It is as sinful to doubt God's willingness to save me as to doubt his existence.' Certainly he spoke of the judgment we deserve, but he knew it is the knowledge of God's love that draws and wins. He could say to his hearers: 'You know well what Christ is – you have been in his company – you have tasted that he is gracious – your experience has taught you that he does sympathize . . . Come then to Him with all your sorrows.' Prominent in all his preaching was the following note, 'Our salvation depends not on the question – What are my sins and my back-

---

Catholicism. The official *Catechism of the Catholic* Church (1994) teaches, 'The children of our holy mother the Church rightly hope for *the grace of final perseverance and the recompense* of God their Father for the good works accomplished with his grace in communion with Jesus' (p. 438). But legalism, Hewitson believed, was by no means confined to Roman Catholicism. In a letter of 1841 he wrote to a friend: 'I relish exceedingly the gospel-views of Christ which your letters so markedly bring out, and in such broad contrast to the law-views of a Judaistic spirit, which, for want of clear discernment of Christ, pervades the preaching of many even regenerated ministers.'

[6] *Miscellany of the Wodrow Society*, vol. 1 (Edinburgh: Wodrow Society, 1844), p. 12. I have modernized spelling in this quotation.

sliding? But on the question – What are Christ's merits, and the Father's promises.'

Andrew Bonar said of Hewitson, 'He was the likest to Robert M'Cheyne of any I knew.' Undoubtedly much of the resemblance lay in the way the tenderness of Christ shone through both men. Yet Hewitson saw himself as far short of what he ought to be: he was still saying at the end of his short life, 'I should be far more tender.'[7] He had not attained *the* likeness he sought, yet he was heard to confess, 'I am better acquainted with Jesus than I am with any friend upon earth.'

3. After all that can be said about this remarkable period, one thing especially compels attention. It is *the great love of Christ for his people.* The lives of so many on this island in the Atlantic were changed in accordance with his own words, 'Other sheep I have, which are not of this fold: them also I must bring, and they shall hear my voice' (*John* 10:16). Just as it had been in Antioch, the awakening came to Madeira because Christ was there (*Acts* 11:21). Kalley had wanted to go to China, and M'Cheyne had wanted Hewitson in Dundee, but Christ had another purpose for them. As in all conversions, the explanation lay in the God, 'who is rich in mercy, for his great love wherewith he loved us'.

Further, it was the same love that sent the blessings that permitted the persecution. First the new church in Madeira was sifted by suffering, and then the dispossessed Christians were uprooted and scattered for greater purposes. They were to form immigrant churches in the West Indies, and then in

[7] Hewitson paid one visit to his former flock in Trinidad. He became minister of the Free Church of Scotland at Dirleton, East Lothian, where he died on August 7, 1850, age 37. There is no longer a Free Church at Dirleton but a fine plaque to his memory is in the little museum in the gatehouse of the Church of Scotland.

the United States. It was while Kalley was visiting the Madeirans in the United States that a book came into his hands that pointed in a new direction. Daniel Kidder in his *Sketches of Residence and Travels in Brazil* described the spiritual destitution of that vast Portuguese-speaking country. It led to Kalley's arrival in Rio de Janeiro in 1855. What he had known in microcosm in Madeira was now visible to him in millions – poverty and religion, crucifixes without a risen Saviour, Roman superstition but no living Christianity. This was where Christ intended him to be for the next twenty-one years.

But Kalley could do little without helpers and, instead of turning to fellow countrymen, he appealed to three of the key Madeiran leaders who had settled in the United States. Not long established with their families in their new homes, it was a hard invitation to accept, yet all three did. One of them replied, 'I have always wished to work for my Saviour.' Another said that if he did not go all the pleasure in life would be lost.

In this way the foundation stones for a Protestant church in Brazil were put in place. Kalley and his assistants were chosen by Christ for a great work. With little or no formal education, they were well-schooled in 'the sufferings of Christ for his body's sake'. Their witness to Christ was compelling and their testimony fearless. Prevented from reaching their fellow countrymen in their island home, the Madeiran Christians would prepare the way for the gospel to spread across Brazil. The hymns first sung by the few Christians in Rio are today sung by millions in that land.[8]

[8] A number of these hymns were written by Kalley's second wife, Sarah Poulton Kalley. Robert Kalley died in Edinburgh in 1888, the funeral being taken by his friend, Hudson Taylor. The grave is in the Dean Cemetery.

Thus in this world, and in the pages of history, do we see the love and the power of Christ. And yet it is all only a foretaste of what will be:

> After this I beheld, and, lo, a great multitude, which no man could number, of all nations, and kindreds, and people, and tongues, stood before the throne, and before the Lamb, clothed with white robes, and palms in their hands; And cried with a loud voice, saying, Salvation to our God which sitteth upon the throne, and unto the Lamb (*Rev*. 7:9–10).

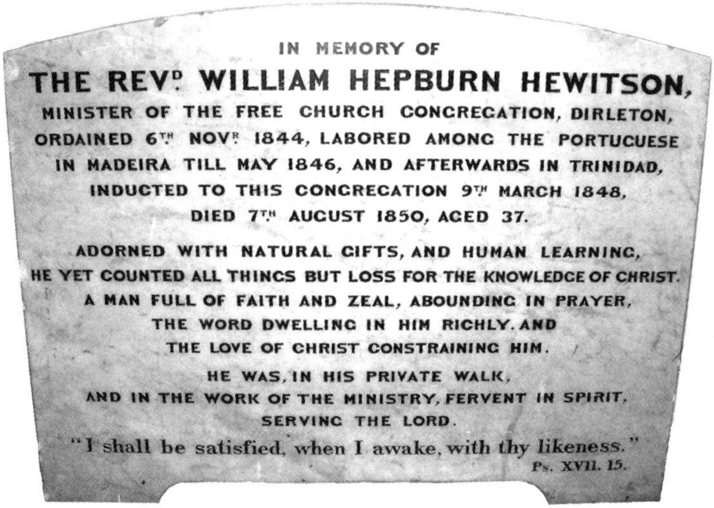

Plaque in Dirleton Parish Church, East Lothian

6

CHARLES & MARY COLCOCK JONES: ANOTHER VIEW OF THE OLD SOUTH

Charles Colcock Jones (1804–63)

To

THE MEMORY OF

Charles Colcock Jones, D. D.,

WHO, WHETHER
HIS WORK AS A MIS-
SIONARY TO THE BLACKS,
OR THE WIDER INFLUENCE OF
HIS EXAMPLE, AND WRITINGS IN
THEIR BEHALF, BE CONSIDERED, IS
JUSTLY ENTITLED TO THE NAME OF THE
APOSTLE OF THE NEGRO SLAVES; AND OF HIS
MANY FELLOW WORKERS IN THE GOSPEL MINISTRY
UPON THE SAME FIELD, ONLY LESS CONSPICUOUS, SELF-
DENYING AND USEFUL; AND OF THE HOST OF MASTERS AND
MISTRESSES, WHOSE KINDNESS TO THE BODIES, AND EFFORTS
FOR THE SALVATION OF THE SOULS OF THE SUBJECT RACE
PROVIDENTIALLY PLACED UNDER THEIR RULE AND
CARE, WILL BE READ OUT, WITH THEIR NAMES,
IN THE DAY WHEN "THE BOOKS SHALL BE
OPENED," AND "GOD SHALL BRING
EVERY WORK INTO JUDGMENT,
WITH EVERY SECRET THING,
WHETHER IT BE GOOD OR
WHETHER IT BE EVIL,"

THIS BOOK IS REVERENTLY AND LOVINGLY DEDICATED.

R. Q. MALLARD, the dedication in his book,
Plantation Life before Emancipation, 1892.

On summer's evenings in 1833, when the sun was low in the tops of the trees, a young woman would sit in the porch of the plantation house of Montevideo, straining her eyes for the sight of her husband returning on horseback. Mary Jones was twenty-seven-years old, and a native of Liberty County, coastal Georgia, where, three years before, she had married Charles Colcock Jones. Both came from prosperous families of planters, and the young couple were inheritors of over nine hundred acres producing rice and sea-cotton. Here, at Montevideo, they built what Mary called 'this beautiful new home'. At first the site was no more than 'a rough and uncultivated field'. On one side was the North Newport River, and on the other more than twenty acres of sweeping lawns were in preparation, interspersed with plantings of groves and avenues of live oak, cedars, pines and magnolias. In due course two more plantations would be added to their properties: Arcadia, with nearly two thousand acres, and Maybank, with seven hundred acres, fifteen miles away on Colonel's Island, where sea breezes made a second home a favourite retreat in high summer. All this land was worked by between one and two hundred slaves, or 'servants,' as they preferred to call them.

The late homecomings of Charles Colcock Jones at this date had nothing to do with agriculture or cotton. Such work had ended hours earlier. Far less had they any relation to socializing. Rather he was away on various plantations, from three to ten miles distant, for the purpose of preaching to slaves. This had not been the lifestyle of the couple at the time of their wedding in 1830. Five months later, on 31 May 1831, he was called to the charge of the First Presbyterian Church of Savannah where he was ordained as pastor and gave 'eighteen months of earnest, laborious, and successful work for the good of both races'.[1] Charles and Mary Jones might have continued to live useful lives in Savannah, but an overriding constraint pulled them in another direction. In November 1832 he gave up his ministerial income, returned to Liberty County, and consecrated his life to the spiritual welfare of the African-American people.

It was probably without precedent for a plantation owner to become a missionary to slaves. Nor was any other Presbyterian minister in the South employed in such work. To understand how this happened we must take the story further back.

Liberty County and Its People

Charles Colcock Jones was born at Liberty Hall, his father's home in Liberty County, on December 20, 1804. The surrounding population owed its origin to two sources. First, to the Puritan forbears who had led a migration initially from New England to South Carolina; then in 1752, some 350 of

[1] 'Memorial of Charles Colcock Jones' by John Jones in *Memorial Volume of the Semi-Centennial of the Theological Seminary at Columbia, South Carolina* (Columbia, SC: Presbyterian Publishing, 1884), p. 196.

their number had moved again into coastal Georgia where Britain had established its latest colony at Savannah in 1733. Members of this group settled the land, later to be known as Liberty County, between the Medway and the South Newport Rivers. As the main meeting-point of their lives, they early built the Midway Church, so-called on account of its position halfway between Savannah and Darien to the south. The white population in the County numbered 1,544 in 1830.

The second and larger source of population had origins more distant than New England. Some fifteen hundred slaves of African descent had come into Georgia with their white owners in 1752. Others were later to arrive, as trade in slaves between the South and Africa continued until finally abolished on January 1, 1808. The change at that date did not affect the slave status of the nine hundred thousand already in America. Those living in Liberty County in 1830 numbered 5,729, working on plantations. Better than any, they knew every part of the flat coastland. In some parts the ground was rich and fertile, in others it was sand and swamp, with creeks and marshes that ran into the sea. A minority of these slaves would be found in the gallery of the Midway or other neighbourhood churches on Sunday mornings.

Liberty County gained its name from the spirit with which its white leaders (still with Puritan instincts) had resisted the forces of the British crown in the Revolutionary War (1775–81). In that struggle, which turned the thirteen colonies into a nation, Major John Jones, grandfather of our subject, died on the American patriot side, along with others from the Midway Church. The church building itself was burned during the conflict, to be replaced by another in 1792. It survives to this day. Two of the signatories of the Declaration of Independence also came from the Midway congregation.

Despite the family alignment in the War, it is said that John Jones, Jr., father of Charles Colcock, loved everything English, and combined the planting of rice and cotton with the lifestyle and interests of an English gentleman. It was while hunting deer that a riding accident ended his life in 1805 at the age of thirty-two. His only son, our present subject, had been born only a few months earlier. Five years later Charles' mother, Susannah Hyrne Girardeau, of Huguenot descent and 'a woman of singular piety', also died; and, thereafter, he and his older sister were brought up among relatives, under the guardianship of their uncle, Captain Joseph Jones. Captain Jones was their paternal grandfather's younger son and 'a gentleman of large wealth and a most successful planter'.[2]

After local schooling at Sunbury Academy, where his teacher was the Scots-Irish minister, Dr William McWhir, Charles was sent the thirty-five miles to Savannah in 1819. Here, at the age of fourteen, he began a six-year apprenticeship in the counting house of Joseph Pelot. It was judged that a merchant's career would combine well with plantation ownership.

In the opinion of his cousin and brother-in-law, John Jones, 'a bright business career prospect was before him'. But other possibilities for his future life were also before the teenager. At this date all white males in Georgia received occasional military training, and in this Charles Colcock Jones so distinguished himself that 'an opening was presented

[2] C. C. Jones, Jr., quoted in *The Children of Pride: A True Story of Georgia and the Civil War*, ed. Robert Manson Myers (New Haven: Yale University Press, 1972), p. 1573. I am immensely indebted to the monumental work of Dr Myers in editing this volume of the Jones' family letters. Susannah Girardeau (1778–1810), was of the same family as John L. Girardeau (1825–98) who gave so much of his life to ministry among people of African descent in South Carolina.

him for entering the military academy at West Point'.[3] It was just as these varied ambitions were before him in the year 1822, that one of the desolating epidemics which periodically took away hundreds visited Savannah. Charles was himself brought very close to death. At the age of seventeen, this 'was the instrument in God's hands of his awakening and conversion'.

The ambitions of the apprentice were now changed forever. On 22 November 1822, along with twenty-six others, Charles Colcock Jones confessed Christ, and became a communicant at the Midway Church in the district of his upbringing, thirty-five miles from Savannah.

Southerner in the North

Several qualities in Charles Jones drew the special attention of his minister at Midway, the Rev. Murdoch Murphy. The change in the young man's life was evident to all. On returning to Savannah he took up teaching Sunday School at the Independent Presbyterian Church, and in this role he made regular visits to the homes of his pupils. He also joined in a society for those who wanted to 'live near to God', and in his personal reading he was studying such authors as Jonathan Edwards. It is not then surprising that the minister of Midway soon urged Charles Jones to consider the Christian ministry as his calling. Jones' own mind was being drawn in the same direction, and it was probably a meeting with Dr Ebenezer Porter, President of Andover Seminary, and a frequent visitor to Georgia, that turned his thoughts to studying in Massachusetts. Thus on May 12, 1825, Charles C. Jones arrived at Andover, the oldest theological seminary in America, in its

[3] John Jones, *Memorial Volume*, pp. 195–6.

rural setting in northeast Massachusetts. His first two years were to be spent at Phillip's Academy, a four-storey building across an elm-lined road from the Seminary. Latin and other subjects occupied him for up to eight hours a day; but physical exercise was evidently not neglected for there were times when he walked as far as Plymouth, a distance of forty miles.

After a visit home in 1827, Charles Jones commenced at the Seminary. At Andover the spirit of an earlier generation in New England still survived in Ebenezer Porter. He had played an important part in the Second Great Awakening, and his *Letters on Revival* gave evidence of enduring importance on the nature of the Spirit's work.[4] From him Jones heard first-hand what a revival was and his admiration of Porter would be life-long.

'With this president,' Jones's son-in-law writes, 'he was upon the most intimate terms; and he has been heard to say that, visiting him at all hours, there was not one in which, at some time, he had not found this godly man upon his knees.'[5] A sentence from a chapel address that Jones gave in February 1828 allows us a glimpse of what he was as a student: 'No man has ever risen into permanent eminence in any profession without *uniting* an ardent attachment to an extensive knowledge of the profession.'

One subject not on the Seminary's curriculum was now beginning to take up a good deal of his thoughts. He could say in 1829 that he had always been hostile to slavery, but the newspapers, the debates and the very ethos of strongly-anti-slavery New England were now forcing him to face questions

[4] Currently in print (Edinburgh: Banner of Truth, 2004).

[5] R. Q. Mallard, *Plantation Life before Emancipation* (1892; repr. Harrisonburg, VA: Sprinkle, 2005), p. 94.

in a way he had never done before. It was not only a thousand miles that separated Liberty County from Massachusetts, where the holding of slaves had been abolished in 1781. Jones thought often of the number on his own land, employed to provide him with the 'conveniences of life', and it troubled him deeply: 'I have spent many an anxious thought upon the subject of slavery,' he wrote to his cousin Mary. The subject of New England and Georgia recurred in many letters to her, as in the following of September 8, 1829:

> Admitting that Georgia has a fine climate, and as beautiful scenery, which she certainly has not, yet the curse of Slavery, would give New England an incalculable superiority. Were you my dear Mary to reside a few months only in a *free* community – you would see more clearly than you do now the evil of Slavery. There is a calmness, an order, a morality, a general sentiment of right and wrong, a justice, an equality, in this society which is not to be looked for in ours. Here, no duellist can live, – no injustice be tolerated. Every man has his rights and the community will see to it that they are not invaded.

But the remedy for the evil of slavery was by no means clear to him. By the summer of 1828 he had come to give his support to the African Colonization Society; and, after speaking for that Society at the South Parish Church in Andover on July 4, 1829, he gave cousin Mary an account of the Society's proposal 'to remove from the United States the Coloured Population, bond and free, as far as this may be practicable, to the Coast of Africa'.

The motivation for this venture was higher than the mere wish to resolve a problem. The hope was, he wrote, that the people thus emancipated and, under the influence of the gospel, resettled in their homeland,

> will form a powerful Republic, civilized and Christianized, to suppress the slave trade on the western shore, and if possible on the eastern – to open extensive trade with the nations in the interior of Africa to send them Teachers & Missionaries to reclaim them from their heathenish condition. What bright hopes may we not safely entertain for the conversion of Africa, that long neglected, long despised and persecuted & cruelly treated Country? What bright hopes of the suppression of the horrible traffic, the slave trade?

The qualification, 'as far as this may be practicable', was significant. For what if the venture was not 'practicable'? Then he saw only two alternatives: either, the sudden end of slavery in the South by means that could threaten the whole social structure, or the enlightenment of the slave owners by the same Christian means as had enlightened him.

The former was the 'abolitionist' option that was finding growing support in the North, although not all northern states had followed Massachusetts in that regard. Charles Jones knew some in the abolitionist circle. He referred in a letter of June 20, 1829 to Catherine Beecher, sister of Harriet Beecher Stowe, the author of *Uncle Tom's Cabin* (which was to bring thousands to that cause) as 'my old friend'.

But while he could contemplate the emancipation of his own slaves, he regarded the idea of an enforced emancipation as representing a radicalism which would not be for the immediate betterment of black or white. It was the Christian faith that was the *first* need of both races. He had no enthusiasm for giving democracy to a people not first prepared by Christianity:

> The question whether a people can govern themselves, is not yet answered. Whether an affirmative answer will be given to

> it, depends upon the nation's becoming a *Christian* nation, – and this depends under God, upon the active intelligent zeal of Christians – Christianity only, will save us from ruin.[6]

The strain caused by the differences between North and South was affecting Jones before he entered his final year at Andover. Despite aspects of society that he admired in Massachusetts, he could write home in the summer of 1829: 'I am tired of living here. My impressions of being a *stranger*, have not worn off during four years of residence and perhaps never would.'

This feeling plainly entered into the proposal he put respectfully to his guardian, Joseph Jones, on July 20, 1829. He wished, he told him, to take his final year at Princeton Seminary, where society would be 'a little more southern, or at any rate, not so entirely northern'. There were southern students at Princeton, where the senior professor, Archibald Alexander, was himself a Southerner, and, 'To graduate from Princeton will help my popularity (if that is to be considered) at home more than to graduate at Andover.'

There were no objections from Joseph Jones and October 1829 saw his nephew established at Princeton Seminary, 'in a warm, well furnished, and carpeted room, with *separate bedrooms*'. His pleasure in the new surroundings was mixed. While he found his fellow students 'a clever sort of folks', and 'pleasant' to him, on January 1, 1830, he wrote of his loneliness: 'All my acquaintances are new . . . I have no friend among them, in the strict sense of the word.'

[6] To Mary Jones, July 9, 1829. Some of Charles' letters for this period survive in his Papers, preserved at the Howard-Tilton Memorial Library, Tulane University, New Orleans. For my quotations from them I am indebted to the unpublished thesis of Eduard N. Loring, 'Charles C. Jones: Missionary to Plantation Slaves 1831–1847' (Vanderbilt University, Nashville, TN, 1976)., and to Erskine Clarke, *Dwelling Place: A Plantation Epic* (New Haven: Yale University Press, 2005).

Jones's hesitations over the slavery issue gave him something of an identity crisis. For some he was 'half Yankee – half Southerner'. One Southerner (a Virginian), with whom he discussed the slavery question on a stage coach journey from Philadelphia, even told him, 'You *Yankees* always express a great deal of feeling on this subject.' But whereas the anti-slavery spirit in New England was 'Yankee', at Princeton Jones would have been required to think with more discrimination on the subject. The position of the Faculty at Princeton was in accord with the recent decision of the Old School General Assembly of the Presbyterian Church. The Assembly had answered the question whether slave holding should debar persons from church membership with these words:

> It is impossible to answer this question in the affirmative without contradicting some of the plainest declarations of the Word of God. That slavery existed in the days of Christ and his Apostles is an admitted fact. That they did not denounce the relation as sinful, as inconsistent with Christianity; that slaveholders were admitted to membership in the churches organized by the Apostles; that whilst they were required to treat their slaves with kindness, and as rational, accountable, immortal beings, and, if Christians, as brethren in the Lord, they were not commanded to emancipate them . . . This Assembly cannot, therefore, denounce the holding of slaves as necessarily a heinous and scandalous sin, calculated to bring upon the Church the curse of God, without charging the Apostles of Christ with conniving at such sin.[7]

[7] Quoted in John Murray, *Principles of Conduct: Aspects of Biblical Ethics* (London: Tyndale Press, 1957), p. 260. The statement represents the position of Charles Hodge who was teaching systematic theology while Jones was at Princeton Seminary. 'He was equally out of sympathy with the pro-slavery men who regarded the institution divine and to be perpetuated as good in itself, and with the "Abolitionists", who held the holding of slaves to be sin in itself . . . He was in hearty sympathy with the many Southern Christians who strove to follow the will of Christ under the

Even though Jones accepted the force of this argument, it did not lessen his concern to urge the needs of black people. In January 1830, with the approval of his professors, Archibald Alexander and Samuel Miller, he formed a 'Society of Enquiry Concerning Africans'. The purpose was to gather and spread information, and to lead those students who planned to minister in the South to consider 'by what course of conduct the best interests of the Coloured population and the approbation of the whites may be secured'. On February 15 he first spoke to this new Society – the majority being 'Southern and Western men'. At a later meeting his address extended to an hour and a quarter on 'The Condition of the Coloured Slave Population of Georgia'. He reported to cousin Mary, 'It was rather long but the whole subject was new and my audience honoured me with their attention to the end. It excited considerable interest.'

Charles Jones had become known in the Seminary as an effective speaker, and he was asked to speak for the 'Society of Inquiry respecting Missions' at an end of term meeting on May 14, 1830. This was one of the Seminary's best-known societies and numbers gathered to hear him speak on African Slavery in the United States.

May 18, 1830 was the end of term at Princeton Seminary, and the start of his last break in the North before a final term to begin on July 1. He spent much of the intervening time in Philadelphia, Washington and Baltimore, meeting with men who were leaders in the African Colonization Society or in other movements for the betterment of slaves. There were also engagements in the capital, including preaching in the

providential conditions he had imposed upon them.' A. A. Hodge, *Life of Charles Hodge* (London: Nelson, 1881), pp. 333–4.

presence of President Andrew Jackson. The latter left immediately after the service and Jones was not disappointed in not meeting him. 'Standing in the presence of God', he wrote to Mary on July 23, 1830, 'to deliver the truths of his word to dying men, I found neither time nor inclination to gaze after the man.'

With the end of his Princeton studies at hand, the question of his own future in relation to African Americans was uppermost upon his heart. How and where he could do most good for slaves was by no means clear to him; the possibilities included settlement in Georgia, an itinerant ministry, or working in an existing missionary organization. His last term at Princeton included Pastoral Theology with Archibald Alexander, Composition and Delivery of Sermons with Samuel Miller, and a weekly recitation of Hebrew with Charles Hodge. Before term ended his mind was made up. His 'General Plan' he wrote to Mary on September 18, was

> to attempt on my return home to introduce a system of religious instruction by word of mouth into our County, for our poor degraded slaves, and thus if the plan succeeds and God opens the door to me, to devote my life to missionary labours among them.

The following week he obtained his Seminary diploma, and his five years study in the North ended on September 27, 1830. After travelling by ship to Charleston at the beginning of November he was finally home in Liberty County.

It was not only Jones's thinking on the race issue that had developed in the years away. On a visit back to Georgia in 1827 he had noted 'my two pretty cousins', Mary Jones and Mary Robarts. It was the former who really had his attention, for, as he was later to say, he had been 'attached' to her before he ever went north in 1825. Mary Jones, a vivacious eighteen-year-old, was finishing her education at a Savannah academy in 1827, and about to stay at home with her father and step-mother at their two plantation houses, Sunbury (on the coast, and favoured in the summer) and Retreat. As her father, Captain Joseph Jones, was Charles Jones' guardian, the two cousins had often been together from childhood, sometimes under the same roof. After Charles' visit in 1827 the correspondence between them was regular and increasingly affectionate. The event which determined the relationship for Charles was Mary's becoming a serious Christian in the winter of 1827–8. She wrote to tell him of Christ satisfying 'an aching void within': Christ crucified 'was life . . . and I am now enabled to exclaim, "Thou art my God!", to rejoice in Christ Jesus as my friend.' The two cousins now understood each other on every level. When he came home for a second visit in 1829, there were long walks and rides together, books shared, and finally the proposal of marriage that Mary accepted. One hurdle remained. Captain Jones was known to disapprove of cousins marrying. That same night, May 29, 1829, Charles wrote to him:

> I can no longer conceal what perhaps you have already discovered – namely, *my attachment to cousin Mary*. You may be surprised that I entertain *more* than what ought to exist between those so nearly connected by blood relationship, but it is nevertheless true . . . I know the family connection existing between Cousin Mary and myself makes the matter more difficult – It is nearer than I ever expected to approach you in matrimonial relation – and therefore beg your opinion & direction.[8]

[8] Quoted by Erskine Clarke, *Dwelling Place,* p. 79.

It seems Joseph Jones was not surprised, and when he raised no objection, the wedding was planned for December 1830. First the final year at Princeton had to intervene and with it another problem. There was considerable doubt in the mind of Charles over his uncle's reaction when he learned the couple meant to spend their lives in missionary work among the black people. While his daughter was a committed Christian, this was not yet the case with the owner of Retreat; like other nominal Christians, he attended the Midway Church without being a member or making any confession of Christ. In his 'General Plan' letter to Mary from Princeton, Charles had urged her to say nothing of what they had in view. 'You will appreciate at once', he wrote in that letter, 'that it will be somewhat unpopular, and may excite much opposition against me, and I shall need great judgment and prudence.' Once the proposal was known, he feared that the hostility could be such that 'it might prove inexpedient for us to marry at the appointed time . . . You will therefore take care of *this* letter & keep to yourself this plan of mine.'

These fears were not realized. We do not know at what stage Joseph Jones heard of the 'Plan', but the wedding went ahead at Retreat on the evening of December 21, 1830, the day after Charles Jones' twenty-sixth birthday. His old friend and school teacher, William McWhir, performed the ceremony.

All we know of Charles' twenty-two-year-old bride confirms the statement that she was 'a woman of decided piety and uncommon strength of intellect and character . . . always in fullest sympathy with him in his intellectual pursuits and his missionary labours'. In all the years ahead she would be his main helper. It is true, as her father had warned, that she could be 'self-willed', but love bound them:

In wintry morn, with deer and gun
We walked in fields and leafy wood
Or drove along the level roads.
An evening fire our chamber warmed,
With books and work our circle formed,
Most pleased of all *to be alone;*
Most pleased to feel that we were *one.*

These words of Charles, written on an early wedding anniversary, expressed what was to be an ever-deepening relationship. There were four children from the marriage, three of whom survived infancy: Charles, Jr.. (1831), Joseph (1833), and Mary Sharpe (1835), who was to marry Robert Quarterman Mallard. Mallard's books remain a valued source of information on the family. The fourth child died at birth in September 1840. Family life was divided between Montevideo and Maybank. The latter, inherited in 1834, on a coastal island connected by causeway, was the favoured summer residence. Wherever they were, the structure of every day included prayer, praise and Scripture, with the holiness of the Lord's day especially prized. If cards, dances and novels were pastimes on many Southern mansions, they were not to be seen at Montevideo. Both Charles and Mary were eager readers. 'Books abounded in the home, and were treated as honoured guests or cherished inmates. Only the choicest had admittance and hospitality.'[9] Among their favourite authors were William Romaine, Thomas Scott and William Jay. Jonathan Edwards on *The Will* was even part of their reading on their honeymoon.

[9] R. Q. Mallard, *Montevideo-Maybank: Some Memories of a Southern Christian Household in the Olden Time; Or, the Family Life of the Rev. Charles Colcock Jones* (1898; repr. Harrisonburg, VA; Sprinkle, 2005), p. 15.

Indoors there were also cats and a dog, and outdoors they saw creation as full of sources for enjoyment. The children were schooled at home with private tutors and regular parental involvement. Charles, Jr. recalled in later years, 'No son could have had kinder or more indulgent parents, or fuller opportunities for indulging those pastimes which a plantation life affords.'

'The Gospel to Every Creature'

Despite his 'Plan', how Charles Jones intended to proceed at the time of his marriage is not entirely clear. Before he left the North he had been licensed to preach by the Presbytery of New Brunswick, New Jersey, at Allentown, but he would need to be called to a pastoral charge before he could be ordained to the Presbyterian ministry. On his return to the South, 'For a period of four to five months he preached as opportunity offered.' At the same time he was evidently active in expressing his concerns with sympathetic planters, and this gained enough response for him to arrange a meeting at the courthouse at Riceboro (between Montevideo and the Midway Church) on March 10, 1831. At this meeting there was interest in his hope of an association to bring the gospel to plantation slaves, and he was asked to enlarge on the whole subject at a next meeting appointed for March 28. This he did, taking for his text the words of Mark 16:15, 'And he said unto them, Go ye into all the world and preach the gospel to every creature.'

From this text Jones argued that evangelism is a primary duty of every Christian; that its scope must include the black people who are 'creatures of God, and like ourselves are moving onward to the retributions of eternity'. For that future, he went on to show, so many of them were unprepared: 'Numbers of them do not go to church, and cannot tell us who Jesus Christ is, nor have they ever heard so much as the Ten Commandments read and explained.' They were 'a nation of Heathen in our very midst'. He then went on to prove the responsibility of planters professing Christianity to see that the gospel was heard by all their people. They condemned, he reminded them, the Roman Catholic Church for not giving the Bible to the people, yet were guilty of the same sin, and should they continue in such neglect 'our neglect might not only shut their souls out of heaven, but our own.'

Objections were then examined, before he outlined a plan as to how the need should be faced. It put the main duty on the planters themselves. Wherever possible, they should take up the work of teaching, augmented, as necessary, by other teachers to be appointed by an executive committee. Further, 'Where it is practicable, a missionary may be employed to take a general supervision of the whole.' This he envisaged as his role. The object was to present 'the Christian religion as understood by orthodox Protestants,' in 'as systematic and intelligible a manner as possible'.

Among the possible objections, Jones raises this one in particular: 'Instructing the Negroes will do no good; it will only make them worse hypocrites and worse men.' Such a view, he responded, is virtually a denial of the gospel. Wherever it is faithfully preached, 'the result is favourable to the piety and morality of the people . . . And from whence did *we*, with all our piety and morality spring? From a people once as degraded as Negroes. And what lifted us so far above our progenitors? *The Gospel*, and nothing else.'[10]

[10] This address was published as *The Religious Instruction of the Negroes. A*

Despite this emphasis on the gospel, Dr Erskine Clarke has written of the meeting of March 1831 as though the main thrust of Jones's speech was the benefit – not least 'the economic advantage' – that would come to slave owners from higher moral standards among their servants. Jones, he writes, directed attention to 'the behaviour of blacks that offended white sensibilities, that called for remedial action. It was an approach that would appeal to white planters, for it meant a major concern would be to socialize the slaves of Liberty County into a southern society of morals and "manners".'[11] Clarke quotes Jones as saying that 'the grand objective' was that souls be saved, and credits him with believing what he said, but he argues that this 'covered his life and his work with grand illusions'. 'His work would never be free from the suspicion that at its heart it was guided by economic motivations, that it was an attempt to increase the profits of the planters.'

According to Clarke, Jones had ceased to be exercised about the real issue that had troubled him while in the North: 'It was no longer a question of slavery . . . Perhaps answering the doubts of his own heart so recently changed from anti-slavery sentiment, Jones declared that slavery itself could be justified if one soul were saved.'[12] This is a serious misrepresentation. Jones accepted a distinction that Clarke does not recognize. His whole life would be a commitment against the

Sermon, Delivered before the Association of Planters in Liberty and McIntosh Counties, Georgia.. A 4th edition was published at Princeton (D'Hart & Connolly, 1832). It was not the first item published by Jones. The first was *An Address Delivered before the Liberty County Temperance Society, May 14, 1829* (Andover, Mass.: Flagg and Gould, 1829).

[11] Erskine Clarke, *Wrestlin' Jacob, A Portrait of Religion in the Old South* (Atlanta: John Knox Press, n.d.).), p. 23.

[12] Ibid., p. 24, 27.

abuses of slavery, but, as he had been reminded at Princeton, slaveholding *as such* is not necessarily sinful. I will return to this subject below.

At these meetings at Riceboro the first 'Society for the Religious Instruction of Negroes' (the 'Association' for short) was formed in Georgia. Within a few weeks twenty-nine planters had signed the constitution and paid a membership fee of $2.00. Practical steps followed with the division of the County into districts and the appointment of teachers (chiefly the planters themselves). More significantly, the Midway Church Missionary Society (an organization already in existence), called Jones to be 'missionary to the Negroes', in connection with the Association. It was thus a joint venture, for members of the Executive Committee of the Association were also members of the Midway Society. Beginning on April 17, 1831, it was arranged that Jones would preach to the whites on two Sundays of every month and two Sundays to the Blacks, with additional preaching to the slaves during the week.

The next development was surprising. Little more than a month after the April date, on May 31, 1831, Jones received a call to become the stated supply of the First Presbyterian Church in Savannah and immediately accepted it. It was not discouragement that induced this change of plan. He was later to write: 'The short period of my preaching to the Negroes before removing to Savannah, convinced me of the fact, that there was a great field of usefulness among them, and one wholly unoccupied, at least in the manner designed.'[13]

[13] *Tenth Annual Report of the Association for the Religious Instruction of the Negroes, in Liberty County, Georgia* (Savannah, 1845), pp.15–16. Between 1834 and 1848 Jones prepared thirteen Annual Reports, each describing the work in the previous year, and with other reflections. But what should have been the fourth was never fully prepared and was not published. For access to the published Reports I am indebted to the Presbyterian Historical Society at Montreat, NC.

Two things appear to have led him to the decision. First, the scheme of planters as teachers was not working. However willing some of them were, they were without teaching experience, and their hearers soon proved it by their disinterest and their disinclination to attend the meetings.

For Jones himself his first endeavours on various plantations had brought home to him the truth of the advice he had received in Washington the previous summer. An experienced man had cautioned him that he should be well prepared before he attempted to evangelize the slaves. Jones, despite, he says, 'much encouragement', learned in those first weeks of plantation preaching that he was not yet ready for the work. It was to be one of his main convictions in later life that churches made a great mistake when they thought that a minimum of gifts and preparation were necessary for effective preaching to black people. This misjudgement, he believed, had partly arisen because, in a number of places, slaves attended public worship on the Lord's Day and their quiet demeanour suggested that they were benefiting by what they supposedly heard. The truth too often, Jones came to see, was that the sermons were not adapted to their comprehension and that little good was being done. On this subject he later wrote:

> To know the extent of their ignorance even where they have been accustomed to the sound of the Gospel in white churches, a man should make investigation for himself – the result will frequently surprise and fill him with grief . . . Some white ministers and teachers, in their simplicity, beholding their attention to the preaching of the Gospel come to the conclusion that they are an unsophisticated race; that they form one of the easiest and pleasantest fields of labour in the world; and that they are a people 'made ready, prepared for the

> Lord;' – nothing more being necessary than to carry them the Gospel and converts will be multiplied as drops of morning dew. Experiment shortly dissipates these visions, and well it is if the sober reality does not frighten the labourer away in disgust and disappointment. He who carries the Gospel to them encounters depravity, entrenched in ignorance.[14]

While Charles and Mary Jones settled in Savannah in the summer of 1831, it was with the intention that the main calling of their lives was only postponed, not abandoned. 'I accepted a call to the First Presbyterian Church in Savannah with the understanding that, whenever I felt prepared, I might withdraw from the church and return to my chosen field.'[15] And once established in Savannah his primary mission was still included as part of his work. Sunday afternoons were given to a service for the blacks of the city, and in the course of a series of sermons on Romans, for March 31 to October 5, 1832, he lost no opportunity to tell his white hearers of their duty, as for instance in these words from his notes for April 14:

> No, we are not only not awake to our responsibilities to the Heathen abroad, but, to the *Heathen at Home*. Our servants. – Lamentable – criminal apathy . . . We have delayed long enough. It is high time to awake out of sleep.[16]

A second reason for his response to the Savannah congregation may have been that he could not be ordained in the Presbyterian Church without a call to a particular charge, and without ordination he would have less opportunity to influ-

[14] Charles C. Jones, *The Religious Instruction of the Negroes in the United States* (Savannah, 1842; repr. New York: Negro Universities Press,1969), pp. 126–7.

[15] *Tenth Report* (1845). The Reports usually refer to the work of the previous year, the Tenth was more comprehensive in its history of the Association's work.

[16] His notes from this date are with the Jones Papers at Tulane University; I am indebted to Eduard N. Loring for this quotation from 'Missionary to Plantation Slaves'.

ence his denomination. At this date he was still a licentiate under the supervision of the Presbytery of New Brunswick. The position changed when he was ordained at the Independent Presbyterian Church in Savannah on November 27, 1831.[17] He was now a minister of the Presbytery of Georgia, and as such he was present, the following week, in Columbia, South Carolina, for the annual meetings of the Synod of South Carolina and Georgia. This was probably the first occasion on which Jones was to plead the need of the black people in a Synod debate and it led to the brethren recording their support for endeavours to carry the gospel to 'our coloured population'.

Little is known of Jones' Savannah ministry. He had three services every Sunday, a Wednesday Bible Class, and a Friday night Lecture. How that work ended he later recorded in the words: 'The ends for which I went to Savannah, being in my judgment accomplished, after a residence there of eighteen months, I relinquished the charge of the Church and returned to the Negroes.'[18]

Opening the Plantations for the Gospel

It was in November 1832 that Jones exchanged his pulpit in Savannah for the dirt floors of cotton houses, sheds, and makeshift plantation chapels. R. Q. Mallard, his son-in-law, explained: 'He was constrained by a sense of duty to devote himself entirely to the great work of his life, to which his attention had been turned while a student at Princeton.' Jones himself remembered the milestone in these words:

[17] The First Presbyterian Church of Savannah was sharing the same building as the Independent Church before obtaining one of their own. The minister of the Independent Church at this date was another native of Liberty County, Daniel Baker.

[18] *Tenth Report*..

> I commenced my labours on the 2nd of December, 1832. The Lord had opened the door. A great work was to be done, but to me it was almost entirely new. There were no precedents in our country to which I could look for encouragement and instruction.[19] The work was one of exceeding delicacy. A slight impropriety might ruin it, while on its success the spiritual welfare of multitudes might depend.[20]

The danger to which he referred in these veiled words was that of incurring the opposition of the plantation owners. Without the co-operation of owners access to their slaves would be impossible. In some quarters there was criticism from the outset. All kinds of evils, it was said, would result from encouraging black people to gather in numbers on their own on Sundays; still more so, if there were to be such meetings mid-week. No good could come of giving such special attention to servants. It would lead to insubordination and unrest. 'The Negroes were doing well enough.' In the eyes of some, Jones was in danger of acting as 'an incendiary'.

The fears of some of the slave owners were increased by recent history. In the previous ten years there had been slave revolts in some places, and literature calling for such action was gaining circulation. A tract urging the black people to violence was found in Savannah in 1829. Numbers of whites

[19] In speaking of 'no precedents' Jones is referring to witness in plantations in Georgia. There were, as he says elsewhere, five black churches in the state at this date, and in his book, *The Religious Instruction of Negroes,* he gives a full account of mission work proceeding among the black people in the South before the 1830s, attributing its rise to the outpouring of the Holy Spirit at the end of the eighteenth century by which 'a new and mighty impulse was given to religion. In the South it awakened many to see the spiritual necessities of the Negroes' (Ibid., p. 63). I have written of the Second Great Awakening in *Revival and Revivalism: The Making and Marring of American Evangelicalism 1750–1858* (Edinburgh: Banner of Truth, 1994).

[20] James Stacy, *History of the Midway Congregational Church* (1899; repr.. Newnan, GA, 1951), p.214. This is a valuable work by a discerning author.

regarded these dangers as sufficient warrant for the enforcement of laws across the South that forbade the teaching of reading to the African-Americans.

The measure of support that Jones had at the outset of his work in 1833 is not altogether clear. Dr Loring[21] considered the twenty-nine planters who subscribed to the Association in the Spring of 1831 'a small number'. In relation to the total number of plantations, between 100 and 125, the number was small. But many of these plantations had only part-time owners in residence or no white person in residence at all.[22] Even if Jones lacked support in numbers, the character and resolution of some who stood by him made up for it. Among these individuals he mentions, in particular, some women 'of rare talents and accomplishments'. In illustration of the role they played, he continued:

> I well remember one of brilliant wit, of unfeigned piety and glowing zeal, of uncommon forethought and prudence, rich in experience and observation, and of a masculine energy, who exerted for many years, at home, over her own family and household, and on the neighbourhood around her, and through the wide circle of her acquaintance, the happiest influence on this subject. In the early days of my ministry to this people, with a few other very near and beloved friends, she was a strong supporter to my faith, and inspirer of my zeal. I look back upon our long winter evening conferences, in the quiet bosom of our respective families, when we all met and took counsel together in the Lord, as among the most delightful and improving, and happy hours of my social and Christian life.[23]

[21] See footnote 6, above.

[22] In 1847 there were 24 plantations with permanent owners or managers; 41 with part-time residents; and sixty with no white person. *Twelfth Report.*

[23] C. C. Jones, *Suggestions on the Religious Instruction of Negroes* (Philadelphia:

The fact that Jones was himself a planter, and appreciated the minds of fellow-planters, enabled him to act in a way that disarmed the fears of some. Liberty County was divided into three 'Districts', numbered 15th, 16th and 17th. Apart from some 300 slaves, all the remainder, 4,577, were found in the 15th District, an area 25 miles long by 15 broad. This was the District Jones committed himself to serve, with six stations appointed for Sunday services in different neighbourhoods. In this work he had other assistants, and his three 'principal stations' became Midway ('hard by the old mother Midway'), Newport, and Pleasant Grove. The most original part of his work was the weeknight meetings for 'religious instruction' he now introduced on various plantations. These required the permission of the owners, whom he encouraged to build a 'small house' for the meetings. Before long nearly fifty plantations were open to him, with what became known as a 'praise house' on numbers of them. For the same purpose, at Montevideo Jones erected what his son-in-law described as 'a neat plastered building, with belfry and bell'. These mid-week plantation meetings were carried on through the seven months of the year when the Joneses were at Montevideo (their 'winter home'), and were the cause of the late home-comings already described.

Whenever the plantation owner was willing, he was asked to superintend a gathering on his land where Jones gave

---

Presbyterian Board, 1847), pp. 37–8. (This work is not to be confused with his book of the same title but lacking the words '*Suggestions on*' first published in 1842). He goes on to name the woman in question as Anne Clay of Bryan County who had died by the time the words were written. On her death in 1843 Jones preached her funeral sermon. *Sketch of the Life and Character of Miss Anne Clay: Delivered at Her Funeral Service, in Bryan Church, Georgia* (Boston: Crocker and Brewster, 1844). Christian and Southern modesty deterred him from naming his own wife for her part in the work.

the instruction. This would take various forms. While he held preaching in high regard, he knew it was not enough. Passages of Scripture had to be memorized and hymns learned. There needed to be interaction between people and teacher, and he made regular use of a question and answer method, preparing his own catechism for that purpose.

A first meeting of the rejuvenated agency for which he was the missionary was held in November 1833; and Jones' Report, the first of thirteen as already mentioned, was subsequently published. In this he described his first year as one of 'experiment and discovery'. There were two things, in particular, he said he had wanted to learn: first, whether, 'after so long a period of neglect', the attendance and interest of the black people could be gained and sustained (there being no question of any coercion); second, whether he was himself qualified for the labour.

On the second he offered no comment but on the first any doubts were gone. On forty Sundays he had preached, twice a day, to gatherings of black people exclusively, at six different 'stations' in rotation, as well as instituting meetings for children and inquirers. At one location in the winter there had also been a Sunday afternoon 'class of instruction for professors of religion of all denominations', and at another place, mid-week, 'a common Lecture, with this difference that the audience is *catechised* on the subject of the discourse'. There were also the mid-week plantation meetings (still in an early stage of development) which, he said, 'we deem *highly* important and, in some respects, more efficacious than those held on the Sabbath'.

Many were in attendance at these meetings – 'over 400', for instance, at the class for 'professors,' and between twenty-five and fifty at a class of children on one plantation. More important than the numbers was the increasing attentiveness among his hearers:

> I have endeavoured, with all plainness, to communicate to them the truths of Christianity; and the effect in several instances has been singular and gratifying . . . No doubt rests on my mind, that if God spares our lives to continue our labours, we shall see a moral elevation in the character of servants, which we have never yet witnessed either in this County, or in any other part of the Southern country . . . *The conversion of souls is the great, the all-important object we aim at*; and we have reason, I trust, to believe that, in this respect our labours have not been in vain, though they have not been attended with any remarkable blessing.
>
> I cannot describe the peculiar and joyful feelings that have possessed my mind, when I have seen penitents from this long neglected and degraded people, inquiring what they must do to be saved. It is not building upon another man's foundation. You are in the high-ways and hedges. You gather the first fruits yourself, and the undivided joy takes full possession of the soul.[24]

The spiritual needs of his hearers were not isolated from their general condition:

> I scarcely need suggest the necessity of paying special attention to the comfort of the Negroes in their houses, food, clothing, etc. Unless we attend to the improvement of their *physical* condition, our efforts to improve their *moral* condition will be abortive; for we shall practically deny what we preach. In order to this, we must moderate our desires for the accumulation of property, which is the sin of us all, and

[24] *Annual Report of the Missionary to the Negroes in Liberty County, GA, Presented to the Association, Nov. 1833* (Charleston: Observer Office, 1834), pp. 9–10. This was the first *Report*, although not named as such.

a sin, the indulgence of which carries no small discomfort to those through whose labour we obtain what we desire. They should have a share in the enjoyments of life as well as we.

The *Annual Report* quoted above for 1833 made mention of a 'children's class'. This was a new development arising from Jones' observation that few between the ages of six and eighteen were present at meetings or services. Traditionally, 'Sunday was the high day for their fun and frolic'. A first Sunday School was begun on August 18, 1833. The innovation, he noted, 'electrified the people . . . it formed a new era.' Later their teacher would describe some of the first occasions when the children met for this purpose:

> They were wild and scary, stupid, sleepy, rude and uncouth: they rushed in pell-mell, squabbling as they came, crowding and pushing upon the seats, dressed in every imaginable manner and some with very little dressing at all. They repeated the questions instead of the answers . . . They sang the tunes and never articulated a syllable of the hymns . . . Yet in a little time, their minds began to act and some of the most unpromising became excellent scholars.[25]

It was not only from children that difficulties were encountered. His adult hearers were at liberty to come and go as they pleased, and how they sometimes exercised this freedom is illustrated by an incident that occurred in the early years of the mission:

> I was preaching to a large congregation on the Epistle of Philemon and when I insisted upon fidelity and obedience as Christian virtues in servants and, upon the authority of Paul, condemned the practice of *running away*, one half of my audience deliberately rose up and walked off with themselves,

[25] *Tenth Report (1845)*, p. 26.

and those that remained looked anything but satisfied, with the preacher or his doctrine.

At the close some were heard to complain that 'that there was no such Epistle in the Bible'. Others said it 'was not the gospel'. And to his face it was said that he 'preached to please the master' (that is, their owner), and that they would not come again. But Jones was careful not to preach a one-sided version of Christian duties. In a *Catechism* prepared for the instruction of his hearers, he had much to say on the duties of 'Masters'. These included the following questions, answers, and proof-texts (to be repeated aloud and memorized):

Q. Is it right for the Master, to overtask and to punish his Servants cruelly?
A. No. Exod. 2:20–27; Prov.29:19–21.

Q. Ought he to require them to do what they are unable to do; or what would be unlawful for them to do?
A. No. Matt. 25:14–15; Exod. 20:8–11.

Q. What are Masters commanded to forbear?
A. Threatening. Eph. 6:9.

Q. Does God show favour to the Master more than to the Servant, and just because he is a Master?
A. No. Eph. 6:9; Job 31:13–15.[26]

An application of the teaching regarding Masters followed in two columns, from which I will only quote extracts:

1. It is the duty of Masters *to provide* for their Servants, both old and young, good houses, comfortable clothing, whole-

[26] C. C. Jones, *A Catechism of Scripture Doctrine and Practice for Families and Sunday-Schools, Designed Also for the Oral Instruction of Coloured People* (Philadelphia: Presbyterian Board, 1852), p. 126 . It was first published as *A Catechism for Coloured Persons* (Charleston: Observer Office Press, 1834).

some and abundant food; to *take care* of them when old, and infirm and crippled . . .

2. It is their duty *to protect* their servants from abuse or ill-treatment . . .
3. It is their duty only to lay upon their Servants *that labour only which is just*; allow them time to enjoy the comforts of life and to do something for themselves . . .
4. Masters should make allowance and be patient . . . by decision tempered with a kind and condescending manner, invite the regard and confidence of their Servants.
5. In the *correction of faults*, let the correction be *certain*, but *just* and *merciful* . . .
6. Especially must Masters regard the *salvation of their Servants* . . .
7. Masters *have a Master in heaven*, to whom they shall give account for the manner in which they treat their servants. God is no respecter of persons.

This *Catechism*, originally published by Jones in 1834 for his missionary work, was no mere abridgement of Reformed catechisms already existing. It is fuller than the *Shorter Catechism*, more directly evangelistic; with the notes added to every part showing how the truth is to be applied to the conscience. The doctrinal teaching is clear and also safeguarded against error. It appears there was a tendency to fatalism among his hearers which he addressed as following:

Q. Why do *not* all men who hear of Christ, believe on him to have eternal life?
A. Because *they will not*. John 3:19,20; Matt.22:1–14; 23:37.

Q. Repeat what the Saviour says, 'Ye will not come.'
A. 'Ye will not come to me, that ye might have life.' John 5:40.

Q. Is God willing that any should perish?
A. No.
Q. Repeat, 'The Lord is longsuffering to us-ward, not willing that any should perish, but that all should come to repentance.' 2 Pet.3:9; Comp. 1 Tim. 2:4.
Q. Repeat, 'As I live, saith the Lord, I have no pleasure in the death of the wicked: but that the wicked turn from his way and live.' Ezek. 33:11 . . .
Q. Whose fault will it be, therefore, if we are lost?
A. Our own fault. Isa.3:10,11; Prov.1:24–33; Mark 16:16; Matt.25:41–46; Hos.13:9.[27]

As the law forbade slaves to read, the *Catechism* was designed for memorization rather than for personal use, although Jones was not supportive of that law and the *Catechism* itself taught, 'Those who would keep the Bible from their fellow creatures, are the enemies of God and man. The Bible belongs of right to every man.' But memorization proved effective, and two years after the start of the Sunday Schools he reported that classes were able to recite twenty to thirty pages of the *Catechism*. The general value of the book was demonstrated by the demand for successive reprints in 1837, 1843 and 1852.[28] It was also adopted for use in foreign missions, being translated and published in Syria (in Armenian) and China. In a Preface the author added advice to teachers that reflected his own practice:

[27] *Catechism* (1852), p. 70.

[28] Scripture texts were more fully added after 1834. The 1843 edition included a lengthy Preface which, among other things, defended the Catechism from the charges of long-windedness and over-preciseness in theology. 'It were to be wished,' Mallard wrote in 1892, 'that some liberal-hearted Christian could be induced to furnish the means to publish an edition of this most valuable Catechism.' *Plantation Life before Emancipation*, p. 119. The Sprinkle reprint is bound in one volume with Mallard's other work, *Montevideo-Maybank*.

> Let the exercises be varied, from one kind of instruction to another, to preserve attention and interest; and to prevent weariness, alter the posture – sometimes let it be that of sitting, and sometimes that of standing. Let the manner of the teacher be lively, and spirited, without irreverence; sober without austerity; and his language plain and intelligible, without being foolish and inaccurate.

In his *Annual Report* of 1833 Jones already knew that he had 'as much and more than he could do', but the work was to multiply. By 1835, besides his other labours, there were eight Sunday Schools with 250 scholars. Wherever he could, Jones enlisted aid in teaching and twenty-five men and women assisted him with the Schools. He also upheld the existing practice of encouraging trustworthy black leaders and preachers, known as 'watchmen', to occupy an office of leadership. These men, normally slaves themselves, could hold plantation meetings, and take on various other duties; all of which he discussed with them at a monthly 'watchmen's meeting'. Without doubt Jones learned from them, while they learned from him. The leader among them in 1833 was 'Sharper' in whose witness to his fellow countrymen, said Jones, there were 'the most fearless exhibitions of Divine truth, and exposures of their wickedness'. But Sharper's great themes were the love of God and the death of Christ. After one of Jones's early sermons it was Sharper that he asked to pray, and we read:

> The old man went down on his knees, with the whole congregation, in the sublimest and most overwhelming descriptions of God and address to Him, drawn from the Bible, and the deep feelings of his own soul, he brought God down in our midst, he placed us, bowing in his awful presence, as our God, Creator, King, Redeemer, and final Judge. The silence

of death reigned; we had impressions of the Divine Majesty and glory during that prayer, which we never had before.[29]

Within months of the beginning of Jones's work Sharper went home; and, not without tears, his white friend preached at his funeral service beside the Midway Church, in the presence of between three and four hundred black people gathered in the moonlight.

Despite 'watchmen' of this calibre, who themselves might take plantation meetings, the load on Jones was a heavy one, in private as well as public, for constant preaching did not lessen the hours he gave to preparation. His cousin, John Jones, remembered: 'His work commenced in the closet and study. His preparations for the Sabbath were made most carefully, with critical examinations of the original Scriptures. His sermons were often expository and universally impressive.'[30] Mary Moragne, who heard him in 1836, commented, 'His manner was calm, and impressive, and his discourse sensible and connected.'

From February 1837 to December 1838 Jones's mission work was interrupted as he took on the work of Professor of Church History at the Theological Seminary of the Presbyterian Church in Columbia, the state capital of South Carolina. The invitation had come to him more than a year before, and was pressed both by friends and the synod itself. In the opinion of his brother-in-law, John Jones, 'his scholarly attainments and wonderful power over young men eminently fitted him for his new work'. It was also urged that he could

[29] Quoted from Jones' 'Journal of a Missionary to the Negroes in the State of Georgia,' by Erskine Clarke, *Dwelling Place,* pp. 154–5.

[30] Writing of the need for careful preparation, Jones was to say: 'If any minister is of the opinion that *any kind of preaching* will do for the Negroes, let him try it, and he will presently be of another mind.'

do more to address 'the great and appalling subject' of slavery from that city than where he was. Christian opinion in the South would thus be challenged more widely. The need for this was evident; for numbers (confronted by the radical Abolitionist propaganda in the North) were ready to defend all aspects of slavery, even while professing to be Christians; in reality, as Jones wrote to his wife, these men were 'infidels . . . though many of them pretend to approve religion'. Mallard believed it was the call for the wider evangelization of the negroes that influenced his move to Columbia. Certainly his commitment was unchanged. He preached to the blacks of First Presbyterian Church, Columbia, on Friday nights, and taught a Sunday afternoon class there of over two hundred. But there was another reason for the removal to Columbia, and it comes out in an address Jones gave to a senior class of students. In the course of speaking of their future duties as ministers of the gospel (which included 'the work of the religious instruction of the Negroes') he warned:

> Engage in no *secular* business as a source of emolument; especially, be warned of engaging *in Planting and the management of Negroes*; for this business, either by inheritance, or family or marriage relations, you may, more than to any other, be exposed. If God in his Providence has given you this property, attend to their religious interests, but manage them through friends or responsible persons, if it be within the bounds of possibility. Not that you cannot manage them and maintain your piety, but you cannot manage them and maintain your standing and influence as Ministers . . . As soon as you begin to watch the changes of the heavens for the early and the latter rain, and to converse freely of seasons, and soils and prices; and to show yourselves as anxious as other men are for full returns from your fields; as soon as you have

> your head and hands filled with the nameless and numberless cares of a Plantation, then will the Minister be merged into the Planter: then will the millstone be fairly hanged about your necks, to drown your Ministerial career in destruction and perdition.[31]

One can only conclude from these words that Jones wanted relief from his own plantation commitments in Liberty County. A statement in a later letter to his eldest son gives confirmation: 'I am certain my necessary and unavoidable connection with the management of Negroes and the conduct of planting has been a most serious drawback to me.' He went on to speak of attempts to 'rid myself of the drawback'.[32] The move in 1837 was one such attempt.

The address to the departing students was given on July 10, 1837; and thereafter, there being no more seminary sessions till the October, the Joneses went back home to Liberty County. In the weeks of high summer that followed, it is not likely that plantation oversight took a major part of his time. We know that he was both preparing lectures for his classes and preaching among the black people. In the summer of the next year, 1838, he was home again, intending to follow the same procedure. This time providence dictated otherwise. Before he was due to go back to Columbia in October a stirring and attention to the gospel began among the black people such as he had not seen before: 'A few inquirers presented themselves for instruction, and a considerable degree of solemnity appeared from Sabbath to Sabbath.' He would later write, 'A revival of religion, taking its rise in the summer of 1838, continued well until the close of 1842.'[33]

[31] *Address to the Senior Class in the Theological Seminary, Columbia, July 10, 1837* (Savannah: Thomas Purse, 1837), pp. 9–10.

[32] *Children of Pride*, p. 110. See also p. 553.

[33] *Tenth Report* (1845).

The result of what happened in those summer months of 1838 was that he returned to Columbia in October of that year to give in his resignation as Professor of Church History, seeing it his 'duty to return to my old field of labour'. I believe it was this spiritual awakening that is the explanation of the seeming contradiction between his action and his warning to the students only one year earlier. One thing is certain: it was not financial self-interest that took him back to his plantations. At the beginning of his work as missionary for the Association the question of compensation was raised: 'I replied that my labours should *be wholly gratuitous:* and they have been to the present hour without any expense whatever to the inhabitants of this county, either white or black. In the year 1841, which was my seventh entire year in the field, the executors of the estate of John Lambert presented me with four hundred dollars, which they have continued yearly since.'[34] His brother-in-law wrote: 'He laboured for years in the ministry at his own charges, and gave liberally of his substance to the poor and every benevolent cause.'[35] In later years his wife could say: 'He expended his fortune in devoted efforts to benefit the Negro race.'[36]

Although it was necessary for him to give time that he grudged to plantation work and oversight, this was not where his satisfaction lay. 'I cannot describe the peculiar and joyful feelings that have possessed my mind, when I have seen penitents from this long neglected and degraded people, inquiring what they must do to be saved.' He was now to know much of that joy.

[34] Ibid.

[35] *Necrology: The Dead of the Synod of Georgia*, Atlanta: Franklin, 1869, p. 195.

[36] *Children of Pride*, p. 1286.

'The Great Revival'

In writing of Jones's return to Liberty County in December 1838, his cousin and brother-in-law, John Jones, remembered: 'The coloured people received him with open arms; and his return seemed to receive the divine sanction by an immediate work of the Holy Spirit, which continued four years.'[37]

As already seen, this is not quite accurate, for an unusual work of the Spirit had clearly begun in the previous summer. Nor had the work stopped when Jones was in Columbia. Watchmen and other black Christians, who had long been church members, were 'active in their efforts on their respective Plantations, and during my absence of two months, greatly promoted the good work'. At the same time, the sermons of the two pastors of the Midway Church 'were highly beneficial to the people, in the way of awakening the careless and deepening the impressions of those already under conviction of sin'.[38]

Once back in his old work, Jones immediately drew up a plan of sermons to be preached at the various stations of the black people. At Midway he would speak from the Old Testament on God's dealing with the church, and her eminent leaders; at Newport there would be exposition of the book of Acts; and at Pleasant Grove a doctrinal series. But soon the plan had to be adjusted:

> The opening sermons of the series, both at Midway and Newport, were received with respectful attention; and very shortly at Midway our congregations increased in size and interest;

[37] John Jones, *Memorial Volume*, p. 199.

[38] The pastors were the Rev. Robert Quarterman , who succeeded Murdoch Murphy as the minister at Midway in 1831, and the Rev. I. S. K. Axson.

> the number of inquirers multiplied, and I was forced to turn aside frequently from the proposed course, and present subjects calculated, to the best of our judgment, to deepen the impressions of the convicted, to awaken the careless, to inspirit the Church, and lead all to the justifying righteousness of Jesus Christ our Lord.

What James Stacy, historian of the Midway Church, called 'the Great Revival', had begun. As Stacy himself entered the ministry in Georgia in the 1850s, and knew of events first hand, we regret that he provides only glimpses of what happened. We learn more from Jones's Annual Reports, especially the Tenth from which I am presently quoting. But these Reports were intended chiefly for the white supporters of the Association who lived in the area and who knew already much of what was taking place. Jones attributed particular significance to the prayer meetings that were instituted for three quarters of an hour before the morning service on Sundays:

> I conducted the meetings, but the prayers were offered by the watchmen and prominent members of the Church. There has never been an instance of a person declining to pray, when called upon to do so. Many of their prayers although uttered in broken language, have been of great fervency, compass and impression. I can never forget the prayers of Dembo, a native African, for many years a member of Midway Church. There was a depth of humility, a conviction of sinfulness, and inability to do all good; an assurance of faith, a sense of the Divine presence, a nearness to God, a flowing out of love, which I never heard before or since: and often when he closed his prayers I felt as weak as water, and that I ought not to open my mouth in public, and indeed, knew not what it was to pray.

For the idea that less confidence could be placed in the Christian profession of black people, Jones had no sympathy. In view of the spiritual disadvantages under which they have long suffered, he wrote,

> I apprehend that our surprise will be, not that there are *so* many spurious conversions and *so* many defections, but that there are so few. Considering their condition and circumstances, and comparing them with the more improved and favoured class of white members, I could not say that the amount and degree of piety were remarkably in favour of the one over the other. I have seen the Scriptures abundantly fulfilled amongst the Negroes – 'Hath not God chosen the poor of this world rich in faith and heirs of the kingdom, which he hath promised to them that love him' (*James* 2:5).

Among the intercessions of the black Christians, Jones would hear pleas for the conversion of plantation owners. Who can say that these fervent prayers did not enter into what soon happened? Jones reported: 'During the revival of religion among the Negroes, which had now been in progress over three years, the Whites remained in a state of indifference to it, and partook not at all of the precious influences descending so copiously around them . . . At the close of this year [1841] we enjoyed a remarkable outpouring of the Spirit of God upon the White congregations of Midway and Newport.' Stacy writes of what happened at Midway:

> In the month of December 1841, Messrs, Quarterman and Axson, still co-pastors, held a meeting at Midway, in connection with their Fall communion season, which resulted in glorious things. It shook the strong holds of Satan, bringing into the church such old veterans as Col. William Maxwell, Capt. Joseph Jones, Mr Irwin Rahn, John Andrews, Joseph

> M. Quarterman, and many noble ladies.[39] People were so enthused, that during the meeting they seemed loth to leave the place after the services of the day were closed. I saw scores of them standing around the church door in a drizzling rain talking of the great things God had done for them and theirs. One might go into the graveyard during the intermission of services and he would see ladies in little groups on their knees in prayer. At the next communion in February, 1842, including the coloured people, there were between fifty and sixty accessions to the church.[40]

Jones spoke of how this work of God brought 'one of the strongest bonds of union' in society, uniting the hearts of masters and servants, and constituting a fulfilment of the words of the apostle, 'For by one Spirit are we all baptized into one body, whether we be Jews or Gentiles, bond or free; and have all been made to drink into one Spirit.'[41] This experience was part of the reason why, in advising others of undertaking mission work, he wrote: '*It is not advisable to separate the blacks from the whites.* It is best that both classes meet in the same building, that they be incorporated in the same church, under the same pastor, having access to the same ordinances, baptism and the Lord's Supper, and at the same time and place, and that they be subject to the same care and discipline.'[42]

Meeting together was not, however, always possible, especially at Midway when the revival multiplied the numbers

[39] Of the notable men leading the above list, Colonel Maxwell was married to a half-sister of Colcock Jones, and Captain Joseph Jones was, of course, his former guardian and his father-in-law. Captain Jones, who became a generous supporter of the Association, was killed in 1846 by a fall from his buggy, the horse having run away with him.

[40] Stacy, *Midway Church*, pp. 258–9.

[41] *Seventh Report* (1840).

[42] C. C. Jones, *Suggestions on Religious Instruction*, p. 38.

wishing to attend. The church building was 60 feet by 40, but the gallery was quite insufficient to accommodate the slaves who wished to attend. Mallard has described the crowds he saw at this date, particularly on 'Sacrament Sunday' when a carriage would take him with his parents and family the 'short mile' to church:

> As we roll along the broad highway, we find the servants clean and neatly dressed and in their best, some on foot and others in Jersey wagons, crowded to their utmost capacity with little and big, and drawn by 'Marsh Tackey's' [coastland ponies] – all moving in the same direction; those on foot carrying their shoes and stockings in their hands, to be resumed after they shall have washed in the waters at the causeway near the church . . . We are among the first to arrive, but every moment we hear the thunder of vehicles rolling across the half-dozen bridges of the swamp causeway near at hand, and the neighing of horses; and here come the multitude, from distances up to ten miles and more.[43]

In the gallery there would only be room for the black communicants. The service begun, white and black candidates for baptism, who had previously been examined by the elders, 'advance together' to the font, and are received as new members. At length, after praise, preaching and prayer, the bread and wine are distributed. In the scene, as Mallard recalled it:

> The number of black communicants is so large, that Toney Stevens [a watchman] comes down from the gallery to replenish the gold-lined silver goblets from the basket of wine in bottles near the pulpit; and as the wine is poured out, its gurgling in the solemn stillness smites distinctly upon our young ears, and the whole house is filled with the aroma of pure imported Madeira.

[43] Mallard, *Plantation Life*, p. 83.

Those who could not get into this service were not forgotten. Another service in the open air had already been planned:

> Immediately at the close of the communion service a great volume of musical sound, mellowed by the distance, comes up from the African church, in the edge of the forest, where godly Toney Stevens, the carpenter, is about to hold forth to his dusky charge.

Early in the 1840s a large wooden structure was erected at Midway for the slaves who could not find seats in the old church. Jones wrote of a week of special meetings in November 1842 when such was the planters' sympathy with what was happening that even those who were not church members left their slaves free on the Friday and Saturday to attend. Sunday was always a free day. 'Services were held on Friday and Saturday, twice a day for Negroes in their own Church. The house could not contain the people: more were *without* than *within*. On Sabbath they attended from all parts of the County . . . Such a congregation of Negroes had not been assembled in the county for many years . . . all seemed anxious to hear the gospel.'[44] One service, in particular, is described by Jones. For years 'concerts of prayer' had been held for foreign missions. Now Midway was to send her own first missionaries to the foreign field. They were the Rev. Richard Q. Way and his wife, the daughter of Rev. Robert Quarterman, Midway's senior minister. A farewell service took place on August 27, 1843, shortly before the couple were to leave for Bangkok. There could be no assurance they would be seen again. Silence pervaded the building as the missionary spoke from the words of Paul in Acts 20:21:

[44] *Ninth Report* (1844).

> The Negroes in the gallery, who had risen up as the interest in the service increased, leaned forward with the tears running down their cheeks, the congregation all below bowed with emotion; the weeping became audible. We remained in this state for about a minute, when Mr Jones concluded by prayer in which the missionaries were solemnly and earnestly commended to God. On being dismissed I observed the ministers and members go up and shake hands with them in tears. No words were spoken, and we separated in silence. It was a day long to be remembered in this church.[45]

Colcock Jones was well acquainted with the history of revivals, and from the outset in Liberty County he was on guard against anything that could tend to promote mere excitement and emotion. 'As it was somewhat of an extraordinary season,' he noted, there were those who 'looked for something extraordinary in the public services of the sanctuary.' News from the North of how sudden 'conversions' had been multiplied by means of 'the altar call' had reached Georgia, and Jones speaks of hearers who expected preachers to 'call them up to be prayed for'. He was convinced such a practice confused a physical action with conversion itself. Certainly he was no opponent of genuine emotion, but attempts to employ emotion to get results he regarded as 'madness': 'Wherever the Negroes in the Southern country are trained up to shouting and groaning, and kneeling to be prayed for, and such like things, there is confusion and fanati-

[45] Reported by Charles Colcock Jones in a letter dated August 29, 1843, which he wrote anonymously to the *Charleston Observer*. Richard Way and his wife eventually reached China, not Bangkok, where they served at Ningpo for sixteen years. A memorial still visible in the Midway Church graveyard marks the death of one of their children, aged nine years, in China. The two missionaries were joined in China by Mrs Way's brother, the Rev. John W. Quarterman, who was responsible for the translation of Jones's *Catechism* into Chinese.

cism and spurious religion.'[46] 'I have resorted to no means but the common means of grace, as seen in our Churches from Sabbath to Sabbath.'[47] As Stacy noted, 'He depended entirely upon the earnest preaching of the word.'[48]

The same motivation led him to discourage 'boisterous', thoughtless singing. The natural exuberance in music of the African people he well understood, but he believed that when grace comes to a person or community it changes singing as well as every other part of life. The worship of God is much more than a matter of human enjoyment and entertainment:

> For the promotion of intelligence and piety, the public worship of God should be conducted *with reverence and stillness on the part of the congregation* . . . Nor should the minister – whatever may have been the previous habits and training of the people – encourage demonstrations of approbation or disapprobation, or exclamations, or responses, or noises, or outcries of any kind during the progress of divine worship; nor boisterous singing immediately at its close. These practices prevail over large portions of the Southern country, and are not confined to one denomination, but appear to extend to all. The extent to which they are carried, depends upon the encouragement given by ministers and denominations. I cannot think them beneficial. Ignorant people may easily be excited, and they soon fall into the error of confounding things that differ essentially. The appearance is put for the reality; the sound for the substance; feeling in religious worship, for religion itself. And so false and perverted may they

[46] *Ninth Report* (1844).

[47] *Annual Report, 1833*, p. 9.

[48] Stacy, *Midway Church*, p. 232. Stacy deplored revivals which were 'periodical and annual', commenting, 'There is such a thing as "Reviving a church to death"' (p. 204).

> become in their notions, that the absence of any outward signs and sounds, is in their view an evidence of the absence of religion; and so accustomed to these things they may become, and so fond of the excitement connected with them, that they will choose such meetings where they are practised, before all others! And this, as it is manifest to all who will judge righteous judgment, to their most serious injury! Let the minister in attempting a reformation, be forbearing, prudent, kind and patient.[49]

Reverence in worship was to be regarded as no mere white custom. In the case of both white and black, Jones constantly cautioned against the premature admission of individuals into church membership. Membership statistics figure in his *Annual Reports*, but they gain no great prominence. He noted that from the autumn of 1838 to the same time in 1840, '250 and 300' were received into the different churches.

While he remained a member at Midway, Jones was careful not to direct converts to particular churches, and he guarded them against 'sectarianism'. This he defined, not as the conscientious preference for one denomination above others, and a promotion of its interests, 'but when that preference is carried to the extreme of bigotry, intolerance and self-righteousness,' then it becomes 'destructive to true piety. I am inclined to the opinion, that where sectarianism prevails among ignorant masses of religious people, it does not ordinarily originate with them; but they are taught it by means of intelligent heads and leaders, and by them it is mainly perpetuated.' Missionaries, he insisted, must be ready to serve blacks with Methodist, Baptist, Congregational, and Presbyterian connections, and be ready to supply recommendations for membership to churches 'not of *their own* denomination'.

[49] *Suggestions on Religious Instruction*, p. 15.

These several denominations all supported his work. It is said that, during the years of his missionary labours, 677 blacks became members at Midway. Stacy wrote: 'As the result of the labours of Dr Jones and his co-adjutors, multitudes of coloured people were brought into the churches.' In 1846 a total of 1,133, nearly one-fourth of the whole Negro population of the district, was in membership at various churches. The figure included 161 at Sunbury Baptist and 543 at Newport Baptist.[50]

What Jones looked for as evidence of the work of the Spirit of God was permanent moral change. This commonly began with conviction of sin. One previously careless hearer confessed how, at the end of a service: ' I was as weak as water. I was afraid to die and be lost; I felt very wicked; I felt I needed assistance. I could not save myself.' Another said: 'I felt very mean on account of my sin; I felt I needed a Saviour. That feeling made me go to Christ.' And again, another exclaimed to the preacher, 'Ah! sir; my heart and the Bible are *not one*.'

Sometimes the first sign of change was antagonism to the preacher. One woman complained that he had told the congregation what she was doing on Saturday night and that everybody knew he was talking about her. In reply she was assured that *he* did not know everything about her: '*But the Word of God did*; and by the way you speak now, it *fits* you exactly; and so it proves itself to you to be the Word of God that knoweth all things, and, instead of being *vexed* with the Word of God, you had better *straighten* your ways and be at peace with it.'

[50] Stacy, *Midway Church*,, p. 221.The figure for black members at Midway was 377. Sunbury Baptist had 161 and Newport, Baptist, 543. According to the tax returns, the black population of the district stood at 4,212, in 1846. The figure excluded those not of taxable age.

Lasting conviction and genuine conversion mean a change of disposition and nature – from lying to honesty; from promiscuity to marital faithfulness; from selfishness to compassion for others. One Christian planter, hearing of the changed character of slaves he had long known, exclaimed, 'It cannot be.' Assured that it was the case, he said; 'It is the most glorious news I have heard in my life; only see the power of God!'

Another white man, contrasting conditions in 1845 with ten years earlier, affirmed, 'That there has been a great and manifest improvement, is evident to everyone, even the casual observer. Drunkenness, theft, falsehood, profaneness, and even lewdness (that hitherto crying sin among them) though not wholly banished, do now exist to a very limited extent, in comparison to what they formerly did.'[51]

Included among the changes noted was the concern of converted slaves for unbelieving Masters. During the 1840s daily prayer and praise meetings were common on many plantations, with few owners forbidding them. Mallard quotes the conversation of one black servant:

> You know my Master. It is in his power to forbid all prayer and praise on the place; to stop *the voice*. But it is not in the power of man to destroy *love in the heart;* to make us hate the God we love. We can *love* in silence. But my Master stops no man in religion. He says he will stand in no man's way. We ring our bell and hold our prayers continually. I only wish he were a Christian. But I live in hope, I think I see an alteration. When he speaks now of the business of the plantation he says, 'If we live,' 'If Providence permits,' we will do this and that; in times past, he did not use to speak so.

[51] Ibid., p. 222.

The last annual Report of the Association – the thirteenth – in 1848 marked the end of the ten years of life that Charles Colcock Jones poured into his mission. He had come to the conclusion that his part in it, at least, had been fulfilled. His hope was that the work was now firmly established. Whereas there had only been three preaching stations in 1838 there were now enough to be able to hold two thousand people, and, 'Comparing this district as it is at present, with what it was seventeen years ago . . . it may be said that the purposes contemplated in the beginning, have been, to a gratifying extent, realized.' 'The capabilities of the Negroes of intellectual, moral and religious improvement' had been demonstrated. What gospel preaching, 'by the favour of God', could accomplish among them was now evident. Instead of the mission leading to the disturbance of society, as some had predicted, slaves in numbers of cases were now 'better servants and better men'.

Something much wider than the change in Liberty County had also happened in these years. In part due to the news of Jones's work and writings, the attention of the wider Christian public across the South and beyond had been drawn to the needs of the black people.[52] His name was now well known. From 1846, when he was given an honorary doctorate by Jefferson College, he was commonly known as 'Dr Jones'. The following year the General Assembly had sought to appoint him as their agent for their Board of Missions for the South and Southwest.

There seems to have been another reason why Jones laid the work down in 1848. The previous year the state of his

[52] For instance, the *Biblical Repertory and Princeton Review* carried news of him in the volumes for 1845 and 1848.

lungs (one of which was injured in childhood) had compelled him to give up weeknight visits to plantations. 'It has been long, laborious work', he said briefly in his final Report. From other sources we know a little of what lay behind those words. In addition to the weight of his Sunday labours, and the oversight of Sunday Schools with some 500 children, it had been his habit for seven months of the year, to ride from three to ten miles, perhaps three times a week, to plantations. John Jones, his brother-in-law, wrote:

> His labours were confined to a warm, damp, and exceedingly depressing climate. The plantation work was particularly drastic. Frequently he would ride home in mid-winter, and at mid-night, with feet and clothing thoroughly soaked from watery roads and night dews. From such exposures and unremitting toil, his constitution received a shock which resulted in a premature decay of vigour and the going down of his sun, even before the autumn of old age.[53]

Even so, Colcock Jones was to write in the last *Annual Report*, 'It has been a pleasant service to me . . . I would not recall one hour, one day, one Sabbath of it; but crave God's pardon for the evil, and give Him the glory for the good.'

Columbia and Philadelphia

Instead of taking up the Assembly's call, Jones, on the advice of his presbytery, returned to Columbia in September 1848 to prepare another generation of students at the Seminary. John Jones said of his cousin Charles, 'He was greatly attached to the Seminary.' Once again, concern to widen support for the gospel among the black people entered into the decision, yet there were differences between this and the earlier move

[53] *Memorial Volume*, p. 198.

to South Carolina in 1836. On the first occasion the trek to Columbia had meant a five-day journey by horse and wagon. Now it was a ship to Charleston, a few nights at the Charleston Hotel, and then a 9 am train which reached Columbia at 5 pm the same day. The age of the 'iron horse' had begun in the South. More important was the difference in conviction with which Jones took up work again at the Seminary. He wrote: 'My present removal to Columbia differs in its circumstances materially from my removal there just ten years ago. Then my own mind was not materially satisfied on the point of duty, and I yielded to the opinions of a large body of brethren in the ministry and friends. I shortly came back to my mission work, believing that the experiment *had not been fairly wrought out* . . . Now it appears to me, if I am not deceived, *this necessary and preparatory foundation has been laid,* in conjunction with many other labourers in the field all over the South.'[54]

The Joneses found a new home near the Seminary. He thought the town 'much improved', with gardens flourishing and 'much grown up' from former days. The trees 'improve the appearance of the streets wonderfully'. At this date Columbia had also two of the most distinguished preachers ever known in the South, B. M. Palmer at First Presbyterian, and J. H. Thornwell at the College of South Carolina.

Even so, it seems Jones found it hard to settle. A variety of reasons accounts for this: spiritual conditions were not flourishing; the Seminary struggled financially; Mary was sick for a period in 1849; and the condition of his plantations (left in the care of managers) needed guidance which he could only give by letter. Perhaps, too, he was uneasy at aspects of the

[54] *Thirteenth Report* (1848).

theological teaching of his colleague A. W. Leland.[55] A recent writer surmises that Jones felt 'slighted' in Columbia, supposing he was esteemed more as 'a missionary' than a competent intellectual. The alleged evidence I find unconvincing.[56] But there is no doubt that, despite Thornwell's presence, there were educational problems that affected his two sons now in critical years of schooling at the College of South Carolina.

Whatever truth there be in any of these reasons, it is certain that a providence that occurred in the early morning of April 18, 1850, made him reconsider his whole position. The preceding day had been a difficult and sad one for them. Jack, their faithful family servant for forty years had just died. Long before Mary had given him a large-print Bible that he would often read to her children – an indication of how the family did not obey the law when it offended the law of God. That day Jack's body lay in a coffin in their home awaiting burial. Jack's wife was also very ill, and their own daughter, Mary Sharpe, was sick. The Joneses were late and exhausted getting to bed on the night of the 17th, only to be awakened after 1.30 am by the cry that their house was on fire. They found the bedroom already filling with suffocating smoke, and half-dressed and with only a few items, such as watches, which could be picked up in their hands, they all escaped. With the house in flames, priority was given to getting Jack's coffin and his dying wife removed to safety. Everything else was burned to the ground. 'We saved nothing but our lives, through the tender mercy of our God. Looking over the ruins

[55] B. M. Palmer, who was in a position to know, said that in the mid 1850s Columbia Seminary, despite its fine building, was in 'the crippled condition in which she had existed from the beginning'. He also spoke of the students being 'dissatisfied with the instruction received in theology', and how this led to the appointment of J. H. Thornwell to that chair in 1855.

[56] See Clarke, *Dwelling Place*, p. 273.

of the study the next day, I picked up part of a volume of John Howe's works. It was compact, but charred like a coal; and there lay open upon its face, distinctly legible, his sermon on "The Vanity of Man as Mortal"!'[57]

In the days which followed, Jones writes of how 'the good people of Columbia' surrounded them with kindness and sympathy, and how his clerical brethren 'condoled with me particularly on the *loss of all my library and papers, lectures, and sermons, etc., of every kind – the accumulation of some twenty years or so. A great loss indeed! Can never be restored.* I am in respect of *ministerial* stores burnt out!'[58]

Jones had no thought of what posterity lost in his loss, but 122 years later we were given some means by which to judge it. In 1972 Yale University Press published an immense volume containing over 1400 pages of correspondence written by Charles and Mary Colcock Jones and by other members of their family circle. The book, *The Children of Pride,* edited by Robert Manson Myers, contains letters covering the years 1854–68. An additional volume of their letters, from the same editor, *A Georgian at Princeton,* gives correspondence from April 1850, the month of the fire, to June 1852. These letters are far more absorbing than fiction, and Mary's letters are equal to those of her husband. The worth of what survived *after* the fire indicates what we might have had if many letters and papers from the prime years of their lives had not

[57] C. C. Jones, *The History of the Church of God during the Period of Revelation* (New York: Scribner, 1867), Preface.

[58] *A Georgian at Princeton,* ed. Robert Manson Myers (New York: Harcourt, Brace, Jovanovich, 1976), p. 11. Jones could write further on April 23, 1850: 'My mind has been and was calm. It was the hand of the Lord! It was mine *to use*, not *to hold* nor *keep*. He took but what He gave – but what was His own. It all resolved itself into *a question of time only*. The time was coming when I must be taken from all that was consumed. It pleased God to take all from me and leave me alive.'

been lost.[59] The later correspondence, now so fully published, makes the reader a member of the family circle in a manner that can have few parallels in Christian literature.

The fire cast a new uncertainty over the Joneses remaining decision. When the General Assembly of the Presbyterian Church convened in May he was elected, in his absence, to the position of Secretary of the Board of Domestic Missions. With an office in Philadelphia, it was one of the most responsible positions in the Church, involving the supervision of some four hundred missionaries. Along with the letter of invitation, came mail from friends who urged him to accept. It would give him 'lever', it was said, for gospel work across the whole country and, not least, for 'your own beloved work, the religious instruction of the blacks'. Archibald Alexander of Princeton similarly assured him that the post 'would open a wide door of usefulness to that part of the population among which your labours have been hitherto bestowed'.[60] The retiring Secretary wrote to him:

> You are well qualified to fill this office. You have good business talents, good preaching powers, can think clearly and express your thoughts that others can understand you; you know men and things, and with your easy and pleasant manners will be an acceptable companion or guest in any society. You have, I believe, the entire confidence of the churches.[61]

When this invitation arrived, Mary Jones was visiting Montevideo, and by letter husband and wife discussed how they should act. He writes to her:

[59] Also lost in the fire were journals (with record of his earlier work), correspondence and another catechism 'upon the historical portions of the Bible almost ready for the press'.

[60] *Georgian at Princeton*, p. 29.

[61] Ibid., p. 22.

> If I know my own mind and heart, I have no objections to remaining in Columbia, no objections to going to Philadelphia, no objections to returning to Liberty County and my old work: for to me it is work everywhere, and my only desire is to know what is agreeable to God's will.

In response Mary reviewed the many things on her heart. Against going North there were such considerations as his health, and their own attachment to the South: 'I am Southern born and Southern reared; my hopes, my desires, my sympathies and my interests are with the land of my nativity.' Something particular troubled her: 'The condition of our poor servants! What will become of them when no master, no mistress, comes at least once a year to inquire into their temporal wants and to provide for their spiritual necessities? It cannot be duty to leave them to live and die like the heathen . . . The interests of our plantations will necessarily decline if we are removed from them for a series of years.'

None of these things, however, were the main issue for Mary Colcock Jones. It was, she wrote, 'What is the divine will? Where shall you do most good? Where best glorify God?' She assured him that she meant to support him. 'Wherever the Lord inclines you to decide is for the best.'[62]

The outcome was that they went North by boat and train and arrived in Philadelphia in early October 1850, their two boys, Charles, Jr. and Joseph, going to Princeton to resume their studies. Adjustment to the change was not easy. Their first accommodation was at the America Hotel from whence Mary wrote to her sons, 'I hope we shall soon get suited, for my head is almost crazed from the noise in the street.' For Charles the change of routine was perhaps even greater. The

[62] Ibid., pp. 25–6.

office business, including correspondence from near and far, demanded his attention from 8.30 am to 2 pm, and again from 3 till 6 pm. Opportunities for study had gone. In addition he was expected to travel and also to preach locally. With regard to preaching he determined what he would treat as the priority. On one occasion faced with three invitations to preach, he noted, 'I am weary; if I preach at all, it will be, God willing, to the Negroes.'

Away from home, in May 1851, he preached to large black congregations at Louisville. After one such service, with five to seven hundred blacks as his hearers, the local minister said to the congregation: 'We have long heard of Dr Jones, and of his great success in *reformation*. But we could never understand the mystery before. Now the mystery is solved. He preaches the *pure gospel*.'[63] Something additional to preaching was necessary to account for the influence of his speaking. 'The more I mingle with men and with God's own people and have to do with the affairs of His Kingdom,' he wrote to Mary at the same date, 'the more do I feel the hourly need of the teachings of the Holy Ghost.'

From Louisville, Jones went on to St Louis. He had never been so far west before and wrote graphic descriptions to Mary of the scenery and the developing nation. After which he concluded:

> But after all, I seem rather to prefer the older portions of our country. The great West is more pleasant to visit than to dwell in. So much mixture of people from all places; so much driving, speculating, selfishness; a world of strangers, a world of changes; moving, pushing, sickening, dying.

His main reason for being at St Louis was attendance on the General Assembly of the Presbyterian Church where he

[63] Ibid., p. 134.

spoke for an hour and a half – 'I did not read but *delivered* it,' he wrote to Mary, 'I was much assisted. The assembly in very many members confesses that the subject of domestic missions was never so presented nor understood before.'[64]

Along with the excursions expected of him, Jones laboured faithfully at his post. We are told, 'He infused new life into the operations of the Board of Domestic Missions, and he awakened the national church to the plight of the Negro.'[65] But by the summer of 1851, with a suitable house for rent still to be found, and in the midst of incessant demands, it is clear that both husband and wife looked back wistfully at their previous labours. In Philadelphia there was no pastoral tie to people or to students, nor was public worship, Mary felt, the same as they had enjoyed in Georgia. On a visit back to Liberty County in December 1851, she wrote of the difference on Sundays to Charles, 'I know it is not another gospel, but oh, it seems as with peculiar unction that the Word is dispensed here.' On one occasion while she was away, Charles in Philadelphia confessed to her: 'Had a real touch of depression yesterday: lonely; no friends to go to see; none to come to see me; bound up in the office; load to carry every day; no respite; warm; tired; feet ached.'

It appears that the denomination had left Jones almost single-handed in administering the affairs of the Missions. By the beginning of 1852 enquiries were coming to him as to whether he would take a call back to Seminary life – to Union Seminary, Virginia, or perhaps to Princeton Seminary (in succession to Archibald Alexander who died in 1851). He did not consider himself free to consider any such invitations;

[64] Ibid., p. 146.
[65] *Children of Pride*, p. 17.

he wanted to see the affairs of the Board of Missions 'more in order and in greater prosperity'. Yet he let it be known that 'the situation was too confining, and it was a question if my general health could stand it'.[66]

The Shadows of the Closing Years

It was Jones's health that finally settled the issue. The disease incurred in earlier years, says Mallard, only needed 'the confinement of office work in Philadelphia, and pressure of responsibility and wearing toil (for he was a man who put his whole soul into whatever he undertook) to complete'. By the late summer of 1853 he was so broken in health that resignation could not be delayed and thus, after three years in the North, they returned to Montevideo in October 1853. He was forty-nine.

The year 1854, the first year home, was peculiarly difficult. The upkeep of his plantations had suffered in their absence; and while efforts at recovery were in progress they experienced the worst hurricane in Liberty County since 1804. Illness was also widespread and a yellow-fever epidemic struck Savannah. 'I never knew such a year of general affliction and sorrow,' Jones wrote on October 5, 1854.

It was hoped that rest would lead to a recovery in his health, and on October 18, 1854, we find him writing, 'I preached at Dorchester last Sunday for the first time for a long, long time, and have an engagement, D.V., for Sunbury the coming Sabbath.' Following that next engagement, Mary reported to one of her sons: 'Your dear father was enabled to preach with great feeling and power from 1 John 3:1–2. A large congregation of Negroes. I trust some good was done. I

[66] *Georgian at Princeton*, p. 293.

felt that it was good to be there myself . . . Sometimes I have hope that your father is improving; then again I am much discouraged.' In January 1856 he was well enough to write to his daughter: 'Our people [the slaves] are generally well. Have commenced my old regular plantation meetings with them. It is old times come back again.'

But any hopes of recovery, and of a resumption of former labours among the black people beyond his own servants, were unfounded. Referring to her husband, Mary wrote on November 20, 1856, 'He is more unwell than for a great while: the nervous inaction greatly increased.' His health, described as a 'wasting palsy', would never be restored; rather he became progressively weaker, especially in his chest and throat. In 1857, for a while at least, doctors forbade him to preach. Thereafter public work was more infrequent. When he did speak it was usually at the Midway Church. Yet it is apparent that he was able to continue some work among his own servants for, on January 24, 1861, he noted that fourteen of them had come to him for spiritual instruction that evening, and had just left at 9 pm. He added: 'A long time since we have had such an awakening on the plantation. May it prove a genuine work of the Spirit!'

Mary Sharpe, the Joneses' one daughter, had returned to Montevideo with them in 1853. She had been a Christian from childhood and in 1857 became the wife of Robert Q. Mallard, the Presbyterian minister of the Walthourville Church, some ten miles inland. Her two older brothers, Charles, Jr. and Joseph, were at this time advancing their careers in law and medicine respectively. Joseph, the younger of the two, professed faith in Christ in 1858, by which date he was a professor in the University of Georgia.[67] He became an

[67] *Children of Pride*, p. 414, where his mother writes of her joy at the news.

active worker in the Sabbath School and his faith was evident ten years later when, with his own family, he escaped death in a night fire.[68]

With regard to Charles C. Jones, Jr. the position was different. While he was good-living, with regard for his parents, his youth passed without any evidence of his knowing Christ. The family letters to him, from both father and mother, are very numerous. Along with family news and affection, there is a strain of grief that he was closer to the world than to Christ: 'Do not put off making your peace with God. You stand in danger of eternal ruin every hour you live without repentance and faith in the Lord Jesus Christ!' (6 September 1854). 'My dear son, I pray the Lord to open your eyes and open your heart to see and feel your need of a precious Saviour' (16 February 1858). 'When, my son, will you seek the Lord? *Why are you not a Christian?*'(3 October 1859).

In 1861 Charles, Jr. was Mayor of Savannah, and in that year he suffered the death of his young wife and their eldest child. Along with deep sympathy, the pleas of parents intensified. His father writes, 'You have been living without God, without Christ . . . feeling in your prosperity that you could never be moved, and making family and fortune and friends and earthly pleasures your happiness and trust' (20 July 1861). Shortly after, his mother added: 'My beloved child, do

[68] Ibid., p. 1422. Joseph Jones became distinguished as a doctor and scientist. Although an elder in Presbyterian churches, it may be that the interests of his career dimmed his Christian commitment for a period. Near the end of his life (1896) he joined the church of his brother-in-law, who records: 'I had a most tender interview with him, in which he recalled his religious past, and sought, of his own motion, through me, a transfer of membership to my church. It seemed to me he regarded it in the light of a solemn renewal of his Christian profession.' Mallard adds that among Dr Joseph Jones's last literary works were 'a brilliant series of articles in confutation of evolution . . . He was convinced that the chasms between the species are too wide and deep to be bridged over by any laws of natural selection, and environment, and survival of the fittest.' *Plantation Life before Emancipation*, pp. 80–1.

not let the world draw you away from the one great design of this *deep, deep affliction.* Seek and you shall find your long neglected Saviour! May the Divine Spirit bring you to Him at once! There is no other rest for the weary and heavy laden.'

The last major public address given by Jones was at the General Assembly of the newly formed Presbyterian Church in the Confederate States in December 1861 held in Augusta. On the sixth day of the Assembly he was helped to walk to the church by Mallard, his son-in-law, and then, too weak to stand, he spoke seated for an hour on the need for evangelistic work among the black people. 'Powerful in its feeling appeals', we read, his address was 'listened to with profound attention'. The Assembly asked him to prepare further material for the next annual Assembly but he declined. In the year that followed, although all his mental powers remained, he became increasingly feeble. To his older son he wrote on 4 December 1862:

> Few men have been more blessed than I with dutiful and affectionate children, and with a wife whose tender kindnesses know no remission; and could relief have come through all your devotion and constant efforts, I should long since have been restored to perfect health. But such has not been the will of God, and to that will it is my desire and prayer to submit cheerfully.

By this date there was sadness in the South such as had never been known before. The issues between North and South, which Jones had first heard debated in the 1820s, were now being settled by force of arms. For years Jones had feared that the controversy would result in the break-up of 'the Union'; and when war engulfed the whole nation in the Spring of 1861, it was unquestionably the darkest event of his lifetime. The conflict of the Northern 'Union' with the Southern 'Confederacy' was to claim six hundred thousand lives before the latter surrendered, exhausted, in 1865. This is not the place to comment on the causes of the tragedy. Even the very name of the war remains a disputed matter. Suffice it to say that the emancipation of the slaves as the alleged reason for the bloodshed is a considerable over-simplification; such defenders of the South as Robert E. Lee, a leading general in the Confederate army, owned no slaves. And there were many Christian supporters of the war in the South (the Joneses among them) who were not committed to the permanence of slavery and looked for 'the gradual emancipation of the negro'.[69] What united them in opposition to the invasion of the forces of the North was their belief in the constitutional liberty of their states. Conviction about the righteousness of their cause united the South: 'I can look extinction for me and mine in the face,' wrote Mary Jones, 'but *submission* never!'[70]

Mary's words equally represented her husband's feelings. In spirit Charles Colcock Jones was intensely involved in the war, and Mary noted the effect of the anxieties upon his declining health. In the last year of his life, when Confederate arms had considerable success, a number in the South were still hopeful of a speedy end to the strife. He was not optimistic. 'We have nothing but war before us,' he wrote on

[69] See, for instance, B. M. Palmer, *Life and Letters of J. H. Thornwell* (repr. Edinburgh: Banner of Truth, 1974), p. 482. Mary Jones referred to Thornwell as 'one of the master minds of the age'. *Children of Pride*, p. 1013. Other Southern military leaders who held no slaves were 'Stonewall' Jackson, J. E. Johnston, A. P. Hill, and J. E. B. Stuart.

[70] To understand this it needs to be remembered that the original thirteen British Colonies were independent of one another before the Revolution of 1775 brought them together in a common cause. It was never, however, accepted in the South that the union annulled the right of states to act independently when they judged their interests required it.

30 September 1862, and on December 8, 'Every prospect at home and abroad is for a *protracted struggle*.'

There was only one way that Jones knew to face this sorrow; he believed that faith in Christ and his deity can brighten the darkest hours. From 1822 he had seen this life as a pilgrimage – 'no durable home here; and our own life is but a vapour'. Not to this world did he look for true happiness. As he wrote on 25 December 1861, 'What a vanity is all earth without the present favour of God and the hope of glory with Him hereafter.'

When the war came it was this faith that led him to look past the external to the sovereign hand of God. Men were only secondary things; the war was his judgment and they must humble themselves before him. 'The Lord's people must be careful not to be led away from their Bibles and closets, and from Him who rules over all' (13 December 1860). 'We are in the Lord's hands; He is dealing with us' (4 July 1861).

In February 1863 Dr Jones was present for the last time at the communion services at Midway. Forty years had gone by since he had first professed his faith at the old church. On March 16, he rose and dressed as usual, walked a little on the lawn in front of the house but returned exhausted. In his study after lunch he talked with Mary about the promises of God. 'In health,' he said, 'we repeat these promises, but now they are realities.' She replied, 'I feel sure that the Saviour is present with you.' To which he answered, 'I am nothing but a poor sinner, I renounce myself and all self-justification, trusting only in the free unmerited righteousness of the Lord Jesus Christ.' Asked if he had any message for his sons, he said, 'Tell them both to lead the lives of godly men in Christ Jesus, in uprightness and integrity.' Sensing the end near, his wife suggested he should go to the bedroom. With assistance this was done and, closing his eyes, he lay down in his customary manner with one foot over the other. Then, 'without a groan, without a single shudder', he 'fell asleep in Jesus, as calmly as an infant in the arms of a loving mother'. The body was taken to his study, where it lay for two days, 'surrounded by the authors he had loved in life', before burial in the graveyard of the Midway Church. On the stone the words are engraved,

> He walked with God, and was not, for God took him.

Mary Jones and the Aftermath

Jones was right in his expectation of protracted war, and the worst tragedies for the South he did not live to see. The fall of Vicksburg to the Union forces; Lee's failed invasion of the North at Gettysburg; the capture of Atlanta, which exposed Georgia to the destructive march of General Sherman through its heart to the sea; the final Confederate defeat at Richmond, and Lee's surrender in April 1865 – all this, and much else, still lay in the future. Before the end almost every family in the South had given their sons for the conflict. The Joneses' eldest son, Charles, went into the Chatham Artillery defending Savannah, and rose to be a Colonel in that regiment. Their younger son, Joseph, although now a qualified doctor, joined the Liberty Independent Troop – one of the state's oldest regiments. Even for those who stayed at home occupations were changed. Mothers now made uniforms, blankets, even cartridges, and collected rags for bandages. Shops were made into hospitals.

While Georgia was initially far from the main battlefronts, its coastline left it exposed to raids and invasion from the sea. From the family letters it is apparent how life was distracted by the reports, rumours, and fears which circulated everywhere. Old Midway Church saw a new sight – the building crowded with soldiers for a service before leaving to join comrades in Virginia. Eventually there were no more men to give, and when Sherman's army swept down into coastal Georgia in December 1864, those who remained were helpless in the face of the ensuing destruction.

From Sherman's army, it was General Kilpatrick's Cavalry which reached Liberty County and Montevideo. For several weeks, into January 1865, the Joneses' home was entered and ransacked. The only whites on the plantation were women and children. Mary Sharpe Mallard (her husband now a chaplain with Confederate forces) was there and expecting her first child, so was Kate, a relative. Charles Jones, Jr. was with what was left of his regiment; and of the whereabouts of Joseph his mother had no idea. When Montevideo was searched and pillaged, food supplies, clothes and jewellery were all seized. Mary noted in her Journal for December 13, 1864:

> It is impossible to imagine the horrible uproar and stampede through the house, every room of which was occupied by them, all yelling, cursing, quarrelling and running from one room to another in wild confusion. Such was their blasphemous language, their horrible countenances and appearances, that we realized what must be the association of the lost in the world of eternal woe.

On one occasion a Christian among the Union soldiers offered them protection, but for the most part the abuse continued until January 1865. So little food remained that Mary and the family were forced to eat before dawn when they were least likely to be interrupted and to have it taken from them. One of their faithful servants, Cato, was accused by the soldiers of hiding food to give to 'that damned old heifer in the house', and told they would blow out his brains if he gave Mary a morsel more. At the same time, pointing to the chapel, soldiers demanded to know what house it was. Cato replied: 'A church which my master had built for the coloured people on the place to hold prayers in the week and preach on the Sunday.' On which his questioners exclaimed: 'Yes, there he told all his damned lies and called it preaching.'[71] When another servant attempted to stop the theft of valuable books from the study, urging that her former master had laboured for the good of the coloured people, she was met with the reply, 'He was a damned infernal villain, and we only wish he were now alive; we would blow his brains out.' On one of these occasions, 'Mother and Kate trembled from head to foot', Mary Sharpe noted in her journal.[72] They knew what a cousin meant who wrote to them about this time, 'I have almost forgotten how to laugh.'

Almost everything living at Montevideo – from horses and mules to chickens – was removed or simply destroyed: 'Twelve sheep were found shot and left in the pasture.' On one occasion the safety of one of the black women was in question; and, one night, faced with a threat that their house was to be burned down, the family took turns to stay awake. In the midst of all this Mary Sharpe's baby was born.

Years later, Charles Colcock Jones, Jr. was to write: 'The Federal cavalry under General Kilpatrick, in the winter of 1864–1865 occupied and plundered Liberty County, converting a well ordered and abundantly supplied region into an abode of poverty, lawlessness and desolation.'[73]

[71] *Children of Pride*, p. 1232.

[72] Ibid., p. 1231.

[73] C. C. Jones, Jr., *The Dead Towns of Georgia* (1878; repr. Savannah: Oglethorpe Press, 1997), p. 189.

Although she might tremble, Mary's faith did not fail. In the darkest weeks of that winter, she could write such words as the following:

> Helpless – oh, how utterly helpless! And yet blessed be God! We feel that we are in the hollow of His almighty hand. It is a precious, precious feeling that the omnipotent, omnipresent Jehovah is with us, and that Jesus, our Divine Redeemer and Advocate, will be touched with our sorrows (*Journal*, 24 December 1864).

> Sabbath, January 15th [1865]. We have had a day of rest. All the women and young people assembled in the kitchen, and we had a pleasant religious service, singing, reading the Scriptures, and prayer and a selected piece on true faith. They were all respectful and attentive. I strive to keep up the worship of God in the family, and believe that true and undefiled religion alone is the great controller and regulator of men's actions . . . From the presence of our Heavenly Father we feared not to meet the face of man. We must have died but for prayer. However agitated or distressed when we approached the mercy seat, we always had strength given as for our day.

Charles Colcock Jones once told his wife that when he remembered Montevideo it brought the picture of Mary singing to his mind. At this dark time she could still write, 'We engaged in singing and prayer.'

Early in March 1865 Mary Sharpe Mallard left with her baby on a hazardous journey to her husband. She carried with her all that was left of the family silver. This was stolen from her baggage, and when she wrote to tell her mother of the loss, Mary's calm reply was, 'God's sovereignty appears in the minutest events of life.' Mary's faith was to be yet more deeply tested. After a visit to her daughter, she returned to find their home at

Maybank burned down; all their stores of cotton were stolen; and Midway Church was standing open (after being a sheep shelter), with its graveyard overgrown with weeds and bushes. Surveying the scene, she wrote to her daughter, 'We are all bankrupt, and only industry and economy will enable us, with God's blessing upon us, to earn a support.' Later she reported in another letter how some of them had assembled to bring the neglected graveyard at Midway back into order in 'respect and affection to our beloved ones'. These words follow:

> When I had finished I went alone into our old church and knelt before the pulpit and there pled with the God of our Fathers that he would not forsake His ancient heritage, but remember the desolations of His own Zion; and although parted and scattered he would once more be favourable to us, send us help from the sanctuary, and strengthen us out of Zion. I prayed that the prayers and tears of the pious dead might come up in remembrance before the throne; but above all that He who had given His precious Blood for the life of the Church would once more lift upon us the light of His countenance and arise with healing in His wings to our bleeding and desolated church. When I rose from my knees I felt an assurance that God would not cast us off (9 December 1865).

The former slave population of Liberty County was now scattered far and wide; but, with the aid of a minority who remained hidden, Mary set herself to recover the plantation. It was to prove impossible. When, at length, she decided to sell Montevideo, no one was interested. A final blow was David Buttolph's decision to lay down his charge at the Midway Church. Mary wrote to her daughter on 19 November 1867:

> Last Sabbath was a deeply solemn and sorrowful day at Midway. Our beloved and faithful pastor, connected with us for

> thirteen years and four months, broke to us the emblems of our Redeemer's love for the last time, now perhaps for the first time in the history of our venerated sanctuary the living teacher is withdrawn. So far as we are concerned, silence will reign within those consecrated walls, or even a more deplorable end may await them. And our precious, our beloved, our sainted dead must sleep in the solitude and neglect of a wilderness. My heart is as if it would burst at this last great affliction which it has seemed best for the great head of the Church to send upon us.

In January 1868, entrusting once 'smiling Montevideo' to the hands of a few black servants who remained, Mary Jones removed to New Orleans to live with her son-in-law and daughter, who were serving a church in that city.

Before leaving Liberty County she had seen one cherished ambition fulfilled. With the help of her eldest son, volume 1 of her husband's *History of the Church of God during the Period of Revelation* had been published by Scribner of New York in 1867. In substance these were the Old Testament lectures he had delivered to the students at Columbia, re-written and revised after his retirement in 1853. 'Thrown out of regular and active employment in the ministry,' he wrote in a Preface, 'I turned my thoughts to a favourite purpose – the recovery of the History of the Church' [that is, the content of his burnt lectures on that subject]. The Preface was dated December 1860, but the Civil War stood in the way of its publication. With the war over, the main obstacle to its appearance was financial, for the publisher was unwilling to bear the cost. Mary Jones had hoped that sales of the book would provide 'the means of erecting a suitable monument at Midway'. It was not to be. Only five hundred copies were printed, and sales were so poor that the publishing of a second volume (covering the New Testament period) was abandoned. 'Times are very hard,' Mary commented on the subject in 1868, 'and it is difficult to interest friends in good books.'[74]

Despite her trials Mary Jones's thoughts were not locked up in the past. Her great hope was in the future. She thought of the departed not as lost, but only 'fading away like the morning stars into the light of heaven'. Her own work was done. In 1869, as she lay dying in New Orleans, far-off from her beloved Liberty County, and the 'sacred tie' of her husband's grave, her daughter asked if she wished her body to rest beside her husband's. The reply was: 'I have always said, "Where I die, there let me be buried . . . " for at the last day we shall all be raised in a moment, in the twinkling of an eye.' After an illness of less than forty-eight hours, she died peacefully at her daughter's home in New Orleans on April 23, 1869.

At that date it would appear that the prayers of the parents for their eldest son had not yet been answered. Charles C. Jones became an eminent lawyer, and widely known both as a speaker and author. His attachment to his old home, which remained unsold after his mother's death, was undimmed. Once a year he faithfully revisited Montevideo. After one visit in 1882 he wrote of 'the old homestead, sadly marred . . . and yet beautiful under the beams of this calm moon and filled with memories pure and consecrated . . . the influences of inexorable decay become more and more apparent. The garden long since has become wild. The dwelling, once so

[74] Many years later, in 1881, the family received $132 from Scribner – 'a wonderful surprise,' Mary Sharpe Mallard wrote to her daughter, 'for I had no idea there ever would be anything realized upon the book'. With copies of the first printing still with Scribner at that date, and no demand for them, she consoled herself 'that the book accomplished one good end in giving occupation and interest to your dear grandfather's invalid life.'

bright and cheerful, has already grown discoloured, and is in parts sadly out of repair. Even the trees are growing old.'[75]

On a wet day in March 1888, Charles Jones, Jr. gave an address at the Midway Church to some twenty people. 'Behold the changes which have overtaken this venerable church', he told his sparse hearers. 'Surely the buried treasures of the past are here far more conspicuous than the expectations of the present. We feel as though we were walking in a vain show.' The Savannah *Morning News* applauded the address as 'one of the noblest efforts of the orator-historian'. But missing from it were any words of Christian faith and hope. Yet if such words were not then spoken there is reason to think that the realities of spiritual life were not now absent from his heart. On the death of his sister, Mary Sharpe, his brother-in-law writes of the way a letter from Charles, Jr. 'reveals the inward nature of the soul, and gives glimpses of what is ordinarily kept under the veil of reserve'. The letter from Charles included the words:

> So your precious wife and my dear sister has left us to join the saints in heaven. So far as she is concerned, what can we say or think, save in joy, that all pain, feebleness and distress are overpast, and that she has entered upon that rest which remaineth for the chosen of the Lord . . . What a source of unutterable pleasure it is to realize the fact that, far above all earthly shadows and anxieties, she is now, and will forever remain absolutely and unalterably happy, in the immediate presence of the Saviour whom she adored, and in the companionship of the dear ones who have gone before.[76]

[75] *Children of Pride*, p. 1438.

[76] Mallard, *Plantation Life before Emancipation*, p. 84. Mallard, writing in 1898, also noted that the children of Mary Sharpe, Charles, Jr., and Joseph (some of them married by this date) 'are, almost without exception, professing Christians, thus keeping up the blessed succession of piety'.

Assessing Charles Colcock Jones

No assessment would be accurate which did not give a major place to his relationship with the wife of his youth. Mary was so commonly at his side that when, on occasion, she was missing it caused surprise. In times of inevitable separation their letters to each other reveal a relationship ever deepening. Twenty-one years after their marriage, Charles wrote to her from Columbia on May 14, 1851:

> Increase of years has brought its cares, and time is making his lasting furrows upon me; but thanks be to God, my heart does not grow old. My wife is still my *bride,* and I can walk with her under these blue skies and upon this green earth, and our young love shall give brightness and beauty to everything, and she shall be more than all the world to me. Into her lap would I pour the fulness of my best labours for her good; and into her bosom all my heart, that she might have everything, and find her happiness in me, as I do mine in her, and as perfect and complete as our Heavenly Father permitteth us to enjoy in each other here below. I bless Him for my wife; I praise Him for his wonderful mercies and loving-kindness to us all our life long.[77]

After his death Mary would write (29 March 1863):

> He is so constantly in my thoughts and affections that I often look around to see if I cannot meet his eye or hear his voice. I often sit at twilight in his lonely study and wish it were given me to behold his precious face and form once more on earth . . . I have been much struck by a remark of Sue's. Speaking of all the spiritual, religious instruction given by your father to the Negroes, especially his own, she said: 'Our dear master has not left any of us poor; he has given us all our property to live off until our Blessed Saviour calls us home'

[77] *Georgian at Princeton,* pp. 139–40.

> Yesterday was the anniversary of his fifty-ninth birthday, today the thirty-third of our marriage. Life is now to me an empty shadow with the substance gone. Today I walked *alone* on the beautiful lawn. I sat upon the blocks where he used to rest and mount his horse. I stood beneath the trees his own hands had trimmed. I listened to the song of the sweet birds he loved so well; recalled the unnumbered times when, side by side, we walked together over every foot of ground, talking with unreserved confidence of all our plans for future improvement and usefulness. I could see him gazing into the beautiful heavens above, or admiring the brilliant sunsets, or the stars as they shone forth in all their glory. He was never tired of contemplating the wonderful works of God. The whole creation was to his capacious mind, to his sanctified heart, the revelation of divine wisdom and goodness . . . I do bless my Lord and Saviour for the mercy and privilege of such a companionship, of such an association – that my lot was cast with such an eminent and godly minister (21 December 1863).

But this marriage relationship was not simply of importance to themselves. What marriage means entered into his whole ministry. He believed that only Christianity teaches the proper relation between the sexes and is unique in its power to elevate womanhood. On this subject he preached one of his best-remembered sermons, 'The Glory of Woman Is the Fear of the Lord'. Much in that sermon reflected his own experience, beginning with his opening sentence:

> No one thing in social life, more distinguishes a Christian from a heathen country, than the consideration in which *females* are held, and the important and influential station which is assigned them in society . . . What unnumbered benefits have flowed from the prayers, and the faith, the precepts,

and examples, and labours of pious women in all ages of the Church on the earth?[78]

It entered largely into his vision for the uplift of the black people who, in too many white quarters, had been denied the privileges of true family life. The theme is prominent in his *Catechism*: '*Marriage has been ordained of God*; and when it takes place between *proper* persons and with *proper feelings and principles, it is the most comfortable and happy state upon earth.*'[79] In plantation cabins, long familiar with marital unfaithfulness, there was a new message to be memorized:

Q.What is the Duty of the Husband?
A. To love and take care of his Wife. 1 Tim. 5:8.

Q. Repeat the Command, 'Husbands love your wives . . .'

Q. Must Husbands and Wives pray for and with each other, and in their families, and do their best to make each other happy for this world and for the world to come?
A. Yes. 1 Pet.3:1–7.

1. *Wives ought to have for their Husbands a love next to that which they have for God.* They are above all others the individuals with whom they vow to live and die, whatever may be the times and seasons that pass over them.[80]

These quotations lead us back to what is most controversial. Whatever merits be recognized in Charles Colcock Jones, for many today he suffers the condemnation pronounced by many on all who tolerated the continuance of slavery in the South. Dr Erskine Clarke, Jones's modern biographer,

[78] *The Glory of Woman Is the Fear of the Lord, A Sermon* (Philadelphia: Martien, 1847), pp. 5, 57. His comment on the words, 'The heart of her husband doth safely trust in her', is in a true sense autobiographical, pp. 21–2.

[79] *Catechism*, p. 110.

[80] Ibid., p. 124.

believes that on this issue he acted out of self-interest. Clarke claims that, having initially asserted slavery to be wrong in principle, Jones then gave up, 'not his slaves but some of his own freedom and moral vision . . . Moral indignation about the evils of slavery would have little power over the seduction of such a southern home.'[81] Eduard Loring, while frequently sympathetic to his subject, endorses the opinion that 'the support of slavery crippled the gospel, thwarted Jones, and led to war.'[82]

This is a complex issue on which much has been written. That the Joneses were affected by the culture in which they grew up is not to be denied. Their hope was that slavery in the South might finally be removed by the gradual uplift of the black people. As Charles wrote in his first Report of 1833: 'Christianity is ultimately to prevail on the earth, and in due course of time, will reach our servants. And should the particular end [emancipation] . . . come by the preaching of the Gospel, happy are we in believing, that it could not come in a more gradual, in an easier, nor a safer way.' But whether this represented a realistic hope has to be questioned. Certainly much missionary work was done across the southern states before the Civil War. William E. Hatcher, writing more particularly of Virginia, said, 'Let it be understood that it was during their bondage and under the Christian influence of Southern people, that the Negroes of the South were made a Christian people. It was the best piece of missionary work ever yet done upon the face of the earth.'[83]

Far more cautiously, however, Albert Raboteau wrote, 'The effectiveness of the antebellum [pre-Civil War] plantation mission is hard to estimate'; and he goes on to point out

[81] *Wrestlin' Jacob*, pp. 15–17.

[82] Loring, 'Missionary to Plantation Slaves,' p. 358

[83] William E. Hatcher, *John Jasper, the Unmatched Negro Philosopher and Preacher* (repr. Harrisonburg: VA: Sprinkle, 1985), pp. 44–5.

that 'successes were dwarfed by the size of the black population.'[84] In 1859 the number of black church members in the South stood at approximately 468,000 out of a total that ran into millions. When it is allowed that Christian influence often extended widely over those who were not church members, the fact remains that emancipation by this means would have been a long way off.

Nor was the problem in the South simply the ill-preparedness for freedom of the subject people. Endemic among numbers of the white population was belief in the servant place of the black people. Some white slave holders, with no faith in Scripture, did not hide their opinion that Negroes and whites were not of the same blood. In Thornwell's opinion the upholders of that opinion deserved the curse of God. But even a Christian of the stature of John L. Girardeau 'believed that God in his providence had made the negro to be the inferior'.[85] Such opinions inevitably operated as a brake on progress toward emancipation, especially when the abolitionist *furore* in the North began to sanction violence.

But to accept that Jones's hopes of an ultimate abolition of slavery rested on unrealistic expectations, is very different from condemning him for acting out of self-interest. He cannot be identified with those who looked down on the black race. His attachment to those he called 'my friends' was profound and sacrificial. He thought nothing of sitting up all night be-

[84] Albert J. Raboteau, *Slave Religion: The 'Invisible Institution' in Antebellum South* (Oxford University Press [U.S.A.], 1978), pp. 175–6.

[85] G. A. Blackburn, *The Life and Work of John L. Girardeau* (Columbia, SC: State Co. 1916), p. 70. Blackburn says of the Negroes: 'They regarded the white man as superior to the black man; his white skin being God's symbol of superiority and their black skins the symbol of their inferiority.' But where had this belief come from? Yet the main seats in Girardeau's Charleston church were for the black people, and even a hundred years after his death he was remembered affectionately with a stained-glass window.

side the bed of a sick servant. After 'Jack' died, before the fire in Columbia, Jones reported to a friend, 'I was with him night and day, and am worn down with anxiety and watching.'[86]

His custom in that regard was so uniform that Mary could write to one of their children at another time, 'You know the tenderness of your father's feelings, and his ceaseless anxiety when servants are sick.'[87] For him this was simple Christian duty. He was speaking of those whom others called slaves when he wrote: 'The death of old and valued members of our families and households creates losses that can never be repaired. We ought to cherish the spark of life in the aged to the last hour, and pay them every attention, and add all we can to their comfort and happiness. God's command is: "Thou shalt rise up before the old and gray-headed."'[88]

Not often was there anger in Jones's letters, but there was over the conduct of a white man who had enjoyed the hospitality of Montevideo. When Jones discovered that, during the visit, the man had taken a sexual advantage of one of his female servants his indignation was unbounded. He wrote to the session of the man's church, calling for disciplinary action, and reminding them that whites were 'superiors not in character but in station in society'.[89] Indeed, as he reminded a would-be missionary among the black people, superiority in character could be with the latter: 'In the course of his ministry, he will find many who are very pious and far more in advance of himself in the divine life, at whose feet he may learn wisdom, and by whose Christian experience and observations, he may be quickened in zeal and improved in every grace; and to have the favour and the prayers *of such* of

[86] *Children of Pride*, p. 265.
[87] Ibid.
[88] Ibid., p. 443,
[89] Ibid., p. 774.

God's people will be a strong reflection and strong support, and more to him than great treasures.'[90]

In his last public address on the subject, given at the Augusta Assembly in 1861, and to which we have already referred, he gathered together his deepest feelings on the race he had lived to serve:

> They share our physical nature, and are bone of our bone and flesh of our flesh; they share our intellectual and spiritual nature; each body of them covers an immortal soul God our Father loves, for whom Christ our Saviour died, and unto whom everlasting happiness or misery shall be meted in the final day. They are not cattle upon a thousand hills, to be taken, worn out and destroyed in our use; but they are men, created in the image of God. Shall we reach the Bread of Life over their heads to far-distant nations, and leave them to die eternal deaths before our eyes?
>
> They are not foreigners, but our nearest neighbours; they are not hired servants, but servants belonging to us in law and in gospel. They are constant and inseparable associates; whither we go, they go; where we dwell, they dwell; where we die and are buried, there they die and are buried; and, more than all, our God is their God.[91]

James Stacy heard that last Augusta address and, speaking of it in 1899, wrote: 'It may safely be said that no man has ever done more for the coloured race of this country than he. No man was ever more beloved and appreciated by that people, his name being mentioned with reverence to this day.'[92]

[90] *Suggestions on Religious Instruction*, p. 13.

[91] Mallard, *Plantation Life before Emancipation*, pp. 199–200. This address, Mallard says, stirred him to the depths and 'while a lover of the race from childhood . . .', the address 'sent me to my home and charge, determined to work for their salvation as I had never done before'.

[92] Stacy, *Midway Church*, p. 224.

Erskine Clarke does not quote such sentiments, and does not appear to believe them. He questions the reality of affection between slaves and their masters and thinks the relationship of the Joneses to their slaves involved 'deep self-deception'.[93] 'They thought of themselves as kind and benevolent owners,' but, when crises came, these 'proud and pious claims' were 'mere bombast and fraud'.[94] He surmises that when the war began the Joneses must have questioned the whole basis of their relationships with their servants: 'Had it really been built upon shared trust and mutual obligations of responsible masters and faithful servants? Or had they dreadfully deceived themselves? . . . had all this been nothing more than an illusion, a mere façade that hid the raw white power that kept Charles and Mary comfortably situated?'[95]

In advancing this thesis Clarke leaves aside the group of witnesses whose testimony on Jones's life work is very relevant. What would Dembo, and Sharper, and Toney Stevens say to these accusations? They could tell of many in Liberty

[93] Clarke, *Dwelling Place*, p. 356. His claim is built largely on the one known instance of Jones selling a slave family on the grounds of 'the trouble the mother has always given'. Jones qualified the sale with the stipulation that the family remain together, a qualification later broken by others. Clarke also speaks of the sale of Abream by 'his master', without making it clear the master was not Jones. *Wrestlin' Jacob*, p. 169.

[94] *Dwelling* Place, pp. 416, 419.

[95] Ibid., p. 410. The suggestion that such thoughts represented the Joneses' assessment of their lives and work is not true to the facts. Clarke quotes Mary Jones's feelings at a low point in 1865, after emancipation had scattered numbers of their former people, 'I am thoroughly disgusted with the whole race' (see *Children of Pride,* p. 1304), but this is atypical, as many other references could show. When C. C. Jones, Jr., published his *Negro Myths from the Georgia Coast* in 1888 he dedicated it, 'In Memory of Monte-Video Plantation and of the Family Servants whose fidelity and affection contributed so materially to its comfort and happiness.' Mallard's books confirm the existence of this permanent affection between the races; and a non-partisan historian, Samuel Eliot Morison, speaking of the Southern Negro, noted, 'Between him and his "white folks" there often developed mutual affection.' *The Oxford History of the American People* (London/New York: Oxford University Press, 1965), p. 506.

County who came to know the love of Christ by hearing of it and seeing it in his servant. The faith of these individuals was no mere imitation. 'Jack', dying in the home in Columbia – the Joneses' home and his own – could say, 'his Saviour was shedding unnumbered mercies all around him . . . he could not begin to speak of God's mercies to him'. And, parting from his wife, Jack 'begged her no longer to put off her soul's salvation'. 'Old Maria', another slave in the family who lived through the fire in the Columbia home, had liberty to tell her mistress, 'God had sent these afflictions to try your faith and patience and see if you would humble yourself and trust in Him and go on with your duty.'

Repeatedly we hear of servants such as Phillis and Hannah who died conscious of the presence of their Saviour. Bella died unexpectedly and, a few hours before, she told Colcock Jones: 'Massa, if the Lord would come for me this night – this *very* night – I would be freely willing to go, for there is nothing to keep me here longer. I can leave all in His hands.' Then there were the many further afield like the black preacher who, hearing of the death of 'my dear old worthy friend Dr C. C. Jones', looked forward to meeting him again 'in the final assembly'.

And what of all the incidental references in the family letters that were never written for the eyes of others? Mary, after attending one of the black services at Pleasant Grove, Liberty, in January 1852, wrote to Charles in Columbia: 'Oh, how the past rushed over my mind! Many precious hours are associated with you and your ministry there, our departed friends, and the black people. They all inquired and sent unnumbered loves and messages. The long, long years of your toil and unwearied effort in the missionary field is ever before my mind.'

How are such testimonies to Jones's Christian influence among the black people to be assessed? It is here that the deepest division of opinion occurs. One side says that his work was necessarily sub-Christian because he failed to see that slaveholding is a moral evil. It is insisted that slaveholding and the postponement of emancipation was sin. This was the Abolitionist argument. But this claim ran into difficulty with the New Testament. The biblical teaching on masters and slaves is not that the institution was evil *per se*. Paul does not condemn the system as such, but gives commands how Christian masters and Christian slaves are to behave. He does not deny that slaves are to serve their masters. Yet masters are not to regard servants as property, or chattels, which they may dispose of as they choose; rather they are participants in a common humanity and equals before God. This was the distinction which Jones sought to follow, and he believed that in denying it, the abolitionists had an argument with Scripture itself.[96]

For Jones there was no inconsistency in believing that slavery is to pass from the earth and in not making its abolition the priority. While he did not neglect the temporal needs of

[96] This is not a partisan Southern argument. As noted earlier, it was accepted at Princeton, and for the reasons carefully argued by John Murray: 'If the institution is the moral evil it is alleged to be by abolitionists, if it is essentially a violation of basic human right and liberty, if slave-holding is the monstrosity claimed, it is, to say the least, very strange that the apostles who were so directly concerned with these evils did not overtly condemn the institution and require slave-holders to practise emancipation.' Murray rejects the response that the apostles were acting on expediency for the time being, until Christian influence took hold: 'The apostles were not governed by that kind of expediency; they openly assailed the institutions of paganism that were antithetical to the faith and morals of Christianity . . . The line of thought required by the silence of the Scripture, on the one hand, and its positive teaching, on the other, is to appreciate the distinction between the institution and the abuses to which it had been subjected and which have frequently been concomitant. The New Testament explicitly deals with the latter and is overt in its denunciation of them.' *Principles of Conduct*, pp. 94–5.

his people, his first duty as a minister of the gospel was not with the social or the political. He believed in a God-given opportunity to evangelize the black people and to bring them eternal good. He would have preferred to have been only a gospel preacher, not a planter; yet had he not been a planter, and had he preached abolition, the missionary endeavour he led in Liberty County would not have been possible. Mary Jones could write to a Union general at the end of the War of her husband's 'devoted efforts to benefit the Negro race. His record is on high, and the good he accomplished in their elevation and true conversion to God will meet an eternal reward.'[97] She was judging by the same perspective when a few years later she believed it 'not to be extravagant to say, more was done for the solid benefit of the negro, through his instrumentality, than has since been effected by all the *Freedman Bureaus* in the land'.[98] Certainly in later years, across the South many emancipated slaves would look back to their days in servitude as the time when Christ found them. Then it was that they began to look forward to the Saviour's coming in the day 'when the stars begin to fall'. As a Virginian defender of the Old South wrote in 1869:

> We are witnesses for the good names of our fathers and mothers who have gone to glory to meet the spirits of their own slaves trained by them for that glory.[99]

Among that number of ex-slaves we read of Maria Jenkins. She lived into her nineties in the 1930s, and when asked, 'Are all your people dead?' could reply,

[97] *Children of Pride*, p. 1286.

[98] *Necrology*, p. 204.

[99] *Selections from the Writings of John H. Bocock*, with biographical sketch by C. R. Vaughan (Richmond, VA; Whittet and Shepperson, 1891), p. 483.

De whole nation is dead . . . De whole nation – Peggy dead – Toby dead – all leaning on de Lord.[100]

* * * * *

On the character of Jones as a Christian the reader of these pages has already enough to form his own judgment. A sentence from his elder son gives us the great characteristic of his life, 'The Bible was his constant companion, his text book, his acknowledged teacher, his guide, his supreme authority.' That his life was lived Godwards none who knew him could deny. In the opinion of one witness, 'He was the most thoroughly converted man he ever knew.' We close with the estimate of his brother-in-law: 'His chief concern was to please God. He lived and moved under the abiding consciousness that God's eye was upon him. He had the most exalted ideas of the greatness, majesty, glory and holiness of God . . . In his own sight he was nothing and less than nothing . . . He ardently loved the Saviour, and desired that His name should be known and honoured in all the earth.'[101]

Today there are no plantations in Liberty County. The whole face of the land has changed and not a trace of Montevideo remains. 'The wind passes over it and it is gone and the place thereof shall know it no more.'

Yet, alone from the past, the Midway Church of 1792 stands, and close to it the graveyard, as though in testimony to the promise, 'The righteous shall be in everlasting remembrance.'

[100] Quoted in Raboteau, *Slave Religion.*
[101] *Necrology*, pp. 196–7.

The Faithful Guardians of Dr Jones' Tomb

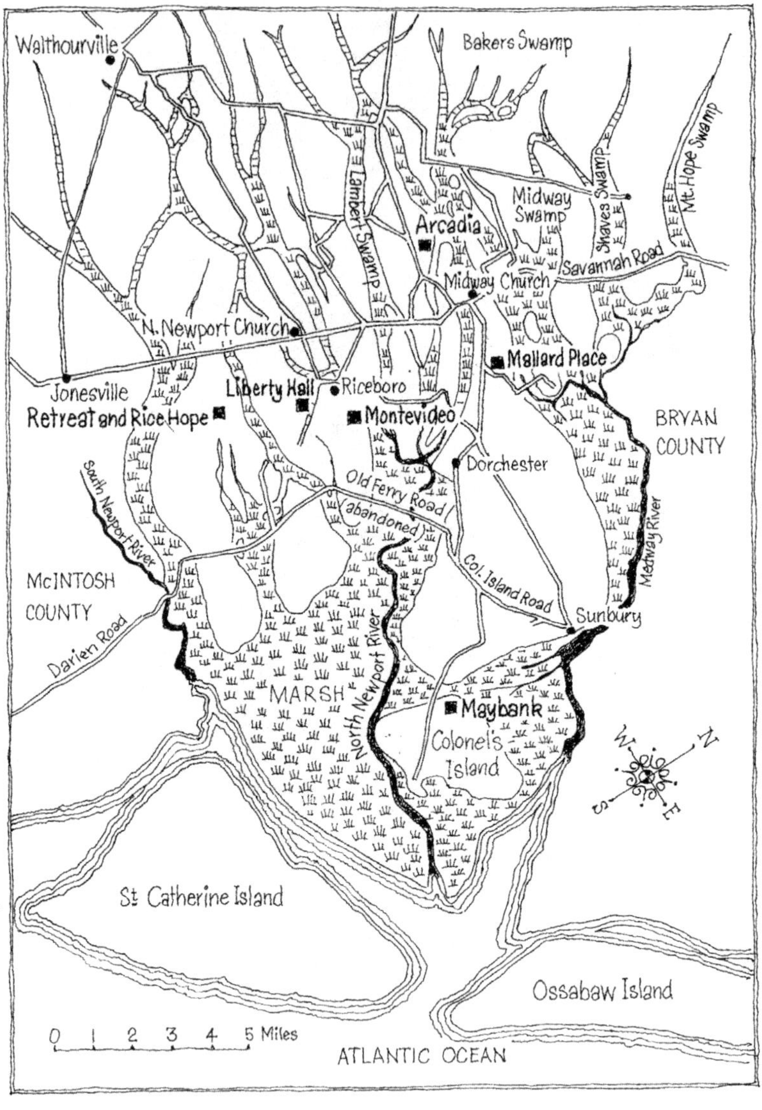

Map of Liberty County, Georgia

7

SPURGEON AS AN EVANGELIST

Charles Haddon Spurgeon (1834–92)

When God's power is moving, there will be a corresponding movement among the people; they will long to hear when God's power is with the speaker. Take it as a significant sign of grace when the houses dedicated to worship are full. Consider that the Lord is about to fill the net when the fishes crowd around the boat.

CHS, 1866

[*On prayer meetings at the Metropolitan Tabernacle*]: One starts in this place every Sunday at seven o'clock in the morning, and another at the hour of ten. A still larger company goes up to the oracle on Monday nights at seven o'clock. Some twelve or fifteen hundred of us are usually to be found in happy fellowship, going up to the mercy-seat on Mondays.

CHS, 1881

The general conduct and conversation of members of a church must always be the best recommendation of the ministry which feeds them.

CHS, 1884

It is a winter's morning, December 27, 1874. Queen Victoria has reigned in Britain for thirty-seven years. In the United States, Abraham Lincoln has been dead for nine years. The day is Sunday, and at the Metropolitan Tabernacle in London, at 10.30 am, a congregation is beginning to fill what was then the largest church in the world. They enter through the side doors, for they are members of the church, and only at 10.50 are the front doors of the building opened to the general public. Soon after that time every seat is taken and some are permitted to stand in the aisles. A sea of people, perhaps five to six thousand in number, now fill the ground floor and the two galleries above. Then, prompt at 11 am, from a door at the front, behind the first gallery, the stout figure of Spurgeon appears and slowly comes down the steps into the pulpit. The service begins with an invocation, then the hymn, 'Come, Thou fount of every blessing'; Ephesians, chapter three, is read; then the main prayer, followed by another hymn and the sermon. The text this morning is Ephesians 3:8, 'Unto me, who am less than the least of all saints, is this grace given, that I should preach among the

Gentiles the unsearchable riches of Christ.'[1] The preacher's opening words were these:

> This is a very remarkable day to me, for, if I am spared to preach this present sermon, I shall have completed twenty years of printed discourses issued week by week.

He was referring to the fact that since January 1855 one of his sermons had been published every Thursday. The publication was heard or read weekly by some twenty-five thousand. On this last Sunday of 1874 Spurgeon said he could find no text that fitted his emotions so well as the words of Paul in his text. I can only give you one or two divisions of his sermon but I do so because I believe they lead us straight into the heart of our subject.

In the first place, he said, the text tells us what *Paul thought of himself*; it was 'very little' – 'less than the least of all saints'. So it ought to be with every preacher. 'I am not content with anything I have done', Spurgeon once said. 'Whatever grace has done for me I acknowledge with deep gratitude; but so far as I have done anything myself I beg pardon for it.'[2]

He went on, *Paul thought very highly of his work*, 'that I should preach.' 'Preaching and teaching, that was the one object of his life . . . This too is our work. The church must see to it that this ordinance be used above every other for the conversion of men.'

[1] *Metropolitan Tabernacle Pulpit*, 1874 (London: Passmore and Alabaster, 1875), p. 709. Hereafter '*MTP*'. The year given immediately after the title is the year during which the sermons were preached.

[2] *MTP*, 1880, p. 333. Speaking to Christian workers in November 1874, it is reported that, 'He did not think that any man that preached with success had any notion that he had begun to preach yet.' G. H. Pike, *Life and Work of Charles Haddon Spurgeon* (London: Cassell, n.d.), vol. 5, p. 140.

'*Paul thought very lovingly of his congregation.* He counted it a great grace that he was permitted to preach *among the Gentiles* . . . Gentile dogs, who were despised by the Jews as uncircumcised and unclean . . . The first chapter of his Epistle to the Romans contains a fearful indictment against the Gentiles, for their horrible vices. They were sunk in a horrible slough of corruption, and yet Paul considered it a great privilege to preach among these heathenish, debased, vicious Gentiles the unsearchable riches of Christ . . . I like to see Christian workers fall in love with their spheres. I never knew a man succeed among his people unless he preferred them to all others as the objects of his care . . . Paul became a Gentile for the Gentiles' sake.'

Such words were preliminary to the main part of his sermon, which had this head, '*Paul thought most of all of his subject.* That he had to preach the unsearchable riches of Christ was his highest bliss.' It has been his own joy, he said, through twenty years:

> This is the most delightful theme of all, to tell poor sinners that there is an unspeakably rich Saviour . . . What have we to say to Gentile sinners? Why, we have to tell them that our Lord Jesus is so rich in grace that he keeps open house all day and all night long, and 'Come and welcome' is written over his palace gates . . . We have to tell you that, though millions of sinners have already come, the banqueting table is as loaded as it ever was; he has as much grace and mercy to distribute as he had eighteen hundred years ago . . . My Master is so rich that he wants nothing from any of you. You need not bring a rag with you, he will cover you from head to foot . . . If you are at the very gates of hell, he is able to pluck you from the jaws of destruction. So mighty is his mercy that no case did ever exceed his power to save or ever will.

When Spurgeon preached these words on that last Sunday of 1874, he was only forty years of age. It was hoped that he had many years before him, yet there were signs that it might not be. Instead of the vigorous 'action' that marked his earlier preaching, he would now speak at times leaning on a stick. He was already suffering severely from gout, a painful disease that caused inflammation of the joints of the body, especially of the feet.[3] Twelve weeks were to pass after that Sunday before he could appear in his pulpit again on March 28, 1875. Yet the ministry was to go on for another seventeen years, deepening as it went, and even after his death in 1892, sermons that he had preached continued to be published weekly right down to the year 1917. In all the New Park Street and Metropolitan Tabernacle Pulpits became a series of sixty-three volumes, an achievement that probably has no parallel. In the year 1903 it was believed that more than three hundred million of Spurgeon's individual sermons had gone out and that if the pages were torn out and placed end to end they would nearly reach from the earth to the moon!

There are different ways of looking at Spurgeon, and this is illustrated in those who have written about him. Let me mention two ways that I believe are misleading.

First, there is the view that sees him as a unique Victorian pulpiteer, a product of his times. Enormously gifted, no doubt, but a man who represented a form of Christianity that has passed away. He left no heirs, or so newspapers said at the time of his death.[4] Eleven years later, a biography of Spurgeon was written by 'One Who Knew Him Well'. In it the

[3] Words quoted by Amy Carmichael from Maltbie D. Babcock (1858–1901) were true in Spurgeon's case, as with many other Christian leaders: 'Where grows the golden grain? Where faith? Where sympathy? In a furrow cut by pain.'

[4] See Pike vol. 6, p. 347.

author said, 'For any permanent and abiding influence upon the theological thought of the Christian Church we shall, however, look to his sermons in vain.'[5] He belonged, this writer believed, to 'a niche by himself'; he shone as a temporary meteor, not 'as one of the fixed stars whose brilliant light abides as a permanent possession for the ages'.

That is one view of Spurgeon and, if it were true, then Spurgeon could not be viewed today as anything more than an historical curiosity.

There is another school of thought on Spurgeon which contains a different danger. Those who belong to this school look upon Spurgeon with admiration and sympathy. They may themselves be evangelical preachers; they delight to read Spurgeon's life and marvel at his gifts. But therein lies the temptation to see him in such an exalted light that we suppose we are scarcely engaged in the same work. The difference between us and him is so great that, while we may praise him, we cannot follow.

I call this thinking dangerous because it is calculated to deprive other preachers of the main lessons to be drawn from his life. Certainly he had unusual natural abilities, and these we are not to try to imitate; but the spiritual factors that made him an evangelist were in no way unique to him. With regard to these factors Spurgeon himself had models: the first was the apostle Paul; the second, in another category, was George Whitefield. He followed them, however, not because of their persons, but because of the way they exemplified God-given principles for effective gospel ministry. Any consideration of Spurgeon as an evangelist has to be a miserable failure if it

[5] *Charles Haddon Spurgeon, By One Who Knew Him Well* (London: Melrose, 1903), p. 121.

does not serve to bring us closer to what we ought to be. The main point in Spurgeon's life is missed by those who are only admirers.

Before we enter more largely on our main subject, I want to set down a few things which Spurgeon did *not* believe about evangelism. To leave out these negatives could be to create a wrong impression.

Three Clarifications

1. *Spurgeon did not believe that evangelism is one man's work*. A first-time visitor to the Metropolitan Tabernacle, seeing thousands listening to one man, Sunday by Sunday, might have supposed the opposite. But one reason the building was so crowded was the presence of many bright Christians who so lived and spoke that strangers were regularly drawn in. A constant emphasis of Spurgeon's ministry was that every Christian should be seeking to lead others to Christ. 'Oh, brethren,' he says, 'do not leave these things to the minister. Too much of that is done, and it is a sort of Protestant Romanism to leave so much to ministers. It is the church – the church as a whole – that God will bless in the conversion of souls when it is really awakened.'[6] 'Great things are done by the Holy Spirit when a whole church is aroused to sacred energy: then there are hundreds of testimonies instead of one, and these strengthen each other.'[7] 'The Christian church should be like a beehive, into which every bee should be bringing honey. All church members should be doing something.'[8]

[6] *Speeches at Home and Abroad* (London: Passmore & Alabaster, 1878), p. 120.

[7] *Lectures to My Students* (1875–94; repr. Edinburgh: Banner of Truth, 2007), p. 425.

[8] *Speeches*, p. 59.

At the end of the year 1874, the membership of Spurgeon's church stood at about 4,800. It is worth remembering what kind of people many of them were. Spurgeon described them on one occasion as 'bricklayers, and carpenters, and working people'. The Metropolitan Tabernacle was not built in an affluent, tree-lined area of London. Rather around the building, in the words of one observer: 'There are whole colonies of streets of small houses, occupied by the poorer order of clerks and non-resident shopmen, artisans, and others who are rarely found on the Sunday within the walls of a church.'[9] It was from such a district that many of the newcomers were drawn. 'His church,' says another witness, 'was essentially a mission church, occupying mission ground.'[10] And Spurgeon's prayer was that all who joined the church should not be mere listeners but sharers in a missionary endeavour. There is evidence that this prayer was fulfilled. A contemporary of Spurgeon wrote: 'Probably no church in modern days ever sent forth so large a proportion of its members as ministers, evangelists, and home and foreign missionaries and workers of all kinds.'[11] There was a still larger number who remained at the Tabernacle as active helpers in the ministry. Lavinia Bartlett, for instance, was asked to fill a vacancy as a Sunday School teacher in 1859. From that date to her death in 1875, it is estimated that between 900 and 1000 members of her class joined the church.[12]

[9] Henry Christmas, *Preachers and Preaching* (London: Lay, 1858), p. 195.

[10] W. C. Wilkinson, *Modern Masters of Pulpit Discourse* (New York: Funk & Wagnalls, 1905), p. 211.

[11] *Spurgeon, By One Who Knew Him Well*, p. 119.

[12] *C. H. Spurgeon Autobiography*, vol. 2, *The Full Harvest* (Edinburgh: Banner of Truth, 1973), p. 79–80. There are records of other such individuals. Spurgeon could say: 'I thank God that we have a great many very warm hearted, earnest Christians in connection with this church – I will make bold to say, such true and lovely saints as I never expected to live to see. I have beheld in this church apostolic piety revived;

There is something to be added before we leave this point. Today the argument is heard that church premises are a poor place for evangelism. It is said that the church building is the place for teaching Christians, while evangelism is better conducted elsewhere. Spurgeon would not have agreed. It is true that he was ready to take opportunities to preach anywhere, in the open air (in earlier years), in hotels, in theatres and such-like places. Certainly he believed every opportunity should be taken up. But the reason he would not agree with the argument was that Christians, consciously gathered in the presence of God, are a convincing authentication of the power of the gospel. Many of the numbers present at the Metropolitan Tabernacle were not there as sightseers or mere hearers; they were *worshippers*, and a visitor, coming into such a gathering, might well be constrained to fall down, 'worship God, and report that God is in you of a truth' (*1 Cor.* 14:25). What happened in first-century Corinth also happened in nineteenth-century London.

2. *Spurgeon did not believe in evangelistic effort to the exclusion of other responsibilities*. The material needs of men, women and children, of the unemployed and the destitute, exercised him deeply. He could say, 'I do not think that the Lord expects people to hear the gospel on empty stomachs. I think he likes to see us doing what he used to do. He likes to see them fed; and whether we feed them first, or preach the gospel to them first, they begin to believe in us; and, perhaps, after believing in us, they may afterwards believe in the gospel.'[13] One evidence of his commitment in this regard was the

I will say it, to the glory of God, that I have seen as earnest and as true a piety as Paul or Peter ever witnessed.' Ibid., p. 82.

[13] *Speeches*, p. 121.

Children's Orphanage for which he was responsible at Stockwell. There were 216 boys in its care in 1874, and the number of children would grow to five hundred.

3. *Spurgeon did not believe that evangelistic preaching is a choice a pastor has to make.* He insisted that an evangelistic ministry, over against a teaching ministry, are not options that may be chosen by the preacher, depending on his preference or gifts. No! He believed that a man without evangelistic passion ought not to be in the Christian ministry. For him it was not enough simply to 'teach the Scriptures' and to trust that in the course of doing so some may be converted. Rather he believed in the necessity of regular, direct, pointed, evangelistic preaching, urgently delivered with the expectation of response. He argued that not all Scripture is equally adapted to the condition of the lost and it is the preacher's business to recognize the texts that God has so often used and to major on such texts.

Spurgeon's Preparation as an Evangelist

We move on, then, to consider how Spurgeon was prepared to be the evangelist he was.

1. *His conversion prepared him.*

I once listened to a panel discussion on a radio programme in which certain unrehearsed questions were being put. One question was, 'What do you think are the qualities that make a good bishop?' The various members of the panel made suggestions in turn. He needed to be a kind man, someone said. He ought to be approachable, was the opinion of another. Then all were startled when someone else said, 'He needs to be *a Christian.*' Spurgeon was a Christian! It happened when he was fifteen, after five years of conviction of sin and three years of praying. The burden and bitterness of sin, the wonder of Christ's love, the doctrine of substitution – all these were great realities to him. He was personally taught, as all Christians are taught, by the Spirit of God. So he could say, 'I live; yet not I, but Christ'. And with the indwelling of Christ came a vital concern for the salvation of others which showed itself first as he taught Sunday School and gave out tracts. 'I often felt,' he said of his youth, 'I could cheerfully lay down my life if I might but be the means of saving a poor old man, or bring a boy of my own age to the Saviour's feet.'[14]

A sound conversion is the basis of all real Christian usefulness. 'There can be no true testimony except that which springs from assured conviction of our own safety and joy in the Lord.'[15]

2. *The theology he learned in his youth prepared him.*

Here we can very clearly see divine providence shaping his life. He was brought up in what was a backwater of rural England. The county of Essex in East Anglia, where he was born, had once been one of the most influential parts of the nation, but it was no longer so in his day. Spurgeon attended no well-known school, and never went to College. Among his best teachers were his mother, and a Mrs Mary King, a cook in Newmarket, who loved 'good strong Calvinistic

[14] C. H. Spurgeon *Autobiography*, vol. 1, *The Early Years* (London: Banner of Truth, 1962), pp. 158–9. In these pages I quote from the edited version of the original *Autobiography*, 4 vols. (London: Passmore and Alabaster, 1897–1900). The editing has excluded some material not from Spurgeon's pen and included some additional information not previously given. See also footnote 12 above.

[15] Ibid., vol. 1, p. 158.

doctrine'.[16] The latest literature and authors to be found in the London bookshops did not reach his home. Yet, in just these restricted circumstances, he was an avid reader; first the Bible itself; then, as he writes, 'I used to rise with the sun that I might get time to read gracious books and to seek the Lord.'[17] What were these books? For the most part they were the books, two hundred years old, that his mother had first commended to him, and which he had found in quantity in his grandfather's old manse. These were Puritan authors, numbers of whom had once ministered in that very part of England. In devouring their works Spurgeon came to believe 'that the Puritanic school embodied more of gospel truth in it than any other since the days of the apostles'.[18]

The reason Spurgeon rated these old books so highly is closely related to our main theme. The main burden of the Puritans was evangelistic. They laboured to see people soundly converted and it was on the subject of conversion and regeneration that Spurgeon believed they were the best teachers in the English language. So while other young men, destined for the Christian ministry, were mostly reading the fashionable religious authors of the day, there was a youth in East Anglia reading Joseph Alleine, Thomas Brooks, William Gurnall, John Bunyan, and numbers of others from the seventeenth century. From this source his mind was stocked with the truths for a lifetime of ministry.[19] One of his first hearers

[16] Ibid., p. 39. In one of his many references to Mrs King, Spurgeon said: 'I learned my theology, from which I have never swerved, from an old woman who was a cook in the house where I was an usher. She could talk about the deep things of God . . . I learned more from her instruction than from anybody I have ever met with since.' Sermon preached in 1889, *MTP*, vol. 39, p. 462.

[17] *Autobiography*, vol. 1, p. 92.

[18] Ibid., p. 387.

[19] 'His acquaintance with our great English Puritans is known to most who know anything about him. Pointing to shelves loaded with the works of these laborious

in London called him an old book in a new binding. When another described him as 'an old Puritan bound in morocco', the country youth replied, 'I am bound in calf, for I belong to Essex.'[20]

It has too often been supposed that for a teaching ministry some good educational background is necessary, while for gospel preaching the need to understand theology is minimal. Spurgeon opposed any such idea. At a later date he would tell his own students for the ministry, 'To be effective preachers you must be sound theologians. Be sure you read Owen, Charnock, and Augustine.'[21]

To miss the theology that shaped Spurgeon as an evangelist is to misunderstand him totally.

The First Controversies

One effect of Spurgeon's theology was apparent very soon after he began preaching in London at the age of nineteen in 1854. He was not in step with any of the main trends in the churches, and that brought him into two considerable controversies, both of which had to do with evangelism. The first of these controversies concerned hyper-Calvinism. During the hundred years before Spurgeon, there had developed in England among numbers of Baptist churches a form of

---

men, he said one day: "I have preached them all".' William Williams, *Personal Reminiscences of Charles Haddon Spurgeon* (London: Religious Tract Society, 1895),p. 34. Assessing the cause of Spurgeon's success, a writer in *The Speaker* found it in two features: his personal character and 'the stern fidelity he showed, from first to last, to the Puritan creed of his forefathers. Never for a moment did he waver in the conviction that the truth he learned as a boy was everything.' Quoted by W. Y. Fullerton, *C. H. Spurgeon, A Biography* (London: Williams and Norgate, 1920), p. 324. Towards the end of his life Spurgeon wrote: 'Out of the present contempt into which Puritanism has fallen, many brave hearts and true will fetch it, by the help of God, ere many years have passed.' *Autobiography*, vol. 1, p. 11.

[20] James J. Ellis, *Charles Haddon Spurgeon* (London: Nisbet, n.d.), p. 55.

[21] Williams, *Reminiscences*, p. 138.

preaching that did not urge sinners to believe in Christ. These preachers feared that if they did so they would be denying the sovereignty of God. They thought that faith cannot be a sinner's duty because the unregenerate are dead in sin. To tell such people to repent and trust the Saviour might imply that they have the ability to do what they cannot do. The blessings of the gospel are only for the elect, and so the gospel cannot be presented as good news for the acceptance of all because God does not have compassion for all.

This teaching claimed to have the credentials of the strictest orthodoxy and many of Spurgeon's early hearers had received it. One of its main exponents had been pastor of the congregation to which the young Spurgeon was called, and so it was not long before he was challenged. Again, then, we note the providence of God. If Spurgeon had not already been familiar with the Puritans, he might have succumbed to the tradition that had become widely accepted and popular in chapels in south London, and if that had happened he would not have been the evangelist he was to become. But his preparation enabled him to recognize this deviation from the truth for what it was, and he did not hesitate to oppose it in a painful controversy.[22]

Spurgeon saw that in the gospel the grace of God is to be set before all men, that God himself entreats sinners to be reconciled, and that those who perish after hearing the gospel will be wholly accountable for their unbelief. It is sin, not divine sovereignty, that consigns men to hell. 'Compel them to come in', is Christ's command. The message is to be pressed upon all, with the certain promise, 'Whosoever shall call upon the name of the Lord shall be saved' (*Rom.*10:13).

[22] I have written more fully on this in *Spurgeon* v. *Hyper-Calvinism: The Battle for Gospel Preaching* (Edinburgh: Banner of Truth, 1995).

No one listening to Spurgeon could be left in any doubt that God is not willing that any should perish. This is how he speaks in a sermon on John 3:14, 'And as Moses lifted up the serpent in the wilderness, even so must the Son of man be lifted up: that whosoever believeth in him should not perish, but have eternal life':

> Sinner, the devil says you are shut out; tell him that 'whosoever' shuts out none. Oh that precious word, 'whosoever' . . . Remember there is the same Christ for big sinners as for little sinners; the same Christ for grey heads as for babes; the same Christ for poor as for rich; the same Christ for chimney sweeps as for monarchs; the same Christ for prostitutes as for saints: 'Whosoever'. I use broad words that I may take a broad range, and sweep the whole universe of sinners through – whosoever looks to Christ shall live.

This first controversy in which Spurgeon was engaged and attacked was largely to pass away. Through his ministry many had their eyes opened to the danger. As a result a new momentum of evangelistic zeal was to be found among Baptist churches and other new churches were established with pastors who had arisen under Spurgeon's influence.

But there was a second controversy in which Spurgeon did not have the same permanent success. On the opposite side of the error of hyper-Calvinism lies Arminianism and, despite Spurgeon, it came to be the prevalent understanding of evangelicals in the twentieth century. True Calvinism teaches that God has a general love for all and a special love for his elect. Popular Arminianism teaches only a general love. It denies any sovereign discrimination on the part of God and claims that all men have the same ability to believe. So the crux of evangelistic preaching lies in getting hearers to decide to become Christians and, to help them make that decision, the method often advocated was the one popularized by C. G. Finney, namely, calling people to show they were responding to Christ by some physical action, such as walking the aisle and coming to the front. It was thought that just as they could decide to walk, so they could decide for Christ.

Given Spurgeon's concern for evangelism, it might be expected that he would be sympathetic to this teaching. Indeed some modern writers have been very surprised to find that he opposed it. The reason he did so was that it contradicted a vital part of the New Testament gospel. Sin is not simply the absence of good, it is the existence of positive evil in human nature. Man is a fallen sinner whose very nature is in resistance to God. 'The carnal mind is enmity against God: for it is not subject to the law of God, neither indeed can be.' 'The natural man receives not the things of the Spirit of God'.

How then is this condition to be changed? Not by the unrenewed human will but by regeneration. There has to be a new birth, a new creation – an event that Scripture likens to a resurrection from the dead. Arminianism does not do justice to the seriousness of our natural condition, and so it makes repentance and believing the *cause* instead of the *result* of rebirth. Regeneration is a change effected by God himself.

> Faith is the work of God's grace in us. No man can say that Jesus is the Christ but by the Holy Ghost. 'No man cometh unto Me', saith Christ, 'except the Father which hath sent Me draw him.' So that faith, which is coming to Christ, is the result of divine drawing. Grace is the first and the last moving cause of salvation, and faith, important as it is, is only a part of the machinery which grace employs. We are saved

'through faith', but it is by grace. Sound forth these words as with the archangel's trumpet: 'By grace are ye saved.'[23]

Someone may ask, If this is true how can an evangelist call men to faith in Christ? Does such teaching do away with the preacher inviting men to Christ? On the contrary, Spurgeon would reply, it is *because God gives life to the dead* that we may preach with confidence. The divine side of conversion is not in the preacher's hand, God must give the capacity to believe, but *what* is to be believed comes by the hearing of the Word of God.

Two things are necessary to a true conversion: grace has to open the heart to receive Christ, and the Word has to give knowledge of the Christ who is to be received. The first part of this sequence, that is regeneration, is hidden from us, but in the second God uses human instrumentality. What first appears to us is repentance and faith, but wherever these are to be found we can be sure something invisible has also happened. If you see iron filings moving across the top of a table, you will recognize, says Spurgeon, that there must be a magnet beneath. So it is with everyone brought to Christ. Spurgeon himself did not recognise this clearly when he was first converted, for his inclination was rather to Arminian teaching: 'I really thought that I could turn to Christ when I pleased'.[24]

[23] *Words of Warning for Daily Life* (London: Passmore & Alabaster, 1895), p. 41. 'Three things must be wrought upon man, before he can come to Christ: His blind understanding must be enlightened; his hard and rocky heart must be broken and melted; his stiff, fixed, and obstinate will must be conquered and subdued: but all these are effects of a supernatural power.' John Flavel, *Works* (repr. London: Banner of Truth, 1968), vol. 2, p. 322.

[24] *Autobiography*, vol., 1, p. 49. Later he says: 'When I was coming to Christ, I thought I was doing it all myself, and though I sought the Lord earnestly, I had no idea the Lord was seeking me' (p. 168).

That fact is important for it is a reminder that a person does not have to be a Calvinist to be a Christian. An evangelist of Arminian persuasion preaches the same Saviour as the Calvinist. Yet as Spurgeon read the Scriptures and the Puritans he saw that the difference between these two positions is of real importance when it comes to evangelistic preaching.

The Bible teaches that conversion commonly begins with conviction, and part of the truth God uses to humble sinners is the fact that they cannot save themselves. The new birth, the Scriptures teach, is 'not of the will of man but of God' (*John* 1:13). The natural man is not half-lost, he *is* both lost and helpless: 'Men need to be told that, except divine grace shall bring them out of their enmity to God, they must eternally perish.'[25] But, it was objected, to tell people of their inability would be to make them despair. Exactly so, Spurgeon replied, that is just what preaching ought to do: 'The preacher's work is to throw sinners down in utter helplessness, that they may be compelled to look up to Him who alone can help them.'[26]

If faith and gospel invitations are preached without teaching on regeneration, then the impression is created that nothing more is needed to make me a Christian than my 'believing'. And if 'believing' is represented as something to be determined simply when and as I choose – just as I may will to walk to the front – then a way of salvation is proposed which contains within it the danger of receiving a delusion. There is a faith that can be created by self-choice, or by the pressure of an evangelistic meeting, but it is not saving faith. The danger of Arminianism for Spurgeon is its tendency to

[25] Spurgeon, *The Soul Winner* (London: Passmore and Alabaster, 1895), p. 20.
[26] Ibid.

streamline conversion as a single event, the decision of a moment that can be instantly registered by the individual and the congregation. In due course, this kind of thinking became so common that, in some parts of the world, a sermon that did not end in telling hearers to become Christians by answering the public appeal to come to the front was not considered evangelistic preaching at all.

Even if Spurgeon never gave such an appeal, it may be asked, in calling people to immediate faith in Christ, was he not doing the same thing? He was not. It is true, faith may receive Christ in a moment, but it is the Holy Spirit's work, not the preacher's, to confirm that the faith is genuine. Spurgeon gave no instant assurance. He knew Christ's teaching that an immediate response to preaching is no proof of a true conversion. Time is needed to show that repentance and faith are ongoing and that the convert has truly been severed from self and is now living for Christ. The truth is that there is no way that true conversions can be multiplied by any human methods or directions. In the course of his ministry Spurgeon became increasingly alarmed at the way the need for conviction of sin and regeneration was being bypassed and conversion made 'easy'.[27] It may be regretted that in speaking of Spurgeon as an evangelist these matters of controversy should be raised, but they underline something basic: *doctrine and theology have a vital part in evangelistic preaching.*

[27] There is a lengthy note on this subject by Spurgeon's contemporary, J. C. Ryle, in the chapter, 'The Cost', in his book, *Holiness.* Ryle concludes: 'The sovereignty of God in saving sinners, and the absolute necessity of preventing grace, are far too much overlooked. Many talk as if conversions could be manufactured at man's pleasure, and as if there was no such text as this, "It is not of man that willeth, nor of him that runneth, but of God that showeth mercy" (*Rom.* 9:16).' So prevalent was the opposite thinking that for fifty years after the death of Spurgeon no prominent evangelist was to be heard striking this note, until the ministry of Martyn Lloyd-Jones who, significantly, was responsible for the reprinting of Ryle's *Holiness* in 1952.

The Content of Evangelistic Preaching

This is the theme which occupied so much of Spurgeon's thirty-eight years' ministry in London and which he could never exhaust. But no small part of his gift was the ability to simplify. He would often summarize the message in just a sentence, such as, when speaking of what man lost in Adam and what we gain in Christ: 'Our fall was by another, and so is our rising again: we are under a system of representation and imputation, gainsay it who will.'[28] 'For as by one man's disobedience many were made sinners, so by the obedience of one shall many be made righteous' (*Rom.* 5:19). Many described Spurgeon's preaching as 'commonplace', that is to say, it was ever going over well-known subjects. Far from disagreeing, Spurgeon insisted that this was the great need. 'We must go to these sinners,' he would tell his students, 'and we must talk to them about such commonplace things as sin, and death, and judgment, and hell, and heaven, and Christ, and his blood. Yes, the blood. We must have that . . . We must hammer away at these: we must keep to these commonplace things, and make every sermon at least to have some part of it in which we distinctly aim at the conversion of sinners.'[29]

In one sense the text he first preached on when the Metropolitan Tabernacle was opened in 1861 was always his text. It was Luke's description of apostolic preaching in Acts 5:42, 'And daily in the temple, and in every house, they ceased not to teach and preach Jesus Christ.' In his further division of that subject the three 'r's were the essentials, 'ruin, redemption and regeneration'. He emphasized these three interlocking truths continually. *Ruin* has to be preached so

[28] Spurgeon, '*Till He Come*' (London: Passmore & Alabaster, 1896), p. 334.
[29] *Speeches*, p. 120.

that men may learn they are condemned. From that position, under divine wrath, only *redemption* by Christ can bring deliverance, and that redemption in its glorious effects brings not only pardon but the gift of the Holy Spirit to make sinners new in *regeneration.*

Certainly at the centre of these subjects, and of Spurgeon's ministry, is *redemption.* Deliverance from the wrath of God and everything we need for eternal life is to be found in the substitutionary work of Christ. Substitution, he never tired of preaching, is the very heart of the gospel: 'Jesus stood in the sinner's place and bore in the sinner's stead what was due to the law of God on account of man's transgression . . . No gladder news could come to man than that the incarnate God had borne man's sins and died in man's stead.'[30]

From one point of view, then, evangelistic preaching is simple. From another it is a burden too great for any preacher. It has to be delivered in its biblical balance and proportions, and with due regard to the different condition of the hearers.

Generalized applications are no use, for there are all kinds of hearers: some defiant, some careless, some doubting, some religious but unconverted, some penitent, some backsliders, some misled by error and so on. Even within such groups there are subdivisions. The defiant and careless, for instance, do not simply need to know they are sinners, they need to be convicted of particular sins and the preacher has to spell them out, and the guilt that belongs to them. But whatever the sin, whatever the need, it is the preaching of Christ that is the final answer:

[30] *MTP*, 1882, p. 316. It is said that it was Spurgeon's preaching that convinced James Denney of the substitutionary nature of the atonement.

> Let a man see God in Jesus Christ and he cannot be unhappy. Is it sin that burdens him? Let him see Jesus Christ bearing sin in his own body on the tree, and let him believe in this same sin-bearer, and that burden is gone. Let him be fretting under the cares and trials of life, and let him get a view by faith of Jesus, an infinitely greater sufferer, sympathizing with him in his sorrow, and surely the sting of his grief is removed. Is he afraid to die? Let him hear Jesus say, 'I am the resurrection and the life,' and he shall be taught rather to long for death than to dread it. Is he troubled about the things to come? Does the awful future lower darkly before him? Let him only hear Jesus say, 'I am he that liveth and was dead, and am alive for evermore . . .'[31]

It is sometimes argued that Calvinistic preaching reduces the comfort of the gospel, for if Christ did not die to redeem all, how can the atonement be preached to all? Spurgeon saw no problem. It is true the sinners for whom Jesus died are not named in Scripture. Nor need they be. The message of the gospel is not, 'Believe that Christ died for you'; it is, 'Come to God through this great Mediator, and you will surely receive all that he did for sinners.' Only after I have come to him am I able to say that the penalty for all my sins has been met by my Saviour, Jesus Christ.

Far from being a problem, Spurgeon believed, on the contrary, that the truth that salvation is wholly of God's grace offers encouragement to all sinners.

> If salvation were of works or of merits then many persons evidently would be excluded from hope, but if it is entirely of grace then none are excluded; and if the power be found in God and not in us, then the same power which can save the most moral young man can save the most dissolute and

[31] Ibid., p. 318.

> debauched person; and the same grace which can save the godly matron can save the impious harlot. The power of God is equal to any miracle. The mercy of God can go any length. Tell it; tell it that Jesus Christ is able to have compassion on the ignorant, and to save those that are out of the way. Out of the way sinners, outrageous sinners, black sinners, scarlet sinners: they too, may pray the prayer, 'Heal me, and I shall be healed; save me, and I shall be saved' . . . If it be of pure mercy, then the utmost guilt need not shut out a soul from heaven.[32]

The Character of the Evangelistic Preacher

For a man to be used in the service of God it is not enough that the content of his message be true. In the effectiveness of preaching there is a real connection between what is said and who says it. Ability and eloquence, combined with orthodoxy are not enough to make an evangelist. Spurgeon believed that Scripture makes clear that God uses instruments of a certain kind, and four characteristics mark them:

1. *Evangelists are men full of faith.* They believe that God has committed his word to writing, in the form of verbal revelation. Therefore they have a message to announce that is not their own, and they are sure of it. To entertain doubt over whether Scripture is all given by inspiration of God is instantly to lose the true authority that is required of a preacher and evangelist. No man will preach the gospel aright who does not wholly believe it. 'We believe and therefore speak.' A modern writer on preaching has said, 'Our great sin in preaching is our little faith.'[33]

[32] *MTP*, 1882, pp. 262–3.

[33] Edmund P.Clowney, *Preaching and Biblical Theology* (Phillipsburg, NJ: Presbyterian and Reformed, 1979), p. 68.

> How often you hear the question put, 'What is the reason of such-and-such a man's power in preaching?' I will tell you the reason of any man's power, if it is worth having. It is not his retentive memory, it is not his courage, it is not his oratory, but it is his faith. He believes God is with him, and acts as if it were so. He believes that his preaching will save souls, and preaches as if he believed it . . . [He] speaks out boldly what God has sent him to speak, knowing that what he says is true and must be received.[34]

The relationship of faith to preaching has many aspects. Faith is essential with respect to the content of the message. The preacher who only preaches to the extent of his understanding is not following the scriptural rule, 'I believed, and therefore have I spoken' (2 *Cor.* 4:13). It ought to be enough that he has Christ's authority for what he preaches.

We are called to declare much that is beyond our understanding. The Trinity and the incarnation of the Son of God involve mysteries above our comprehension. And the same applies to truths at the heart of God's way of salvation. The problem with both hyper-Calvinism and Arminianism is that both seek to understand what Scripture does not explain. Hyper-Calvinism says that it is irrational to say that men are dead in sin, without ability, and then to tell them to believe and live. To which Spurgeon replied:

> Indeed, it would be idle altogether were it not that true preaching is an act of faith, and is owned by the Holy Spirit as the means of working spiritual miracles. If we were by ourselves, and did not expect divine interpositions, we should

[34] *New Park Street Pulpit*, 1860 (London: Alabaster & Passmore, 1861), pp. 376–7. In another place he said to students, 'I would sooner that you believed half a dozen truths intensely than a hundred only feebly.'

> be wise to keep within the bounds of reason, and persuade men to do only what we see in them the ability to do. We should then bid the living live, urge the seeing to see, and persuade the willing to will . . . But, brethren, where is the mighty power and the victory of faith if our ministry is this and nothing more?[35]

In the same way Spurgeon answers the Arminian objection that if God is sovereign in all things then men cannot be responsible for their sins. He asks:

> Can you understand it, for I cannot, how a man is a free agent, a responsible agent, so that sin is his own wilful sin and lies with him and never with God, and yet at the same time God's purposes are fulfilled, and his will is done even by demons and corrupt men? – I cannot comprehend it: without hesitation I believe it and rejoice so to do, I never hope to comprehend it. I worship a God I never expect to comprehend . . . Now, to deny this truth because we cannot understand it, were to shut ourselves out of a great deal of important knowledge.[36]

Faith has other bearings on preaching. It gives the evangelist present evidence of things unseen and makes the content of his words real, and when those words concern the broad way that leads to destruction, and the hell beyond, there will be inward tears and heartbreak. 'Let those preach lightly who dare to do so, to me it is the burden of the Lord, – joyfully carried as grace is given, but still at times a burden which at times crushes my whole manhood.'[37] Spurgeon speaks of times in preaching when 'my whole soul has agonized over men, every nerve of my body has been strained and

[35] *Lectures to My Students*, 2007 edition, p. 420.
[36] *MTP*, 1870, p. 501.
[37] *The Sword and the Trowel*, 1875, p. 7. See next page for more on his preaching.

I could have wept my very being out of my eyes and carried my whole frame away in a flood of tears, if I could but win souls.'[38] Preaching has eternal consequences and where this is not rightly believed something essential will be missing in the pulpit. What was once called 'wet-eyed preaching' will not be seen where faith is weak.

In a yet more important respect faith is essential. It will stop a preacher thinking that he has done when all his notes are on paper and he enters the pulpit alone. He is *not* alone. 'The Spirit of truth, which proceedeth from the Father, he shall testify of me' (*John* 15:26). There is One on whom the preacher is to depend while preaching; One who can give thought and expression that never occurred beforehand; and One who has power over hearts and consciences.

Faith has a paramount place in preaching. How can five thousand men be filled with five loaves and two fishes? Faith knows the answer. How can an immense congregation be sustained through thirty-eight years, without any such attractions as can appeal to worldlings? The answer is, 'He that believeth on me, the works that I do shall he do also' (*John* 14:12).

God gives first place to faith because faith gives all glory to him. In the last paragraph Spurgeon ever wrote to his people he reminded them, 'We would have it so happen that, when our life's history is written, whoever reads it will not think of us as "self-made men", but as the handiwork of God, in whom His grace is magnified.'[39]

[38] On this point, see John Piper, 'Brothers, We Must Feel the Truth of Hell', in *Brothers, We Are Not Professionals* (Nashville: Broadman & Holman, 2002), pp. 113–8.

[39] 'In Memoriam,' an appendix to *The Sword and the Trowel* (London: Passmore & Alabaster, 1893), p. 115.

2. *Evangelists are men moved by love.*

It was observed about Spurgeon's preaching that although he was addressing such large numbers, each hearer felt that he was engaged in speaking to them individually. This was not an illusion, for in a real sense he was. We noted his words in the sermon with which we began, that Paul thought very lovingly of his congregation. So did Spurgeon. He did not see the people before him as just a crowd; they were needy individuals, often from hard and lonely backgrounds. Listen to this revealing sentence in a sermon on 'Herein is Love': 'When I have heard people say, "What is the good of looking after such riff-raff?" I have been saddened. The church of God feels that the souls of the meanest are precious, – that to save the most foul, the most ignorant, the most degraded . . . is an object worthy of the effort of the whole church.'[40] And Spurgeon felt this because, he believed, Christ felt it first. He believed that the Saviour who wept over Jerusalem was present in south London to seek and save the lost. Love and sympathy for all his hearers shines through Spurgeon's ministry. Certainly it was not the attribute of love alone that he preached. He held that warnings and the announcement of God's present and future wrath upon sin are necessary to faithful preaching but that is not enough:

> The spirit of Elijah may startle, and where it is exceedingly intense it may go far to prepare for the reception of the gospel; but for actual conversion more of John is needed, – love is the winning force. We must love men to Jesus. Great hearts are the main qualifications for great preachers, and we must cultivate our affections to that end.[41]

[40] *MTP*, 1883, p. 119.

[41] *Lectures to My Students*, 2007 edition, p. 422.

This is a recurring emphasis in Spurgeon's counsel to others. To pastors he says, 'If we are to prevail with men, we must love them.'[42] 'Love is power. The Holy Spirit works, for the most part, by our affection . . . faith accomplishes much, but love is the actual instrument by which faith works out its desires in the Name of the Lord of love . . . The holy grace of love needs to be more preached among us, and more felt by us.'[43] In similar words he reminded students at his Pastors' College: 'More flies are caught with honey than with vinegar. Preach much on the love of God.'[44]

This leads us to something still more important.

3. *True evangelists are the result of personal fellowship and friendship with the Saviour.*

'Follow me and I will make you to be fishers of men,' said our Lord to those first disciples. 'They have been with Jesus', was reported of them. This is the secret hidden from the world. The promise is, 'He that loveth me shall be loved of my Father, and I will love him, and will manifest myself to him' (*John* 14:21). The true evangelistic spirit comes from communion with Christ, for it is his spirit. Yet Spurgeon sought Christ's company, not for the work's sake, much though he loved Christ's cause. No! He loved the Saviour for who he is. He wanted all his thoughts and desires to be concentrated on Christ's person. To be wholly surrendered to Christ, to please him, to know more communion with him – this was Spurgeon's motivation, and by the grace of God it made him what he was. As an evangelist his thinking was, 'Not I, but

[42] *The Soul Winner*, p. 181.

[43] Spurgeon, *An All-Round Ministry* (repr. London: Banner of Truth, 1960), pp. 192–4.

[44] Williams, *Personal Reminiscences*, p. 172.

Christ', not my preaching, but his speaking through me, not my love, but Christ's great love for men and women. All the grace that became visible in his life and ministry was but the overflow from this divine source. 'God is love; and he that dwelleth in love dwelleth in God, and God in him' (*1 John* 4:16). Living near the fountainhead is the explanation. In the first years of his ministry he set this ambition down in his first book, *The Saint and his Saviour*,[45] published in 1857, and the last hymn that he ever gave out, in January 1892, the month of his death, had the same theme:

> O Christ! He is the fountain,
> The deep, sweet well of love;
> The streams on earth I've tasted,
> More deep I'll drink above.

Spurgeon said: 'The old proverb is, "Every true pulpit is set up in heaven," by which is meant that every true preacher is much with God.' It is as communion with God fails that preaching fails and we grow hard and cold. Then there is no possibility that we can speak aright of Christ's amazing compassion to needy sinners and rebels. Speaking of this subject, Spurgeon says, we are meant to be like the water pipes in a city. The purpose of a pipe is to convey water to the other end and, should it be blocked, the purpose must fail. The love of Christ is given to his servants, not that they should enjoy it for themselves alone, but that it should be conveyed to others: 'If you think thus, you are a pipe plugged up; you are of no use . . . for the system of love-supply for the world requires open pipes, through which divine love may freely flow.'[46]

[45] See, especially, the chapter, 'Love to Jesus'. See also *Till He Come*, pp. 315, 351.

[46] *MTP*, 1883, p. 120.

It was Spurgeon's communion with Christ that enabled him to bring a 'commonplace' message to people with an enduring freshness and wonder.

4. *Evangelists are men dependent on the Holy Spirit and on prayer.*

It is possible for us to consider all that we have covered above and yet only to feel as the disciples did before Pentecost. How far short we fall! Yet we are *not* before Pentecost. 'Another Comforter' has been given to dwell with us, and he is as divine as our Lord himself. He has come to do what we cannot do of ourselves, to help us, to lead us to pray, to teach us of Christ. 'I will not leave you comfortless, but will come unto you.'

If then we ask, 'How can we come to fresh and new communion with Christ? How can we obtain more faith and more love?', the answer is the Holy Spirit. And if we ask how souls are to be saved, the answer is the same:

> It is clear that we must abundantly and continually pray that the Holy Spirit may rest upon us. He will give the Holy Spirit to them that ask him. The Holy Spirit is never backward to work, but all the history of the church goes to show that, in seasons of the greatest operation of the Holy Spirit, there has generally preceded a time of mighty, intense, and earnest prayer. If we are to have souls saved we must pray: we must pray: we must pray.[47]

When we continue to pray, as Spurgeon prayed, 'Oh, that I could have the Spirit of God in me, till I was filled to the brim',[48] something is going to happen.

[47] *Speeches*, p. 115.
[48] *Autobiography*, vol. 2, p. 123.

To speak of Spurgeon as an evangelist without reference to prayer would be unforgiveable. We have the accounts of many who attended the Metropolitan Tabernacle under Spurgeon's ministry, and repeatedly we find them saying a similar thing: they say the singing, the reading of Scripture, the preaching, were all memorable, but often what stood out most of all was the way in which they were led into the presence of God in prayer. It was not the prayer as such that was admired, but something far more.

One hearer wrote that Spurgeon's public prayers, 'have been a means of grace, and a revelation of what prayer might more often be to those who have been unable to hear them without intense mental emotion'.[49] D. L. Moody, recalling a visit to the Tabernacle, said, 'He seemed to have such access to God that he could bring down power from heaven.'[50] Another, who was often present, puts the point accurately in these words: 'It was neither his homely diction, nor his wondrous voice, nor his transparent sincerity that did all this. It was God's will to come near to us in these exercises, and we lost sight of Spurgeon altogether in the reality of the Eternal Majesty and the Infinite Love.'[51]

If such public praying did not arise from what first happened in private it would be mere acting. But no one doubted the sincerity of Spurgeon's words when he said to others, 'If the foundation of the pulpit be not laid in private prayer, an open ministry will not be a success.'[52] 'When we are preparing in secret to serve the Lord in public we shall make poor work

[49] Ellis, *Spurgeon*, p. 50.
[50] Pike, vol. 5, p. 96.
[51] Ibid., p. 98.
[52] *The Soul-Winner*, p. 60.

of it if we do not beforehand draw near to God in prayer.'[53] 'The secret of all ministerial success lies in prevalence at the mercy-seat.'[54]

Spurgeon insisted that every church that prospers spiritually has within it a praying and pleading people. The weekly prayer meetings at the Tabernacle were for him of first importance. But he warned fellow pastors that the way to see a praying people was to follow that course oneself: 'Be much in prayer yourself, and this will be more effectual than scolding your people for not praying. Set the example . . . One of our most urgent necessities is fervent, importunate prayer.'[55]

During Spurgeon's ministry a number of his prayers were taken down, almost certainly without his permission. It was only after his death that they came to be published. I think they take us farther than any other material in understanding why Spurgeon was the Christian and the evangelist that he was. The real history – one could say, the secret history – of the thirty-eight years of his London ministry, lies in those prayers. The petitions, the praise and the pleadings are sure indications of the work of the Holy Spirit. John Bunyan's picture of a provider of oil, hidden behind a wall, who keeps the fire burning with new supplies, was no fiction.

Three Warnings

There are certain dangers confronting the evangelistic preacher, with which we must conclude.

1. *The danger of coveting success and popularity.*

This is a subtle temptation. A faithful preacher wants the work of the gospel to prosper, he wants to see conversions.

[53] *MTP*, 1883, p. 154.
[54] *Lectures to My Students*, 2007 edition, p. 51.
[55] *An All-Round Ministry*, pp. 358–9.

But where success becomes the motive a concern for numbers can slowly begin to take control. So if the simple preaching of Christ does not prove enough then some other aids and attractions had better be added. 'If your gospel has not the power of the Holy Ghost in it . . . you are tempted to have a performance in the schoolroom to allure the people, whom Christ crucified does not draw. If you are depending on sing-song, and fiddles, and semi-theatricals, you are disgracing the religion which you pretend to honour.'[56]

It was this same desire to obtain success, Spurgeon believed, that led to a readiness to make premature announcements on the number of converts. No such announcements were made at the Tabernacle. But the Tabernacle itself could be a misleading example to preachers and Spurgeon insisted that the only thing to be imitated was the Lord's ministry:

> Tell me, then, how Jesus set about it. Did He set about it by arranging to build a huge Tabernacle, or by organizing a monster Conference, or by publishing a great book, or by sounding a trumpet before Him in any other form? Did He aim at something great, and altogether out of the line of common service? Did He bid high for popularity, and wear Himself out by an exhausting sensationalism? No; He called disciples to Him one by one, and instructed each one with patient care.[57]

2. *The danger of grieving the Holy Spirit.*

Evangelists are not simply involved in a battle for truth; every Christian has his own moral battle. Indwelling sin unmortified will make the best grow careless; the world around

[56] *All-Round Ministry*, p. 389.
[57] Ibid., p. 250.

us would have us in its mould; we may lose a sense of how displeasing sin is to God. If these things happen we must fail, for we shall grieve the Holy Spirit. Hence the seriousness of the apostle's injunction, 'Hold fast the pattern of sound words which you have heard of me . . . That good thing which was committed to you, keep by the Holy Ghost who dwells in us' (2 *Tim.* 1:14).

As Spurgeon saw the direction of church history he gave increasing warnings on the danger of orthodoxy without holiness of life: 'The Holy Spirit does not bless that church in which holiness is not regarded.' In particular, it was his fear that evangelical churches were growing more tolerant to the sin of worldliness in its many forms. He did not expect to see conversions in churches where 'the members commonly go to the amusements of the world'.[58] Any sort of amusement that has the least taint of impurity, or the least toleration of ungodliness and bad language, should be shunned by the Christian. The doubtful and the questionable are all to be avoided. 'Only the pure in heart shall see God', he would remind his people.

> It will, indeed, be ill for the church of God if her members should become impure. In these days, we must be doubly strict, lest any looseness should come in among us. Actual sin must be repressed with a strong hand, but even the appearance of evil must be avoided.

He believed that true evangelism becomes impossible when watchfulness against worldliness and all forms of sin is neglected. It would have been incomprehensible to Spurgeon how some evangelicals today can recommend watching the kind of films that appeal to non-Christians on the grounds

[58] *Speeches*, p. 118.

that it will help us to understand how the world thinks. Guidance of that kind was remote from his understanding of the Bible.[59]

3. *The danger of not giving all praise to Father, Son and Holy Spirit.*

Every form of pride and vanity is a peril to us. He insisted to his students that 'the Lord will not use those who will not ascribe the honour entirely to Himself', and gave them this illustration of how glory may be stolen from him: 'You know how many attempt this theft. "When I was preaching at such-and-such a place, fifteen persons came into the vestry at the close of the service and thanked me for the sermon I had preached." You and your blessed sermon be hanged, – I might have used a stronger word if I had liked, for really you are worthy of condemnation.'[60] All good done, every sermon blessed, every conversion witnessed, every church built up, is all of God and, 'To the praise of the glory of his grace'. Spurgeon was no more humble by nature than all the children of men, but he was taught it, and increasingly humility shone in his life. Every one of the sixty-three volumes of the *New Park Street Pulpit* and *Metropolitan Tabernacle Pulpit* carried the same statement on the Dedication page,

TO THE ONE GOD OF HEAVEN AND EARTH
IN THE TRINITY OF HIS SACRED PERSONS
BE ALL HONOUR AND GLORY,
WORLD WITHOUT END,
AMEN.

[59] Of course, screen plays did not exist in his day but the theatre, their forerunner, did, and his convictions on theatregoers who were professed Christians were often stated. See, for example, *Only a Prayer-Meeting*, p. 341.

[60] 'Qualifications for Soul-Winning – Godward', *Sword and Trowel*, 1893, p. 161–2.

The final words that Spurgeon wrote to his people from France, weeks before his death, were these and I give them in the form in which they were later printed:

> THE VISTA OF A PRAISEFUL LIFE WILL NEVER CLOSE, BUT CONTINUE THROUGHOUT ETERNITY. FROM PSALM TO PSALM, FROM HALLELUJAH TO HALLELUJAH, WE WILL ASCEND THE HILL OF THE LORD; UNTIL WE COME INTO THE HOLIEST OF ALL, WHERE, WTH VEILED FACES, WE WILL BOW BEFORE THE DIVINE MAJESTY IN THE BLISS OF ENDLESS ADORATION.[61]

In harmony with these words was the last hymn Spurgeon ever wrote, and which was sung at the last Pastors' Conference he attended. The last three verses read:

Now my soul in praises swims,
Bathes in songs, and psalms, and hymns:
Plunges down into the deeps,
All her powers in worship steeps.

Hallelujah! O my Lord,
Torrents from my soul are poured!
I am carried clean away,
Praising, praising all the day.

In an ocean of delight,
Praising God with all my might,
Self is drowned. So let it be:
Only Christ remains in me.[62]

The bringing of others to sing such a song was the great purpose of Spurgeon's life.

[61] *Sword and Trowel*, 1893, p. 115.

[62] Quoted in R. Shindler, *From the Usher's Desk to the Tabernacle Pulpit* (London: Passmore and Alabaster, 1892), p. 265.

INDEX OF PERSONS AND PLACES MENTIONED

The Banner of Truth Trust originated in 1957 in London. The founders believed that much of the best literature of historic Christianity had been allowed to fall into oblivion and that, under God, its recovery could well lead not only to a strengthening of the church, but to true revival.

Inter-denominational in vision, this publishing work is now international, and our lists include a number of contemporary authors along with classics from the past. The translation of these books into many languages is encouraged.

A monthly magazine, *The Banner of Truth*, is also published and further information about this and all our other publications can be found on our website, or by contacting either of the offices below.

THE BANNER OF TRUTH TRUST

3 Murrayfield Road
Edinburgh, EH12 6EL
UK

PO Box 621, Carlisle
Pennsylvania 17013
USA

www.banneroftruth.co.uk